P.

Sist

Co

Mirrors

Laya Saul has written a book that will give today's generation of Jewish women their rightful inheritance: the role models that reveal our legacy and illuminate our future.

Lori Palatnik,
Founding Director, Jewish Women's Renaissance Project (JWRP)

Sisterhood of the Copper Mirrors is an in-depth exploration of fourteen of the most prominent women in the Hebrew Bible. By focusing on the eternal archetypes represented by each female character, Saul illuminates the spiritual lessons these strong women teach us—lessons that are as relevant today as they were thousands of years ago. Saul writes in a clear, engaging manner, making this book accessible to all Jewish women, whether this is their first introduction to biblical heroines or they've been studying the material for years. *The Sisterhood of the Copper Mirrors* is an entertaining book that is sure to inspire Jewish women of all ages and backgrounds.

Nina Davidovich Litvak,
screenwriter and cocreator, Accidental Talmudist

Accessible and inspiring. Laya Saul tells the epic stories of women of the Torah and brings to life the lessons and values of being a Jewish woman. I am happy to recommend and support such a wonderful book.

Olivia Schwartz,
codirector, Chai Center, Los Angeles

A masterpiece! A beautifully written, easily accessible resource, *Sisterhood of the Copper Mirrors* offers today's women and girls a lifeline connecting us to our holy mothers and other women in the Torah. Laya Saul joyously guides us in realigning our souls with the Godly inheritance that has been awaiting us over the centuries. The holy women of whom she writes are surely dancing in praise of this brilliant accomplishment! *Sisterhood of the Copper Mirrors* is an enlightening and inspiring experience for readers of all faiths.

Miriam Yerushalmi,
author of the *Reaching New Heights* series
as well as several children's books

I have had the distinct privilege to read portions of Laya Saul's new book, *Sisterhood of the Copper Mirrors*, and found it to be a wonderful introduction to the broad subject of women in Jewish tradition. It is well sourced in Jewish text, peppered with fascinating stories, astute psychological insights, and practical advice for the modern Jewish woman. By highlighting famous and influential women in Jewish tradition, the author not only makes these biblical stories come alive but in the process covers almost every issue confronting contemporary women in a spiritual yet practical manner. I highly recommend this book for not only those curious about learning more about their Jewish feminine identity but for all those who want new and refreshing perspective on this important subject.

Rabbi Avraham Arieh Trugman,
Director, Ohr Chadash;
author of fifteen popular books on Jewish topics

Sisterhood of the Copper Mirrors is a marvelous foundational "family history" that mirrors the wisdom, power, and spiritual DNA of the Jewish woman.

Adrienne Gold,
Trip and Education Leader, Jewish Women's Renaissance Project (JRWP)

Our rich legacy of wise Jewish women, a sisterhood that spans the generations, is brought to life with deep but easily accessible stories. Laya Saul, with her warmth and delightful style, takes us into the challenges and decisions that these women faced. You will get to know each woman as her personal story is told and the inspiration she ignites is shared with you, her sister.

Ellyn Hutt,
author, *Living in the Present Moment: A Divine Design*; educator in Jewish wisdom for living for over thirty years

As women, we often find ourselves in need of refueling. As we learn about our own feminine archetypes, we can find a source of strength—sometimes bold, sometimes quiet. *Sisterhood of the Copper Mirrors* is a place to begin, to learn the stories and tap into our inheritance as Jewish women. Read the stories, breathe in the qualities they bring us, and shine the light you're here to shine!

Eve Levy,
Founder, Shine—Inspiring Jewish Women, an initiative under the Portland Kollel; www.ADashOfEve.com

Eloquently, insightfully, and articulately written. Laya Saul makes the legacy of the women of Tanach accessible, inspiring Jewish women to reach their spiritually inherent potential as members from birth in the Sisterhood of the Copper Mirrors.

Rosally Saltsman,
author and journalist

The role models written about in Sisterhood of the Copper Mirrors can be a catalyst to discuss values and morals together. These eternal life lessons can become part of our personal journeys, spurring us on to live lives of fearless dignity for ourselves, our friends, and our communities.

Chaya Bracha Leiter,
co-founder and teacher at Ascent of Safed, Israel

On the cover: The images of the leaves on the cover and throughout this book are from the mandrake plant. Mandrake is the common translation of the *dudaim* plant in the story of Rachel and Leah, said to aid in fertility. May we find a joyful path in our efforts for spiritual fertility, and may we grow in our connections as we bring our spiritual fruits to benefit the world.

Scripture quotations are modified from *The Holy Scriptures According to the Masoretic Text*, published by the Jewish Publication Society in 1917.

Author photo by Rebecca Sigala
Cover artwork by Sara Eidelshtein, Teatree Design
Typesetting and design by S. Kim Glassman

ISBN 9780972322980

Kadima Press
848 N. Rainbow Boulevard #665
Las Vegas, NV 89107

For information about special discounts available for bulk purchases, sales promotions, fund-raising and educational needs, contact:
www.KadimaPress.com

In memory of my father and mother

**Matityahu Mendel
ben Yehoshua Leib HaLevi**

and

Matah bat Shimshon Berish

whose dedication to the path of Torah
has carried and inspired me in infinite ways

To the Jewish women

—and men—

in every generation

who have guarded

and passed on our

sacred tribal teachings

in ways great and small

And to all of us who are seeking

הרב ארי דוד קאהן
השקד 5\3 ת.ד. 443
גבעת זאב 90917

ח' מנחם אב התשע"ח
July 19, 2018

I have known Laya B. Saul for years, and I am delighted to
see that she has completed yet another book, *Sisterhood
of the Copper Mirrors*.

In this work, the author has succeeded in taking
complicated, authentic Torah teachings and presenting
them in a manner that allows even beginners to feel connected to the profundity of Torah. Her target audience,
women who are unfamiliar with the lives and teachings
of Jewish heroines, will undoubtedly be enthralled by
the depth of the ideas and the relevance of the messages
that have been skillfully culled from these fascinating
life stories.

I was privileged to discuss many of the ideas in the
book with the author, and I wish her continued success
and good health. May she continue to inspire her students,
and continue to be inspired by them, and may many more
new students join this special "sisterhood."

בברכה,

Rabbi Ari Kahn
הרב ארי דוד קאהן
מרא דאתרא ק"ק משכן אתרוג גבעת זאב

Rebbetzin Chana Bracha Siegelbaum
Midreshet B'erot Bat Ayin
The Village of Bat Ayin
Gush Etzion, 90913, Israel

רבנית חנה ברכה סיגלבאום
מדרשת בארות בת עין
ישוב בת עין
גוש עציון, 90913, ישראל

I enjoyed reading *Sisterhood of the Copper Mirrors: The Legacy of the Jewish Woman* by Laya Saul. I found the *hashkafah* (outlook) of the book kosher according to the teachings of Chazal (Our holy Sages). It is clear that the author lives the Torah that she is sharing in her book. She frequently quotes Talmud, Tanach, Midrash, Rashi, and other classical commentaries, with an occasional Zohar and even Arizal, giving the book a mystical edge.

Sisterhood of the Copper Mirrors familiarizes the reader with fourteen selected biblical women. From the Torah: Chava, Sarah, Rivka, Rachel, Leah, Miriam, and Tziporah; from the Prophets: Rachav, Devorah, Yael, and Chana; and from the Writings: Ruth, Naomi, and Esther. The way the author uses the concept of the copper mirrors of the righteous women who brought redemption from Egypt as the theme throughout the book, allotting each woman her personal mirror and gift, is very original and speaks to today's women seeking spirituality.

This book is skillfully written, weaving strands of Midrash and commentary into the narrative and using modern terminology that speaks to people of all backgrounds. Similarly, the narrative is interspersed with modern examples and personal stories to illustrate how we can emulate the character traits of our holy mothers. The writing style is personal, somewhat poetic, and easily read. It really brings the biblical women to life for contemporary women.

With blessings of the Torah and the Land,

Chana Bracha Siegelbaum

Chana Bracha Siegelbaum

PHONE: (972-2) 993-4945 | FAX: (972-2) 993-1215
WEB: WWW.BEROTBATAYIN.ORG | EMAIL: INFO@BEROTBATAYIN.ORG

Sisterhood
of the
Copper
Mirrors

The Legacy of the Jewish Woman

Sisterhood
of the
Copper
Mirrors

The Legacy of the Jewish Woman

LAYA SAUL

Kadima Press

CONTENTS

YOUR SPIRITUAL INHERITANCE

A Rich Legacy

Question: If a beggar on the street inherits a million dollars—but does not know about it—does that make the beggar rich?

A beggar who finds food in garbage dumpsters and does not know about any inheritance will continue to eat out of dumpsters. That person's life will not change: the beggar will not eat, sleep, or dress differently. So the answer is no. *Potential is not actual.* If someone does not know about an inheritance, that person is not rich. If someone knows about an inheritance but does not claim it, that also changes nothing! It happens more often than you may think: a fortune is available, but for whatever reason, the money goes unclaimed. In some cases it's because the money is associated with pain, and the heirs don't want it. In plenty of cases, the next of kin don't even know about it.

It is the same for the spiritual inheritance of every Jew. That desire to know more about your inheritance is why you are reading this book now.

This book is an invitation to journey into discovery: a discovery of self, of peoplehood, and of your relationship with the Divine, as reflected in the archetypes of Jewish women. These women's stories are relevant to our lives today. They pulse with life and truth. Jewish rituals serve to bring the spiritual realms into the material world. Some women have never really been given their inheritance, perhaps because of misconceptions or lack of Jewish education. Yet if you are a Jewish woman, this treasure belongs to you. It's up to you to claim it, live it, and celebrate it. With these women behind you, you can shine your special and unique spark into the world. Their wisdom and example will serve you as you weave your own thread into the fabric of your people and world.

What You Can Expect

This book explores the stories of some of the prominent women in the Tanach. Tanach is a Hebrew acronym for Jewish Scripture, made up of the Torah (the Five Books of Moses or Pentateuch), the Neviim (the Prophets, including books such as Joshua, Judges, and Isaiah), and the Ketuvim (writings, including books such as Esther, Ruth, and Job, as well as Psalms, Proverbs, Ecclesiastes, and more). In Christian tradition, the books that make up the Tanach are called the "Old Testament."

Each chapter of this book explores the story of one or more women of the Tanach in three parts:

- **Stories:** understanding the foundation of the biblical stories of our foremothers

- **Gifts:** guiding us to use the tools within us by delving into the qualities of strength embodied by each of the women

- **Reflections:** sharing insights and food for thought that we can bring into our daily lives from the rich heritage of each woman covered in this book

Additionally, there is a mini-guide at the end of the book to help you think about spiritual pathways that may resonate with you as you claim the gifts of your heritage.

Some Things to Consider

As you journey to understand the legacy of the Jewish woman, consider the following ideas.

We've been hijacked! There are certain Hebrew words that, when translated, bring up strong and sometimes even bitter emotions. You might even say that the English versions of the concepts described by Hebrew words have been "hijacked" by other religions, academics, or political movements. To reclaim these hijacked concepts, you'll find some of the original Hebrew words have been integrated in this book. Each of these is defined, and there's a glossary you can refer to at the back of this book.

Don't slam this book shut! It is possible that you may encounter something in this book that will bother you. Please, if something in this book annoys you, refer to another source, check the websites in the resources section at the end, or just filter it—we filter all the time—or set it aside; you can revisit the thought later if you want.

One example of a slam-the-book-shut-hijacked-term that raises the hackles of lots of people is "God fearing." It's a translation of the Hebrew term *yirat Shamayim*, which literally means "awe of Heaven." Awe. You can be in awe of an ocean. Awe of an ocean comes with the understanding that with all we may know about it, there is still much more that is unknown. An ocean also inspires awe because we recognize that it is more formidable than any human and should be approached respectfully and appropriately. An ocean is but one small creation in a universe we can hardly conceive of. If we consider the Creator of the universe, what is the awe that might inspire? Someone who has *yirat Shamayim,* heavenly awe, would likely want to approach the spiritual realms with wonder and respect. That person strives to do the right thing even if no one is looking and there is no chance of getting caught. There's an understanding that we take responsibility for our lives and we are accountable for what we do and do not do. Heavenly awe can be as quiet as the whisperings of your own conscience. Heavenly awe can be as tenacious as a mama bear protecting her young. There may be other ideas that seem problematic to you, and we'll explore the fuller concepts inherent in the Hebrew words.

It's perfectly wonderful to come to something you find challenging. Whatever slam-the-book-shut challenges you find, please consider what a dull journey it would be if the pathway were always smooth and no obstacles dared you to grow. If you find there is something in this book that does not speak to you, just skip that thought and move on to parts that nourish you.

A first glance may not always make sense. Some of the things you learn on this journey will be logical to you right away. Some things may seem to make no sense at all. Sometimes an understanding of the time during which the stories of the Tanach take place will help you make sense of its teachings. In addition to the books of the Tanach, other traditional Jewish texts such as the Talmud (Jewish oral law along with rabbinic commentaries), the Midrash (interpretive rabbinic literature), and the many commentaries on these that have been handed down over the centuries will help us dive into and understand the relevance of these stories for today's world.

When someone meets you for the first time, it does not make any sense for that person to judge the complexities of you by looking at your hair or eye color or the outfit you happen to be wearing that day. No one could begin to understand the depths of who you are, your feelings, yearnings, dreams, or strengths at first glance. The women in the Tanach are as complex as you are, so don't expect to understand them at first glance, either. Their stories can't be tied up in a neat bow. In any case, how disappointing it would be if their stories and teachings were so shallow.

All of the stories of the Tanach can be understood on many levels. A four-level system to help us explore and understand the depth of our teachings was developed in the thirteenth century. The Hebrew acronym for this is the word *pardes*, meaning "orchard." That word itself hints at the sweet fruits you can find within the teachings. *Pardes* stands for: *pshat* (literal), *remez* (hinted), *drash* (interpretive), and *sod* (secret):

- **Pshat**, the simplest level of understanding of Scripture, gives us the story at face value, the basic understanding: who, what, and when.

- **Remez**, the next level, shows us the "hints" to deeper understandings of the texts.

❧ **Drash**, inspirational or moral teachings drawn from the body of interpretive rabbinic literature called Midrash, are at a deeper level still.

❧ **Sod**, the deepest level, is known as "secret." This is the realm of Kabbalah, esoteric mystical teachings.

A spiritual secret is not something that I must keep to myself and not tell. It is something that the seeker must actively seek to find and understand. For example, you can read about snow. You can see snow in a photo. But it's not the same as being in a white-out blizzard, or hearing the squeaky crunch as you walk along the street, or standing still in the cold as soft, giant flakes flurry all around you. The "secret" (*sod*) level is earned through your relationship with and study of the Torah.

The process of discovery is the journey. Just because a story or teaching doesn't make sense now doesn't mean that it won't eventually; it just means that it doesn't make sense *yet*. As with anything of value, it takes effort. It's kind of like life: sometimes what's happening clearly makes sense, and other times it takes years to reveal why a certain event had to happen. The same can be true in learning science, or math, or grammar. It's true of gardening, or cooking, or building. It is simply impossible to understand everything all at once. You start with the basics and deepen as you go.

As we seek to understand the lives of our mothers, we see their stories were not simple or easy. No hero came in to save them. These were not fairy tales. No perfection. In fact, the challenging aspects to their stories can be easily *mis*understood. If *our* lives can be complicated, why wouldn't the same be true in other generations? Growth is a constant journey toward deeper understanding. The thing about learning the stories from the Torah is that they are many layers deep, so if something is challenging to understand, trust that your understanding will ultimately deepen on the journey. If this book leaves you with more questions, that's great! Keep asking questions.

If the Torah is a teacher, what's our relationship with her? Another thing to consider is the idea of being in a relationship. How do you build a relationship? How do you build trust? You show up every day. You listen. You share yourself. When people in your life demonstrate that they will show up for you, you will begin to open up. It doesn't happen all at once; it happens in degrees. You can't snap your fingers and expect "quality time"—you have to keep showing up. In a relationship with a parent, spouse, child, or friend, you can talk to the person daily, and while each conversation may not feel earthshaking, the ongoing interaction is meaningful. The trust you build allows for deeper sharing and connecting. Similarly, showing up on your spiritual journey, giving it time and being open to new discoveries, eventually bears fruit.

Torah is a path to elevate your soul and also to bring truth to the world. The Hebrew word used for Jewish law is halachah, which translates as "the way." It's not about black and white; *the way*—our spiritual walk in this world—is about applying these principles and ethics as we make our contributions to this world. It's about building a world that is good and just.

About the footnotes. For those who want to do more research about the stories, there are footnotes to identify Scriptural sources or additional details. There's no reason to stop what you're reading to see what the footnote says. It's important to know who said what, so sources are included in case they are relevant to some readers.

Men are part of the stories. In learning about the stories of the matriarchs, we must also understand something of the patriarchs. Each man and woman brings something to our history, and it is their partnerships that built the nation. So while the focus of this book is on the stories of the women, some of the stories of the men in their lives will be covered as well.

Dare to grow. Learning or walking a spiritual path is not simple. There is a teaching that learning Torah comes with hardship.[1] This journey of learning, as deep and meaningful and full of value as it is, may challenge you to take a risk and grow. Even in our world of fast food and instant gratification, you know that the things that have the most meaning in life come with challenges. Your best achievements came because of your commitment. You know how to do challenges. You've got this!

Keep dancing, keep shining. It's possible that the one and only thing we truly have control of in life is our attitude. Know that the qualities embodied in each of our foremothers are already within you. Becoming conscious of these qualities will strengthen them within you. Going deeper into the purpose of all of life, even into the hard parts, can bring you to a place of greater happiness that you can step into, if you choose it. We may not be able to control all that happens around us, but we can control what we do with all of life's experiences. Taking hold of how we handle life and what we put out into the world is the power of using the legacy we receive from our matriarchs. Enjoy the journey, take it gently, and shine!

---

1. Talmud, *Berachot* 5a, says that God gave the people of Israel three precious gifts (Torah, the Land of Israel, and the World to Come), and all of them are acquired by suffering.

WHAT ARE THE
COPPER MIRRORS?

In the Merit of the Righteous Women

The title of this book, *Sisterhood of the Copper Mirrors*, comes from a story in the Torah as explained in rabbinic tradition that took place when the Children of Israel were slaves in Egypt. In those dark times, the Israelites endured cruelties as horrific as those of the Holocaust. Humiliation, sadistic torture, and evil were the very real experiences that our nation endured. Babies were ripped from their mothers' breasts to be drowned. People were slaughtered so that Pharaoh could bathe in their blood. And that slavery lasted far longer than the Holocaust—it went on for over two hundred years!

When the Israelites were finally released from this slavery in the Exodus—leaving Egypt—it was an event of such magnitude that we continue to tell the story every year at our Pesach (Passover) tables, just as we have done for thousands of years. So central is the Exodus to our communal experience as a people that it forms the basis of the first of the Ten Commandments: "I am the Lord, Your God, Who took you out of Egypt."[1] And our sages give credit for this momentous event to the *merit of the righteous women*.[2]

What does "in the merit of the righteous women" mean? How did the righteous women get the credit for the redemption out of Egypt?

We're taught that during that painful time, the women made extra efforts to perpetuate the Jewish home and family. Though they were also shattered, they would not surrender building their families and their nation. They rose up to go out to the fields to give love and support to their husbands who had collapsed from their labors. The women used polished copper as mirrors to make

---

1. Exodus 20:2.
2. Talmud, *Sotah* 11b.

9

themselves as beautiful as they could be. In these simple mirrors, they looked not only at their external appearance but also searched for the reflection of their innermost beauty, the essential beauty of the spirit, to shine through. In this way they enticed their exhausted husbands, so that they could continue to build the nation, even in the darkness of slavery. When the Jews finally left Egypt, they left with great wealth.[3] Yet the women kept their simple copper mirrors.

Then came the time when Moshe (Moses) journeyed up Mount Sinai to receive the Torah. He was gone for forty days. Some of the men grew impatient. They wanted to create a golden idol to worship. Aharon (Aaron), Moshe's brother who was appointed as the High Priest, tried to stall for time. He told the men to take gold from their wives to make the idol, knowing full well that the women would not agree. Indeed the women did refuse to give their gold to make an idol. Instead the men took the gold from their own ears!

Lest someone think the women refused simply because they were attached to their jewelry, we see later in the story that when Moshe asked the nation to contribute gold, silver, and other materials for the construction of the Sanctuary and the Ark of the Covenant, the women led the way and contributed generously. Along with their gold, silver, and other precious materials, the women passed forward their copper mirrors. Moshe wasn't sure if they should be used to build the Sanctuary; weren't they, after all, tools of vanity? He asked God directly. The response? Use the mirrors, because God considered them sacred and precious.[4] The story goes even deeper regarding the copper mirrors. The Israelites had plenty of resources for everything, *but* there was a limit to how much gold, silver, or other resources would be used. There was an exact amount, for example, that would be used for the Menorah (candelabra), and no more. So if someone didn't contribute fast enough, his or her gold might not be used. With the copper mirrors *every single one that was contributed was used*; not one was turned

3.   Exodus 12:35–36.
4.   Exodus 38:8 and relevant midrash cited by Rashi.

away. These mirrors were used to construct the laver (the copper washbasin and its stand) where the priests would wash before they would be permitted to perform their service to God in the Beit Hamikdash, the Holy Temple in Jerusalem.

If you are a Jewish woman today, you are a direct descendant of the women who used these copper mirrors in Egypt and gave them for use in the Temple. These women not only survived the hardship and pain of slavery in Egypt, but took action to ensure that our nation would thrive. We are the Sisterhood of the Copper Mirrors.

The Value of Seeking

As Jewish women, we can claim our inheritance, but we must actively seek it. The heritage passed down to us by our biblical foremothers is available to us today, if only we take the time and make the effort to connect with it. Think about the most precious things in your life. Most people put their loved ones at the top of the list. Clearly in your family relationships, there is an investment of time, effort, very likely tears, and for sure patience. It makes sense: if we want to have a deeper relationship with someone, there is vulnerability and commitment involved. We have to spend the time. We have to risk opening our mouths to express what's in our hearts and minds so we can be understood, and opening our ears, minds, and hearts in order to understand another. There is so much value in taking that risk over and over as we build deeper relationship with those we love. It's the same on a soul level in the realm of spirituality. It takes effort and risk to connect spiritually and deepen our relationship with that Highest Power that is commonly labeled "God."

In a spiritual journey, in seeking a deeper connection with your heritage and with God, the more Torah you learn, the more questions come up. The more you know, the deeper the mystery of the journey. Walking the spiritual path of the Jewish woman requires that you challenge yourself, your beliefs, and even the source of your beliefs.

The beautiful part is that no one is required to hurry along the way. Everyone is on her own path and travels it at her own pace. The call is not for you to try to become someone else—never! The call is to wake up to know yourself and to brave the challenges of becoming your truest self.

The Foundation

A book about women in the Bible means we are using Scripture as a source. Tanach (as described in more detail in the preface, that's the Five Books of Moses, the Prophets, and specific writings) is about the journey of a nation that struggles to search for, relate to, and serve the Creator—so let's explore this concept of God. The only real way to begin to fathom some aspect of God is to get straight what God is *not*. *God is not an old man with a white, flowing beard sitting on a throne in the clouds.* God is not a man. God is not a woman, either. God is not even Jewish. As soon as a description of the Eternal is put into words, it cannot be true, because words are finite and "God" is Infinite. So, with our limited thoughts and perceptions, we do the best we can within the confines of language.

In the Torah there are many names for God. The most common and powerful of them is composed of four Hebrew letters, which mean *That-Which-Was, That-Which-Is, and That-Which-Will-Be.* The Eternal. This four-letter ineffable name is not pronounced out loud (only the High Priest was allowed to pronounce this holy name, and only in the Beit Hamikdash, the holiest place in the world, on Yom Kippur, the holiest day of the year). When we see the four letters (*yud, heh, vav, heh*), we use the pronunciation Ah-doh-NAI, but we don't even speak that word outside the framework of prayer; it is spoken with reverence and hopefully love. In religiously observant circles, people usually refer to God as Hashem, which literally means "the Name."

The word *God* itself has unfortunately been saddled with many confused associations, not all of them from Jewish sources. In this book, different words will be used to represent this concept of God, Creator, Master of the Universe, Almighty, Eternal.

There's a story about a guy who was talking with a rabbi and said, "I don't believe in God." So the rabbi asked him to describe God. The guy shared what he thought, and the rabbi answered, "I also don't believe in that god." How can we take our concept of God beyond what we thought as children and let go of shallow, naive, or immature ideas?

Take the image of God as masculine. Giving the Infinite-Almighty-Eternal-Divine a gender is a tool we can use to try to comprehend spiritual concepts in some small, human way. Even though it is common to call God "He," it's an important foundation to understand that it's not the whole picture—in Jewish prayer, the Hebrew grammar we use for God is also sometimes in feminine form. We talk about the Shechinah, a (grammatically and spiritually) feminine word that refers to a feminine aspect of God. We must strive to know that God is Oneness, beyond masculine and feminine.

God is also beyond time. We might ask, "What was there before God?" What we cannot comprehend is the paradox that there is no "before" God, because God created time. There are many things we cannot comprehend about the Divine, and this is reflected in the symbolic way we speak about God.

Creator, King, Father, Lover. We use many metaphors to understand in some small way our relationship with God. Each evokes different feelings within, so we can plumb the depths of this relationship. As a people, we have always been defined in relation to God. Even the name of our nation, Yisrael (Israel), means "struggles with God."[5] It also means "straight to God."[6]

---

5. Genesis 32:29.
6. Maharal, *Gur Aryeh*, Bereishit 49:33.

Judaism teaches that each and every one of us is in a relationship with God that is very intimate and personal. A beautiful thought I heard is that the same Creator Who spoke mountains, oceans, and galaxies into being also decreed that the world needs *you*.

If there is one concept to take with you into your daily breath, it is that God loves you. The metaphor of a parent to a child comes in handy here. A loving parent shows affection and also gives discipline, all out of love and commitment to raising the child to be his or her best. Even the rough spots in life have purpose and meaning *from a divine perspective*. Sometimes we don't like the things that we have to experience or see in this world. So how is someone supposed to be grateful or happy when things get hard in life? Is there a way to keep perspective?

There's a story of an old grandmother who was doing a needlepoint project. Her grandson looked up from where he was playing on the floor and all he saw were the knots on the back of the cloth. He couldn't understand how it would possibly be something that would look nice. Day after day his grandmother would explain that he would understand when it was finished. But day after day, he only saw a mess of knots when he would look up at her work. When she was all finished, she lowered the cloth. All the colored threads that seemed just a jumble from underneath were suddenly a beautiful picture.

God has a perspective we cannot understand in this world. Your life experience has already taught you there are situations that don't look so great when you're in them. But with time, we understand how those very experiences shaped us to become better, deeper, more sensitive, or stronger. Disappointments can lead us in a direction we didn't plan on, but in the end turn out better than we imagined. Challenges gift us the opportunity to see what we are capable of; we can use the hard times to build character.

We've been given a guide about how to be in this world; the body of writing called Torah is the manual for life. We're told there are seventy faces of Torah.[7] Begin where you are. Just start talking. Some people call that prayer; others might call it meditation, and there's more on this later. A relationship with God springs from a connection that already exists within each of us, because the creation of life began with God's breath. The Hebrew word for breath, *neshimah,* shares its root with the Hebrew word for soul, *neshamah.* The relationship to the Divine is as close to you as your every breath.

Knowing the Truth of Who We Are

When you picture the women of the Bible—Sarah, Rivka (Rebecca) Rachel, Leah, or any of the others—what images come up? I've asked many women this question, including those who know these stories well. The answer I get is nearly always the same. "I don't know... mid-twenties?" The image is that of a young, smooth-skinned, perfectly proportioned, slender woman.

As you'll see from the stories that follow, the women of Tanach are as young as three years old and as old as 130, and every age in between. Sometimes their influence covers a long period of time, and we see them at different ages, playing their parts in our legacy. This reminds us how important we are at *every* age and stage of life.

There is a blessing that Jewish parents give to their sons and daughters: May God bless you and watch over you. May God shine His face toward you and show you favor. May God be favorably disposed toward you, and may He grant you peace. For daughters, we begin the blessing with, "May God make you like Sarah, Rivka, Rachel, and Leah." Why do we bless our daughters to be like the matriarchs? Each one of them actually grew up in a home of idolatry and immorality. They did not grow up learning how to be good, or even knowing about God. As you will see in the coming chapters, these women honed their characters to become matriarchs of a nation that would have a tremendous positive impact to touch all of humanity.

---

7. Midrash, *Numbers Rabbah* 13:15.

Living in the role of the feminine does not mean being help-less. Our matriarchs did not prick their fingers or eat an apple only to fall asleep to await the kiss of a prince. There was no fairy godmother waving a wand to turn pumpkins into coaches. Sadly, there are no birds to help with the housework. Our stories are about partnerships. Our matriarchs were spiritual giants who survived abductions, famines, conniving relatives, and the pain of infertility, and at the same time, they spread the teachings of oneness while building deeply personal relationships with God that continue to echo meaningfully into our hearts.

To be a Jewish heroine, you don't need to be old enough or young enough. You are never too young or too old to make an im-pact! You can be a convert or be born from a Jewish mother. You can be single, married, divorced, or widowed. You may not have had any Jewish education, or you may have had much. Your lineage may be Sephardic or Ashkenazic. Whoever you are, you count! You make a difference, and no act should be underestimated in its ability to build and redeem a nation! You will see this played out in the stories we'll explore in this book.

Tapping into this power does not happen all at once. You claim it. You step into it, and the nobility crowns you.

With nobility comes responsibility—moral, ethical, and spir-itual. But please don't be afraid! Don't let that stop you from the journey of claiming and reclaiming the truth about yourself. *This is not a path of perfectionism*, as you will see. We are only human, we all fall on our faces! Our nobility and strength come from standing up again, over and over.[8]

You will see as you learn about the women in Tanach that they all made mistakes: laughing at the wrong time, having the right intention but the wrong action, starting off on the wrong foot, or not setting a strong boundary. The mistakes themselves are a kind of archetype. Their lives were not perfect, nor did they live the

---

8.   As it says in Proverbs 24:16, the righteous person falls seven times and gets back up again.

"happily ever after" of fairy tales. They were real women facing real challenges. Like them, we will also make mistakes. We'll stick our feet in our mouths. We'll wish we had kept our mouths closed when we opened them at the wrong time in the wrong way. We'll wish we had spoken up when we were silent.

What vibrates within you is a unique blend of the various qualities of the women of Tanach, our archetypes. The qualities of these wonderful women of Tanach are like the notes that make up the songs of our legacy as Jewish women. Every song is made up of notes: sharps and flats, highs and lows. And each one of us is an instrument, playing these notes in her own special way, adding her own harmony to the symphony to make it richer and more magnificent. You are in this world to sing your song, to put your music into the world. Whether privately or publicly, what you add is significant and important.

In this generation we have another chance to stand up for the truth of who we are as Jewish women today, just as our mothers did in Egypt. The great sixteenth-century Kabbalist Rabbi Isaac Luria, known as the Ari, wrote that the generation before the Moshiach (Hebrew for the Messiah, who will usher in an era of world peace for all humanity) would be the reincarnation of the generation of Egypt.[9] It is said that the final redemption will once again come in the merit of the righteous women. That time is now. Know where you come from. Know the truth about who you are. No matter how old or young you are, no matter your size, education, skin color, abilities or disabilities, customs, or level of religious observance, you—yes, you, dear reader!—matter and are essential. Do not underestimate the light and goodness you bring into this world.

As you read the stories in this book, you are invited to look within your own inner mirror as you explore the beautiful and sometimes complex reflections of your inheritance. Welcome to the Sisterhood of the Copper Mirrors!

---

9.   Arizal, *Likutei Torah* and *Sefer Halikutim*, Exodus 3:4.

chava
Mother of All Life

The Story of chava

Chava, the first woman (known in English as Eve), launched each of her children—all of humanity—on a course that requires us to heal what is wounded and make whole what is broken. The foundation of her story is in the story of creation.[1] In the beginning, God spoke the world into being. Every Hebrew letter carries a vibration or energy, and when letters are put together to form words, those words reveal the essence of the thing. The words for "speak" (*dover*) and "thing" (*davar*) in Hebrew have the same root letters. One of the first lessons in the Torah is the power of speech to create reality.

We learn that God created the world in six days. Perhaps a day was twenty-four hours, or perhaps a "day" in godly timing was millennia. All the elements of the universe were created, and then it was time: God made man. Adam was created, male and female *together in one being*, formed from the dust of the earth. (Earth is *adamah* in Hebrew: *Adam* comes from *adamah*.) This gives us the notion that there is a unity between man and woman. God breathed the breath of life into the nostrils of Adam, infusing that singular being with a living soul. (As we noted earlier, in Hebrew, the word for breath, *neshimah*, and the word for soul, *neshamah*,

---

1. The story of Chava can be found in Genesis 1:26–3:24.

are from the same root word.) Our very breath is an intimate gift. If you have ever witnessed a baby taking its first breath, you know the miraculous majesty in this most basic part of being.

Adam was put in the beautiful Garden of Eden to tend and protect it. In the garden were two special trees. One was the Tree of Life. From that tree, Adam was permitted to eat. The second was the Tree of Knowledge of Good and Evil. Though this tree is sometimes referred to simply as the Tree of Knowledge, it is a misunderstanding that changes the entire meaning of the story. It is the fruit of the Tree of Knowledge *of Good and Evil* that was forbidden to Adam. If all you hear is "Tree of Knowledge," it sounds pretty good. Who wouldn't want more knowledge? But this knowledge was confusing for someone who did not yet understand what evil was.

God made it clear that the consequence of eating the fruit of the Tree of Knowledge of Good and Evil would be death. But it was not called "Tree of Death," which would be the more obvious opposite of Tree of Life. (By the way, you may notice that no mention is ever made of an apple—in fact no specific fruit is named.)

At this point in the story, God gave Adam (who was still united male and female) the desire for a mate. God brought all the animals before Adam in pairs, to name them. Seeing that each animal had male and female mates, Adam got the idea that he would like a companion. So God put Adam into a deep sleep, and from his side (perhaps his rib), created the first woman—Chava. The Hebrew word used to tell us that God created or more literally "built" the first woman—*vayiven*—is related to the Hebrew root *binah*, which means "understanding." Woman was built with understanding. But as we shall soon see, the "understanding" that women were created with can be both a gift and a danger.

Adam calls his new companion "woman" (*ishah* in Hebrew) because she was taken from man (*ish*). He also gives her the name Chava, which comes from the same root as "life" (*chai*), because she was the mother of all life.

Now separate beings, Adam and Chava lived together in the Garden of Eden, a place of complete bliss. There was no such thing as regret. They were naked but not ashamed. There was only love and light and connection with All That Is. It was a good life.

Enter the snake. (Cue ominous music.) Don't picture a garden snake. This was a shrewd being with legs. The smooth-talking hipster serpent slinked up and engaged Chava, saying, "Hey there, didn't God say not to eat from any tree in the garden?"

Chava, wanting to be helpful, clarified that only the fruit of one tree was forbidden. However, she also inaccurately added that God told them they would die if they just touched it. Remember, God told Adam not to *eat* the fruit from the tree—nothing was said about touching it. According to the Midrash, Adam added this extra precaution when he explained God's commandment to the newly created woman.[2] The snake took advantage of her error. He pushed her up against the tree. Once she touched the tree and did not die, doubt came into the picture. He moved in closer and convinced Chava that eating from the tree and gaining the knowledge of good and evil would make her more like God.

Chava knew she was not supposed to eat this fruit, but she was seduced. She saw the delightful fruit and she desired the wisdom. She ate fruit from the Tree of Knowledge of Good and Evil.

She did not want to be alone in her new awareness, so she convinced Adam to eat some of the fruit too. Now their eyes were opened in a whole new way. There had been no evil in the world, but with the tasting of that fruit, they saw things from a different perspective. They were suddenly ashamed of being naked, and covered themselves with clothes made of fig leaves. Did they realize that nakedness would from then on be a potential source of pain and destruction?[3] Reading this story in Hebrew reveals something that the English translation does not. In Hebrew, the snake is described as *arum*, commonly translated as "cunning," and the snake is called

2.　*Genesis Rabbah* 19:3.
3.　Rashi, Genesis 3:7.

the most cunning of all animals of the field. When Adam and Chava find themselves ashamed of their nakedness, the same Hebrew word is used, *arum*. It is an interesting repetition of the theme of nakedness and an interesting connection between nakedness and deception. On one hand, "baring all" appears to be so open and forthright, while in reality, it does not call for depth at all.

They heard the voice of the Almighty and hid themselves from God's presence among the trees.

God called out to them, "Where are you?"

Now, God certainly knew where they were, so why ask? There is a divine kindness operating here. God was not asking for information but creating an opening to connect. God gave Adam and Chava a chance to come clean about what happened. Instead, Adam said he hid because he was naked.

Giving them another chance to be honest, the Eternal asked who told them they were naked, and then asked outright if they ate fruit from the forbidden tree. But neither one took responsibility for their actions. Adam pointed to Chava, reminding God she was the woman He created, and said she brought the fruit to him. When God turned to Chava, she blamed the snake for enticing her.

When you make a mistake, there are consequences. If you break a glass, you might have to pay for it, or at least be sure you clean up all the shards so that no one will be cut. Hurting someone emotionally requires an apology, perhaps learning how to be kinder or to communicate in a way that can be understood clearly. When Adam and Chava ate from the Tree of Knowledge of Good and Evil, the mystical damage was that evil was released into the world. The shattering release of evil that happened with that fateful act is exactly what each of us, as sparks of the original man and woman, is responsible to repair and heal. Since that first choice, humankind has known evil. We have faced it. We battle it in big and small ways within ourselves. But what did that first human know about evil? Some sources suggest that when Chava ate of the fruit, she actually had a deep understanding that if humanity were to battle the evil within them, the eventual return to the Garden of Eden would be even sweeter because it would have been earned.[4]

Adam, Chava, and the snake all had to face the consequences of their actions. Each received a punishment. The snake was cursed with having to crawl on its belly and with eternal hostility with humans. Chava's punishment was enduring painful childbirth and being ruled over by her husband. Adam's punishment was having to labor for his livelihood and then return to the dust from which he was created. The Eternal made Adam and Chava garments of animal skins and clothed them.

Now, speaking to the angels, God said that since Adam and Chava knew about evil, they couldn't be allowed to eat from the Tree of Life and live forever. God banished them (and all mankind after them) from this place of perfection. An angel with a flaming sword was set to guard the way to the Tree of Life. However, while this expulsion looked like a punishment, it was actually a blessing. What if man and woman had consumed from the Tree of Life after they ate from the Tree of Knowledge of Good and Evil? Mankind would have become immortal with the duality of good and evil as an eternal reality. We still live in a world of duality, but there is hope that we will repair the damage done by the release of evil in the world. Evil in the world is not eternal. That is the hope we take away from this story—that we can repair what was damaged and return to the wondrous state of living in the garden. Eating from the Tree of Life at this point would have made *this* reality—with evil existing within us—eternal. We were sent away for our own protection.

What if Chava had never even spoken to the serpent in the first place? Every woman has had that experience of being approached by someone and having a gut feeling that talking to that person would not be a good idea, but doing it anyway because she wants

---

4.   See Chana Weisberg, "Women and the Forbidden Fruit," https://www.chabad.org/parshah/article_cdo/aid/435969/jewish/Woman-and-the-Forbidden-Fruit.htm.

to be nice or polite. A major lesson Chava teaches us is the importance of setting boundaries.

Chava's Gift: Setting Boundaries

Think about your life. There are some things that you can clearly see
are dangerous, no doubt about it, and you'd never think of risking
something so life threatening. We put guardrails on stairways so
people don't fall. We have stoplights to keep us safe on the roads. We
teach our children safety by telling them never to follow a stranger
who wants to show them a cute puppy. When a child is too young
to understand the full danger or extent of evil in the world, we still
try to protect them using terms they can grasp. We protect them
by making a clear boundary.

Not all boundaries are so clear in life, so how do we distance
ourselves from what is dangerous? We build what the Torah calls
"fences." When we know where the edge of a minefield is, we give it
space and put up a fence with warning signs. The idea is to create a
buffer zone to put distance between what is dangerous or what can
hurt us—physically and also spiritually—and what is safe.

One useful guideline is to be clear about what you don't want.
Then, set the boundary—say no to what you don't want. Being strong
about setting boundaries is a problem for a lot of women. We have
been taught to be kind, and we know that kindness is a quality with
the power of understanding and the power to build. At the same
time, there are ideas and actions that must simply be closed off. You
may already know what some of those are for you in your life. There
are times when we can say no politely and kindly, and there are times
when we need to completely cut off the thing that encroaches on the
well-being of our lives and the lives of our families.

For example, a saleswoman approaches you in a department
store and offers to help you pick out a new wardrobe. "No, thank
you" will work as you keep on walking. That was easy. If someone
offers you easy money to set up a crack lab in your living room, the

answer is also an uncomplicated (popular television shows aside) "click"—by hanging up the phone. The next one may not be so easy: an old boyfriend tries to make contact online, but you are married. The popular culture might say that's fine; you should "stay friends" with him. But why is he even trying to connect? If you're not sure, ask the men in your life for insights about his possible motivations. You may find you need to set a clear boundary.

"Just say no" can be a good motto for some situations. There's a problem that can come up, though. When you say no, the asker may gently—or not so gently—prod you, "Well, why not?" *You are not obliged to provide an answer.* When someone doesn't take no for an answer, it could be a sign of wanting to control. Setting the boundary with clarity may involve grace in some situations, and other times it may involve significant adrenaline and determination. Finding your strength, your inner power to hold the boundaries, is important.

If you really want to fine-tune the concept of boundaries, consider that sometimes the boundaries you keep don't have anything to do with other people. What do *you* bring into your own life— your awareness, mind, emotions, and body? What environments are you creating for yourself (for example, what kind of music and friends are you spending time with; are you surrounded by clutter or clear space; and so on)? Are they really serving you? What are you watching online (is it fear based or uplifting, for example)? What are you eating and drinking (is it balanced or excessive)? What inner self-talk is happening (are you putting yourself down or taking leaps in the direction you want to head)? Do you allow yourself to let your thoughts run away with you in negative ways (ruminating on difficult past events or conversations)?

There's a story of a student who went to his teacher and great leader, the Maggid of Mezritch (an important rabbi in eighteenth-century Poland), and asked how he could control his stray thoughts. The Maggid told the student to go to Reb Ze'ev, another of his students. The student went to the home of Reb Ze'ev. It happened that it was just before Shabbat (the Jewish Sabbath, which lasts from Friday at sunset to Saturday after sunset). He heard people bustling in the home as he knocked on the door. No one answered. He knocked some more. No one answered. He finally realized he'd better go somewhere else to settle in for Shabbat, so he went to the synagogue and wound up sleeping there. After Shabbat, Reb Ze'ev invited the student to his home for the beautiful rituals and meal that usher out the Shabbat. They ate and had deep discussions; the environment was warm. Finally, the student spoke up and asked Reb Ze'ev, "Why didn't you welcome me when I came? I don't understand why you were cruel to me! The Maggid sent me to you to teach me how to control my stray thoughts!" Reb Ze'ev said, "Ah, but that lesson I taught you when you first arrived: *Just because there's a knock at the door doesn't mean you have to answer it.*"

You don't have to let every stray thought into your life. You may not be able to stop certain thoughts from "knocking," but you can set a boundary even within your own mind and thoughts.

As with any important quality, finding balance is not an exact science. Being clear about your values will help. What is most important to you? Where do your values come from—what is their source? Sometimes it's not about your values, it's about your energy and resources. One week you may have the strength to go that extra mile, and another week that same activity is simply over the top and will sap you. What are the priorities in your day, week, life? What are the goals that you want to achieve? Only you know, so getting honest with yourself is key. There are times when letting down the boundaries you set is important. Maybe you were sure you didn't want company, but someone you're very close with is in need, so you drop the boundaries this time. Another time, you may have to firmly but kindly tell a person you don't have the energy for whatever is being asked of you. It is always okay to tell people you need time to consider a request before you give an answer. Give yourself the space to do the inner inventory.

We all have fragments of Chava within us. She is the first archetypal woman. We are not just from her; we are part of her.

Chava's story in Torah is not about condemning women. This is about women standing up and taking responsibility to repair the particular things that we can fix in this world. This sounds drastic in a way, but it is exactly what we, as Jewish women, can and must do.

Reflections in Chava's Mirror: The Potential of Sexuality

The human body is an amazing creation: every nuance, every cell, every breath, every strand of fuzzy hair. There is a delicate balance that maintains health from bones and hormones on the inside to eyes and skin on the outside. By filling our senses or moving us about, the body's parts all enable us to create our outer reality. And the most titillating of all the elements of human physicality is sexuality. It sells, it motivates, it is used as a weapon, and it is used as an ultimate expression of loving.

Sexuality is a powerful energy. Like the power of any of the elements—fire, wind, earth, and water—if it is channeled for good and healing, it is good and healing. If it is unleashed and not respected, it will do damage. Some cultures use sexuality against women. There are strong influences in the popular culture today that objectify women's (and men's) bodies and value appearance over character and deeds. Some women are taught that their sexuality is their power, and they use it to manipulate. Sexuality can be about procreation. It can be used as a loving expression. In Judaism, sexuality within marriage has the potential to be a creative force for the highest soul connection.

The question is how you choose to work with this energy. I love the metaphor of a laser. The word *laser* is an acronym for "light amplification through stimulated electron radiation." Hang on—I'm going to explain. A laser basically takes microscopic particles (electrons) in a chamber and stimulates them. The electrons give off light (photons). Because that energy is concentrated, directed, and focused, it can become a laser light that cuts diamonds or performs surgeries!

We have a powerful sexual energy and it is up to us to use the energy in a way that is building this world with laser-like focus. Our bodies are sensual and sexual—not just the reproductive organs but all of us, from our hair to our skin. The soft brush of one hand against another can elicit intense responses. It is no small thing that the Jewish teachings on sexuality understand that power and honor it.

There are so many misconceptions about the Jewish perspective on sexuality. The most damaging falsehood is that Judaism treats women as second class, God forbid! One of the reasons for this book is to tell the truth about the significant and cherished role that women have in Judaism.

The dignity of the Jewish woman—and all women—is paramount. A woman is not a sexual object used solely for the pleasure of a man, nor is she to be used solely for procreation. There are plenty of examples of men in Torah who took women to be used only as bodies, and their heavenly punishment was severe. In Judaism, a woman is a full partner in creating, building, repairing, and healing family, community, and the world. Traditionally, for reasons of modesty, conversations about sexuality are a private, delicate matter, and passed along one on one. In this generation of instant gratification and information overload, our teachings have been twisted and misunderstood. Our traditions and rituals have been confused with the teachings of other religions.

Some religions consider sexuality to be a source of sinfulness, and their spiritual leaders are forbidden to marry and enjoy sexual relations. Some worship sexuality and use it as a form of idolatry. Neither of those is the Jewish approach. In Judaism, sexual intimacy is part of a committed and purposeful marriage between a man and a woman. We're taught that marriage also includes the Divine Presence. The marital bed has the potential to be the holiest part of the relationship. It is the pleasurable union of body and soul.

In the Beit Hamikdash (the Holy Temple in Jerusalem, literally "House of the Sacred"), there was an inner chamber containing the Ark of the Covenant on which the Shechinah, the feminine Divine Presence, would rest. Only the High Priest could enter this sacred inner chamber—the "Holy of Holies." The intimacy between a husband and wife is considered the Holy of Holies within marriage. More than the Shabbat table, more than all the prayer books, this is the place where the highest spirituality and potential for creation can be expressed!

When Adam and Chava were created, they had a relationship that was pure and blissful. They connected in the highest way; it was sublime. The sin of eating fruit from the Tree of Knowledge of Good and Evil brought the struggle between good and evil into their being and into the world. Sexuality is a dramatic place for that struggle to play out: it can be the source of subjugation, horror, and pain; or it can be as it's meant to be, the source of the ultimate pleasure, comfort, and connection.

In Context

Hebrew words can reveal mystical secrets. The Hebrew word for "fire" is made up of two letters, *alef, shin* (אש, pronounced *esh*). These same two letters are the base for the words "man," *alef, yud, shin* (איש, pronounced *eesh*), and "woman," *alef, yud, shin, heh* (אישה, pronounced *eeshah*). The two extra letters, *heh* (ה) and *yud* (י), spell a name for God. This is a hint to the potential relationship between a man and a woman. When God is included in the relationship, the couple is fully "man and woman." When God is removed, it is like a fire that will eventually just burn itself out, leaving blackened destruction along its path.[5]

Sex in the framework of a loving marriage is where the highest potential for the sacred is found. Our Torah teaches that having sexual relations *with the right person, at the right time* is actually a

---

5. Talmud, *Sotah* 17a.

mitzvah (this word is often translated as "good deed," but it literally means commandment)! Under the *chuppah* (bridal canopy), a husband gives his new wife a marriage contract called a *ketubah*. It outlines what *his* obligations are to *her*. He must provide for her. Part of what is written in that contract has to do with providing for his wife sexually. It is called *onah*, which comes from the Hebrew word meaning "answer." A man should fulfill his wife's desires and satisfy her. This is a time of connection and divine pleasure. So the *right person* is your spouse.

Within a Torah environment, there is also a *right time* for a married couple to be together sexually, which has to do with the woman's monthly cycle. When a woman is menstruating and for seven days thereafter, she and her husband are forbidden to each other physically.

There is a natural rhythm or pulse in relationships—drawing close, pulling away, and then drawing close again. The distancing of the physical brings the opportunity to develop and deepen other aspects of the relationship between a husband and wife. It expands the focus to intellectual, emotional, or spiritual deepening. As we all know, people get busy and distracted. Couples can get into routines or go on autopilot. It can be all too easy to become desensitized to each other. Judaism has a mitzvah to resensitize a couple to each other using the woman's cycle.

For one week after her bleeding has ended, the wife counts seven days. (There are other aspects of the counting that are beyond the scope of this book.) On the seventh night the wife will immerse in the waters of a *mikveh* (ritual bath). A beautiful benefit is that the couple can get in sync with each other. In honoring the time of separation (called *niddah* in Hebrew), the physical source of great pleasure is forbidden and, not surprisingly, desire grows! With the cycle of the body comes the cycle of separation, immersion, and then union.

Ritual Waters

Mikveh is a sacred ritual that the women of our tribe have been performing for literally thousands of years. The waters of the *mikveh* have a direct connection to the waters of the Garden of Eden! If you are a Jew today, there is no doubt that your great-great-grand-mothers immersed in the renewing waters of the *mikveh,* and in some generations this ritual was observed at great risk during times of persecution. Ancient ruins in Israel have revealed the biblical standard of construction that we use to this day. The *mikveh* can be a natural body of water, or a constructed, spa-like pool that is connected to a natural source of water.

It is not a bath that you wash up in. Before a woman immerses, she bathes, washes and combs her hair thoroughly, trims her nails, brushes her teeth—every part of her body is cleaned, so that there is nothing between her and the water. No makeup, no nail polish, no jewelry, no belly button rings or lint! An attendant (female) is present to help her make sure she is truly ready. (In cases when certain items are difficult to remove, a rabbi should be consulted.)

It is a time of clearing and cleansing. With the cleaning of the body, a woman can also have the intention of cleaning her emotions or thoughts, letting go of what does not serve her. The preparation itself can be a beautiful time of release.

The most painful misconception about the ritual bath is that women are somehow impure or dirty during or after their period. *Not true.* The High Priest would also immerse in the waters of the *mikveh* before he would go into the Holy of Holies. It was not because he was "dirty." Rather, he needed to purify himself spiritually before undertaking the most elevated spiritual worship. Another time that people used the ritual bath during the times of the Holy Temple was after contact with a dead body. Women use the *mikveh* for a combination of these two reasons. First, a woman after menstruation has had contact with a sort of death: menstrual blood is the sign that the potential of life was lost, as there was no conception. Moreover, the woman is purifying herself spiritually for an elevated spiritual and physical relationship with her husband.

Immersing in the waters of the *mikveh* is a time of blessing. It is a time and place of prayer, connection, and renewal. It's not unusual for a woman to sense generations past and future. Coming out of the water of the *mikveh* has been likened to rebirth from the waters of the womb.

Most *mikvehs* today are beautiful and nurturing places. It wasn't always like that. There were women in Eastern Europe who had to chip through icy rivers in order to fulfill the mitzvah. In Russia, where it was illegal to perform Jewish rituals, there were secret *mikvehs* that very few knew about. Even today, there are women who travel for hours in order to immerse.

All the preparation, traveling, and immersion the woman does for this sacred ritual is not taken for granted by her husband, who has also been keeping track of the days in his own way. The couple both make "*mikveh* night" a special priority for being together on every level.

The time of a husband and wife being together is intended to be an oasis of pleasure, joy, and connection. The love that is shared creates a light that radiates into all aspects of their relationship and ripples into the world to manifest in beautiful ways.

Sadly, not every marriage functions well. Though this short section cannot possibly cover everything about sexuality, it is important to know that there are other times when sexual intimacy is not allowed even within marriage! If a woman is drunk—forbidden! If you're angry with your spouse, or worse, planning to get divorced—no! That is not a time to be together.

All of the Jewish teachings around intimacy are intended to sensitize a couple to each other on every level and bring peace into the sacred territory of elevating physical intimacy. In this way, whether we are literally giving birth or metaphorically bringing life into the world, women have the opportunity to return to the garden and be like Chava, the mother of all life.

Sarah
Beauty and Nobility

The Story of Sarah

When Sarah was born she was given the name Yiska,[1] which means "seer" or "visionary." This name described her well, as she later became a prophetess. She had an especially close relationship with the Divine. It is said that she was a reincarnation of Chava.[2] She came into the world with a mission to bring light where there was darkness and knowledge where there was ignorance. She is also said to be one of the four most beautiful women in the Bible.[3] Her name changed twice during her life, reflecting her growth and evolving mission.

The first time her name changed was when she married Avraham (Abraham), who called her Sarai, which means "my princess." (He was called Avram at the beginning of this story. His name also changes, as will be discussed below. We'll only use the names Avraham and Sarah in the telling of Sarah's story here.)

Who was Avraham? Avraham was our first patriarch, the first Hebrew. Though he was the son of an idol worshipper,[4] Avraham sought truth, rejecting the worship of any one thing (such as the

---

1. The story of Sarah can be found in Genesis 11:29–24:67.
2. Rabbi Yechiel Heilprin, *Seder Hadorot*.
3. Talmud, *Megillah* 15a.
4. Joshua 24:2.

sun or moon or stars) or person (such as the ruler of his time, Nimrod) as a god. He developed a relationship with the Creator of the world. He brought the idea to the world that there is only one God. It could sound so simplistic, but within the simplicity of One is the complexity of all of creation.

There is a story from the Midrash that is commonly taught to young children about the young Avraham that reveals something of his nature to us. Avraham's father was an idol maker. He was minding his father's store of the newest, hottest statues. When people came to buy idols, he would ask them how they could possibly worship something that was just one day old. One time a woman came to bring an offering to the gods. He placed the offering in front of the largest idol, smashed all the other idols in the shop, put a stick in front of the big statue, and told his father that the big idol had destroyed the small ones because it wanted the offering. Of course, his father knew that was ridiculous, and Avraham challenged his father right there.[5]

The lesson of this story—just one of the many stories of Avraham—might sound fundamental to our modern sensibilities. Perhaps as Jews, we like to tell the story of Avraham smashing idols to our children to empower them. We want our children to understand that our Source cannot be limited to the physicality of stone or wood. Perhaps we are empowering our children to seek truth themselves, to beware of the traps of any popular culture, and to seek to know God from within. Our spiritual journey begins as early as when we hear the first stories, so we can wake up to the yearning within.

Avraham's chosen life partner and soul mate was Sarah. She became our first matriarch. The Torah teaches us that Sarah was actually a greater prophet than Avraham.[6]

It is said that when a man and woman unite as husband and wife, they become greater than they could have been separately.

---

5.   Midrash, *Bereishit Rabbah*, 38:13.
6.   Rashi, Genesis 21:12.

Avraham and Sarah knew that they were on a mission—a mission so large it would change all humanity. Their mission was to bring monotheism, the knowledge of one God, into the world. This idea was for the whole world, not just the Jewish nation. Three major world religions honor Avraham as a patriarch. His influence was not by the sword and never by force. Avraham and Sarah were the parents of our nation. Every Jew (*every* Jew, including those who convert) is their descendant.

Avraham and Sarah lived in the desert in tents. But don't picture them camping. They were wealthy, and their tents were large and substantial. They had servants. They were known for their hospitality, always inviting and welcoming strangers. To fulfill their mission to awaken humanity to knowing that there is one Creator, Avraham taught the men, and Sarah taught the women.

Sarah's Tent

Sarah's tent was not some dingy hovel. She was not relegated to hidden or second-class status. Her tent was a place where women were nurtured and taught according to their sensibilities and sensitivities. Sarah's tent was a place known for its mystical properties:[7]

- The Shechinah, the feminine Presence of God, rested over her tent in the form of clouds.
- The Shabbat candles she lit on Friday evenings stayed lit the entire week.
- The challah bread she prepared stayed fresh all week.

These are the same miracles said to take place in the Beit Hamikdash, which became the center of the Jewish nation and Jewish worship. Yet this Temple would not be built for hundreds of years from the time of Sarah. From this we understand that *the home is the primary place of holiness* and that the Temple took its cues from the tent of Sarah, our mother, our first matriarch.

---

7. Rashi, Genesis 24:67.

Sarah's tent is also the model for every Jewish woman's home. To this day, Jewish women around the world kindle lights in their homes before sunset on Friday, the onset of the Shabbat, and prepare braided loaves of bread (which can be a mystical experience in its own right). The love and warmth each woman brings into her home is a spark and reflection of the light of the Shechinah.

God promised Avraham that a great nation would come from him. But Sarah was barren. She was well into old age and had no children. How could she be the mother of a nation if she could not bear a child? Sarah was the first woman of the Tanach who carried the pain of barrenness. She knew God had promised Avraham that a nation would come from him, and yet, she could not conceive.

Journeys

God sent Avraham and Sarah away from the land of their birth into a new land. They left all that they knew for this new place where God told them to settle. On the simplest level, they picked up their stuff and moved. The deeper meaning is that they were being challenged to let go of what they were in order to become something more. As we journey through life's experiences, especially on an awakening spiritual path, we are always being called upon to deepen as well. Embarking on a path of spiritual growth takes courage, and the destination can never be seen or understood from the starting place. Avraham and Sarah had the fundamental strength to journey into the unknown toward something greater. We can walk in their footsteps. Such a journey does not come without trials and ordeals, though. This is a theme throughout all the stories of Torah—that tests and tribulations transform us and refine character.

After a short time in this new Promised Land, there was a famine. Avraham and Sarah left to travel down to Egypt. It was known that the men of Egypt would kill a man to take his wife, but with a brother, they might bargain to purchase her. It was also known that any woman of particular beauty would be brought before Pharaoh (the title given to the monarchs of ancient Egypt). So Sarah hid

during their travels into Egypt, and Avraham asked her to say she
was his sister if she was discovered. Indeed she was, and, being
especially beautiful, she was brought to Pharaoh's palace. Pharaoh
wanted to take Sarah, but she did not fall prey to his evil intentions.
God afflicted Pharaoh, and it became clear to Pharaoh that Sarah was
Avraham's wife. Pharaoh quickly arranged to send them on their way
with generous gifts of wealth. On a mystical level it is written that
Sarah was a reincarnation of Chava, and Pharaoh was a reincarnation
of the serpent from the Garden of Eden.[8] This was an opportunity to
repair Chava's error and preserve the proper boundaries.

Hagar

This pharaoh went even further than rectifying the serpent's evil.
He saw the power and spiritual connection of Avraham and Sarah.
The Midrash tells us that Pharaoh and his daughter, the Princess
Hagar, agreed that it would be a greater experience for Hagar to
serve in the house of Avraham than rule as a princess of Egypt.
Hagar willingly became a student and handmaiden to Sarah. Hagar
was a princess of Egypt who had been steeped in royalty, albeit of a
depraved nature. She courageously abandoned that life to be close
to Sarah, a woman of the truest nobility. How powerful it must have
been for Hagar to be around Sarah!

Avraham and Sarah had been told that a nation would come
from them. How could that happen if Sarah was barren? Do you
think that surrogate parenting and adoption are new concepts? King
Solomon's teaching that "there is nothing new under the sun" is well
known. Sarah thought the nation could be built *physically* through
Hagar while she, Sarah, would raise the child *spiritually*. Sarah
selflessly asked the beautiful Princess Hagar to be with Avraham,
and she asked Avraham to take Hagar as a second wife to conceive
a child in order to begin to build the nation.

Hagar conceived right away. With that conception, something within Hagar shifted. Her attitude toward Sarah changed.

---

8. *Seder Hadorot*, "Adam."

She became haughty. Hagar interpreted the contrast of her quick conception to Sarah's barrenness to mean that Sarah was not as elevated as she. It is very tricky territory when you try to guess God's intentions and plans. Hagar believed she was meant to lead. She was wrong. It was not Avraham alone leading the nation; Sarah was his full partner. Sarah was not replaceable. In letting Hagar know her place and holding on to her own space, Sarah was harsh with Hagar. Hagar was upset and ran away into the desert.

While in the desert, an angel came to Hagar. Hagar may be one of the more misunderstood characters of the Torah. She challenged Sarah, and since Sarah is our mother, it's easy to feel protective of her. Yet, we see here that Hagar saw and spoke with angels! She was surely in an elevated place—just not *Sarah's* place. The angel spoke to Hagar, called her Sarah's handmaid and asked her where she was coming from and where she was going.

If you look closely at this conversation, the angel was not asking where Hagar was physically located. In fact, there they were together in the middle of who knows where, and the angel had no problem finding her! So maybe the angel said it with a meaning more like, "What were you thinking?" It was a question prompting Hagar to consider where she was spiritually, not physically. Hagar told the angel that she was running away from her mistress. The angel told her to go back and to yield to her. The angel, speaking as a messenger from God, continued that Hagar would have more descendants than could be counted. The angel told Hagar she would conceive and exactly what kind of man her son would be: "Behold, you will conceive and bear a son; and you will name him Yishmael, because the Lord has heard your affliction. And he shall be a wild ass of a man; his hand will be against every man and every man's hand against him; and he will reside in the face of all his brothers."

Hagar responded to God's angel in awe and she returned to Sarah. Just as the angel said she would, Hagar bore a son, Yishmael (Ishmael), who would be the father of a nation. There is more to the story of Hagar; we'll get back to her.

At this point, God changed Avram's name to Avraham and told him he would be the father of many nations and that kings would descend from him. God and Avraham had a contract that reaches into all the generations of Jews. He promised Avraham and his offspring the Land of Israel as an everlasting possession. The responsibility of the Jews in this contract is to live in faithfulness to the Eternal Oneness we call God.

God also changed the name of Avraham's wife, to reveal that she had become something greater: she was no longer to be called Sarai ("my princess") but Sarah, the princess of the nation, with the same promise and blessing of nations and kings of nations rising from her.

God told Avraham that Sarah would yet conceive. Avraham *laughed* (pay attention here, we have a theme going on)—with joy. Sarah would have a son the next year, God revealed, and this son would be called Yitzchak (Isaac). The name Yitzchak comes from the same root as the word for laughter! They were also told that the covenant would continue through Yitzchak. God reassured Avraham that Hagar's son Yishmael (whom Avraham prayed for and clearly loved!) would father twelve princes to become a great nation. But Sarah's son, Yitzchak—who would be born by that time the next year—would maintain the covenant and be the next patriarch of the Jewish nation. God and Avraham "cut" a deal—Avraham and all the men in his house circumcised themselves on that day. Avraham was ninety-nine years old at the time. This act established the covenant. To this day, circumcision of boys (usually at eight days old) remains a sign of the eternal connection between the Jewish people and God.

Angels Visit

Three days later, while Avraham was recovering from the circumcision, three angels who appeared as men approached his tent. Avraham ran to welcome his guests. (He influenced his descendants with the quality of enthusiastically welcoming guests with warmth, a mitzvah that many aspire to practice today.) Here is a beautiful lesson from the Torah. Avraham offered them bread and water but actually provided a much grander welcome. Everyone from Avraham's tent got involved in the preparation of food. A lavish meal was served. From this seemingly small aspect of the story, we learn it is best to *say little and do much.*

In the tent, the angels asked Avraham, "Where is your wife?" He answered, "She is in her tent." Two simple lines with deep significance. Why is this small conversation so important to us? The angels knew where Sarah was. So why did they ask? The angels wanted Avraham to note Sarah's great traits. Or maybe the conversation was recorded so *we* would note her traits. Sarah was humble, modest, and unpretentious. Do not read that as weak or cowering. Let's breathe some life into this story and consider the possibility of what was happening behind the scenes. Sarah was in the middle of the desert on a scorching hot day. Guests came and she managed the production of an extravagant meal. Most of us have entertained and know the work involved in hosting a meal, even with help. Sarah was hosting in an era without electricity, food processors, blenders, or grocery stores to run out to and pick something up at the last minute. Oh, yeah, and all the men had just been circumcised and were still recovering! When you do that kind of work, it might be nice to be around for a little credit. But Sarah left the scene of her labor. Make no mistake here. In that generation other nations considered Avraham as the king of the Hebrews; Sarah was his match and soul mate in nobility. She stood as the leader and spiritual guide of the women who were following their teachings. She didn't need the attention of any man to validate her worth. *Is it possible that standing in inner power and confidence is the truest power of all?*

Conception and Misconceptions

Though Sarah was out of sight, she could hear all that was being said. The visiting angels told Avraham that at this time next year

Sarah would have a son. Remember that Sarah was well past her childbearing years. When Sarah heard this, she laughed and said, "After I have withered shall I become rejuvenated? And my husband is old!"

After Sarah laughed, God asked Avraham, "Why is it that Sarah laughed, saying: 'Will I really bear a child? I am aged.'" Did you notice that God only mentioned that Sarah noted *her* age? Was that a white lie of omission from the Master of the World? The very profound and eternal lesson? *Keeping peace in the home between husband and wife is paramount.* God sets the example. How vigilant we must be in choosing our words carefully regarding husbands and wives. How conscientious we must be in keeping peace within our own relationships!

This story also gives important hints to understanding relations in marriage. The intimacy between Avraham and Sarah was still a vibrant part of their lives. Just in case you weren't sure, intimacy is meant to be an expression of great love, in and of itself! We learn from the story of Avraham and Sarah that "conception" is more than a child in the womb. We are taught that Avraham and Sarah conceived the *souls* of all converts to Judaism.[9] They are our first role models in relationships, in honor, in commitment, and in love. Their love was dedicated to radiating spirituality into the world. On a spiritual level, even when the conception of a baby isn't "in the stars," intimacy is still an act of divine creation and conception.

Contrast this loving precedent to the ways some cultures or religions throughout time have viewed sexual relations. Even today, some practice female genital mutilation, destroying a woman's ability for pleasure in intimacy, often causing permanent pain. Some religions require their spiritual leaders to lead a life of separation and celibacy. They turn their backs to the elevation that can come from the pleasure and bonding of intimacy between a husband and wife. Other cultures or societies worship sexuality as an end in itself, allowing women, men, or children to be sacrificed or used as

---

9. *Zohar* 1:79a. See also Ramban, Genesis 12:6; *Shulchan Aruch*, Even Ha'ezer 129:20.

commodities. Judaism sanctifies the relationship between husband and wife. As discussed in the chapter on Chava, we are taught that sexuality has the potential to be an act of holiness. It certainly is a means of creating life, but there are also spiritual elements in relations between a husband and wife.

Abduction Redux

As the story progressed, there was unrest in the region. This was when and where the story of Sodom and Gomorra happened—but that's not for this book. Avraham and Sarah moved to another part of the country, Gerar, to continue their work. There was a repetition of the abduction that happened in Egypt. Unlike Pharaoh in Egypt, this king had a dream to warn him. The king of Gerar captured Sarah anyway, and his household was punished with a plague. Again, Sarah was returned to her husband, along with gifts. Avraham prayed for the healing of the king and his household, and the effects of the plague healed. This plays into what is to follow: though Sarah again avoided being taken sexually (with the help of the plague), she would be accused of being intimate with the king of Gerar.

Finally, Sarah conceived. She gave birth to a son and, as God instructed them, they named him Yitzchak. Because of her advanced age, some people did not believe that Sarah really gave birth to Yitzchak. To prove that she did, women brought their babies so Sarah could nurse them.[10] The Midrash also tells us there were false rumors that when Sarah was kidnapped in Gerar, she had relations with the king, and Yitzchak wasn't really Avraham's son. But Yitzchak was the spitting image of his father, no doubt there! The baby was given a *brit* (covenantal circumcision) at eight days old. Sarah proclaimed that God had brought joy and laughter to her and everyone who heard about this incredible birth, the child of her old age who would be next in line to build the Nation of Israel.

10. Rashi, Genesis 21:7.

Listen to Her Voice

Meanwhile, Hagar's son Yishmael had grown into a young man. It is written in Torah that Yishmael mocked Sarah. He was indeed the "wild ass of a man" that the angel predicted he would be. (If you were to continue your study of this topic through the texts available, you'd find that Yishmael returned to righteousness as an adult, and perhaps even grew close again with Yitzchak.)

It was clear to Sarah that Yishmael would be a wicked influence on Yitzchak. He had to go. Sometimes in life we have to do very hard things, things we would rather not do, but if we don't take a strong stand, more damage will be done. We have all had the experience of knowing deep inside that we should or should not do something. Ignoring clear warnings can have disastrous results. It was clear to Sarah that in order for Yitzchak to grow into the man who could father the Jewish nation, he would need to be in an environment that was uncorrupted and moral. She approached Avraham to send Yishmael away. Avraham clearly loved Yishmael, his son from Hagar. Avraham didn't know how to deal with that sticky situation. So he asked God directly for guidance. God answered, "*Listen to her voice*; do everything that Sarah tells you." How important it is for husbands and wives to understand each other's wisdom and really listen. Sarah's wisdom here was beyond her ego, her comfort, and her love for her son. Her vision was for the building of the Jewish nation, and Yishmael's influence was not tolerable.

Avraham did send Yishmael away, along with his mother Hagar. In the desert, as their water ran out, Hagar left her son so she would not see him die. Yishmael prayed to be saved. The Midrash records that angels argued with God not to save him, knowing what his descendants would be like and the evil things they would do against the Jewish nation.[11] But God judged Yishmael *as he was in that moment.* God opened Hagar's eyes and she saw a well. They were both saved. This is a significant teaching about the way God

---

11. Midrash, *Genesis Rabbah* 53:14.

judges us from moment to moment, in the moment! Where you are right *now* is what matters more than the past or the future.

The Binding of Isaac and Sarah's Death

Next the Torah relates the complex story of God asking Avraham to sacrifice Yitzchak. While not directly the story of Sarah, the story of the "Binding of Isaac," in Hebrew called the Akeidah, is one of the fundamental chapters of Jewish history. It set the tone of what God does and does not require of the Jewish people for all time. The teaching of this story is so important, so critical, that it is read in our daily prayer service. It is also the Torah portion that is read each and every Rosh Hashanah (Jewish new year), the day our souls come before the heavenly court for judgment. It is also during this dramatic event that Sarah passes to the next world.

Yitzchak grew into a young man. God told Avraham to bring Yitzchak to an altar as a sacrifice! It's important to understand that at that time, human sacrifice was the norm for many cultures. On a deep level, Avraham was being tested, challenged to do something that was impossible for him to do. It was not only about his love for his son. How could God tell him to do this after the promise that a nation would be built through this son?

This test wasn't designed to see if Avraham would pass it; God already knew what would happen. But *tests from Hashem reveal to the person who is being tested what they are made of.* In the process, there is growth. Avraham bound Yitzchak on an altar, and only at the moment when he had the knife raised to strike the final blow did a heavenly voice tell him to sacrifice a ram and not his son. The heavenly voice called out the promises of a nation that would be a blessing to all the nations.

There would be no human sacrifice. The core value taught through this story, this precedent that set our nation apart, is the highest regard for human life. We may think this can be taken for granted, but make no mistake: while in many cultures and at far too many times throughout history the significance of life has been disregarded, this value has been upheld within our nation for millennia.

Though the voice of Yitzchak is very limited in this story, our commentaries reveal that he was not a passive victim.[12] He knew full well what was happening and understood the import of his almost-sacrifice.[13]

And where did this take place? Exactly on the spot where the future Temple would be built in Jerusalem. If you visit the Western Wall in Jerusalem, you will be standing near the spot where Avraham bound his son for a sacrifice.

At the end of the story of the Akeidah, Sarah died. Our sages and teachers note that when the Torah puts one event next to another, it indicates a connection, and Sarah's death is no exception. There are several Midrashic stories explaining why she died at this point. Perhaps it was the voice of the Satan causing doubt, or the shock of fear, or even a shock of relief. We cannot know for certain exactly what caused Sarah's death.

Though God had promised the land to Avraham, the Torah goes into detail about Avraham negotiating and purchasing the place he would bury his wife. This ancient place is known today and is called Me'arat Hamachpelah. In English it's called Cave of the Patriarchs, but the Hebrew name tells the full story since *machpelah* means "doubled" and refers to both the matriarchs and the patriarchs. Adam and Chava were buried there, as were Avraham and Sarah, Yitzchak and Rivka, and Yaakov and Leah, whose stories follow. Even today Jews go there to pray to God in the merit of these ancestors.

So Avraham went to bury his wife.

We are given a hint of the depth of love between Avraham and Sarah at her funeral. In this world, everyone suffers and endures pain. It's part of life. Everyone has to grieve. When Sarah

---

12. Midrash, *Genesis Rabbah* 56:4.
13. This is not an easy story. This is a simplified version, and it is worthy of deeper study to discover the complex layers of love and the foundation that was set for our nation!

died, Avraham grieved for her. In every Torah scroll, in the word that tells us that Avraham cried, we find one letter printed smaller than all the rest. This is meant to get our attention, to make us take notice of a message. Through that one small letter, we are taught that there is a world of grief that could not be written about. Who can understand that kind of grief unless they have experienced it? It is a private place between the griever and God.

When someone is grieving, there are no words; only love and being present can comfort in a time like that. My mother shared the story of when her sister died. She sat the traditional week of mourning called shivah in her home. Her rabbi came to visit. She said to him, "I just can't stop crying." The rabbi told her that in those times when the waves of grief come over you, God is coming close to comfort you.

Sarah's Gift: Standing in Dignity

One theme you'll find in this book is that often the Hebrew word for a quality or concept has more dimensions than the English word. This is true for two words that describe dignity: *anavah* and *tzniut*.

Anavah is usually translated as "humility." We could consider this to be the way one feels inside, which is expressed through how we behave in the world. *Tzniut* is usually translated as "modesty." We could consider modesty to be the outward expression (such as how we dress) that reflects our inner world.

The English words fail us when tapping into the power of these concepts. Modesty and humility do *not* mean timid, self-conscious, frumpy, bashful, low self-esteem, mousy, tentative, ashamed, or fearful. No. What are the positive descriptions of modesty or humility? Think unpretentious. The English word *humility* comes from the same root as the word *humiliation*, and that is where it fails, because humility is not about living in a state of humiliation. Someone who is coming from a place of humility is not putting herself in the center of the world, but she does keep herself in the balance. Some people refer to the "me generation." You know the expression: "It's all about me!" When someone is practicing *anavah*/humility and *tzniut*/modesty, she does not put the focus on or call attention to herself. These concepts are about balance, and that leads to a greater good.

Anavah (Humility)

Humility is about understanding your place in the world. No matter how rich, good-looking, smart, or strong any person is, we understand that mankind as a whole and each one of us as individuals are like "the dust of the earth." The whole earth, from a heavenly perspective, is like a speck of dust in the universe. Understanding this helps us to remember not to be too full of ourselves! At the same time, thinking of ourselves as nothing but dust can be depressing.

The balance to this is to think, "The world was created for me!" You are unique and important, and all that happens is designed exclusively for you. The idea is to keep perspective. This balance contains the ultimate in worthiness ("the world is created for me") while keeping the perspective of our place in the limitlessness of the universe and all of creation.

How does humility come into play in everyday life? Consider interpersonal relationships. Positive psychology puts it this way: "You can be right or you can be loving." That means there has to be a nullification of the egoistic self—you'll give up being "right" and humble yourself (like the dust of the earth)—for the sake of being in the relationship with peace. When conflict arises, sometimes people take on the position of being "right." We've all done this, and it's usually disastrous. When you dig your heels in to be "right," you either have to eat crow, or you hurt or embarrass someone else. On the other hand, this is not about dropping all boundaries and being a *shmatteh* (Yiddish for "rag") to be walked all over. It's not about putting yourself down, retreating from your God-given talents, or diminishing your worth. It is a place of profound balance between nullifying the ego's pride and at the same time honoring the integrity of the spark of divinity that animates you.

Let's not confuse being right with being *righteous*. Being righteous is returning a lost object, or being kind to someone who is feeling alone, or saying no to an unethical practice. Having to be right can be about ego and usually comes at someone else's expense: "I'm right and you're wrong." (Hint: that will not build relationships. Would you rather be "right" or living in peace?)

True humility (*anavah*) is perhaps the most powerful balance of ego. When you stand inside yourself in that balance, you are standing in your truest power. If you're out of balance on one side ("I'm no good, stupid, ugly," etc.) or the other ("I'm better, smarter, prettier," etc.), then you are not in your true power. One side represents the power and potential you are born with ("the world was created for me"), the other is the power of the Creator ("I am the dust of the earth"). You are a spark of the Divine! Yes, you are of the Divine. You are a small spark of something great and infinite. It's about perspective!

One way to approach an understanding of humility is to consider the advantages you have in life with gratitude, and at the same time to be compassionate in understanding that not everyone has had your education, connections, or support. There is a beautiful metaphor. We humans are like drops of water compared to the ocean that is God. While one person might seem so much richer or smarter or whatever, the drop that they are isn't all that different from the drop you are.

There's a story about a great rabbi in Jerusalem, in the days when streetlights were just beginning to be installed. He walked outside to see the new streetlight they put near his home. Now, he had moved to Israel from a country in Europe that had streetlights. It was not the first time he had ever seen one. Still, he seemed so intrigued with it, walking nearer to the streetlamp, checking the ground, and looking up. Then he would move farther away, again looking up and looking at the ground. His students wanted to know what he was studying. Why was he so intrigued with a street lamp and his shadow? He explained. The farther you are from the light, the longer your shadow. The closer you are, the shorter your shadow. The shadow is like the ego. That is how Moshe could be the most modest of men;[14] he was so close to God's light.

Sarah was confident enough in herself that she did not need to be in the limelight. We know that Avraham and Sarah were exceptionally wealthy. We know that Sarah was extraordinarily beautiful. But Sarah did not need to *display* her wealth or her beauty. She did not deny who she was. She did not dumb herself down. She did not flaunt her beauty. This character trait sets a tone for us to measure how we hold ourselves.

Tzniut (Modesty)

Standing with dignity is also about how we present ourselves. There are many levels to this: physically, intellectually, verbally, and so on. The value of modesty has been a Jewish theme throughout time. A physically modest woman is one who knows the power and allure of her body and her nature. She chooses a dignified manner of dress that honors her whole self—not objectifying or degrading herself by flaunting her sexual beauty. She stands tall in herself without shame. That is her inner power, and it is even empowering to those around her! An intellectually modest person will be aware of those around her and will not make a show of her wit at the expense of others. An accomplished woman will not brag about all she's done. She may even hide it, depending on the situation. This consciousness is partly about protecting yourself and primarily about caring for those around you with sensitivity.

Here is an extreme example: imagine the most magnificent banana split, complete with hot fudge and whipped cream. Enjoy it! But you don't eat it while you are sitting with someone who is hooked up to tubes and machines in the last hours of her life. It's

---

14. "Now the man Moses was very humble, more than all the men on the face of the earth," Numbers 12:3.

just not the time and place to ooh and aah over ice cream. You get the idea.

How does this work in more subtle areas today? We are so bombarded with the notion that for a woman to have value, she must be young and provocative. The programming starts early. Think Disney princesses, by and large helpless, with inhumanly proportioned features and body shapes. It continues in anatomically unrealistic photoshopped fashion images and department store mannequins that do not represent the true form of a woman. Fashion trends reveal more and more skin and undergarments and call attention to the body in provocative ways through printed designs and words. This reduces women to their body parts. Measuring worth through skin texture, length of eyelashes, or waist and breast size contributes to the objectification of women. Remember, modesty isn't about being dowdy or dumpy—it's about seeking balance. I have seen a T-shirt marketed for young girls with the words "You know you want me." Prepubescent girls do not want to put out sexual messages or invite sexual advances. What message does wearing such a T-shirt wire up in a young girl's awareness about her value as a female?

Whole industries are built on creating provocative images of women and using those images to sell products ranging from trucks and beer to watches and luxury cars. The cosmetic, fashion, and entertainment industries have infiltrated our minds, telling us what is acceptable and desirable. We're told what we need to wear, drive, and carry to be of value. It's not just modern or Western culture that objectifies or seeks to control how women dress. For centuries in China, little girls as young as four years old would have their feet bound. This was an excruciatingly painful process that broke their bones and deformed their feet to keep them small, which was considered a way to render women more erotic. And of course, a woman with deformed feet cannot run away. Perhaps you've seen the striking photos of tribeswomen who wear stacks of thick metal rings that lengthen their necks. The rings actually push down on the clavicles, causing deformity. Is that the beauty of exotic majesty?

Opinions vary when it comes to the idea of modesty, and the word itself can turn up the heat in discussions. This is such an important and foundational issue in Torah. In Hebrew the word for "face" is *panim*. It comes from the word that means "inside," *p'nim*. It is in the eyes and face that one can see what is inside another person. Have you heard about micro expressions? Our faces reveal what is really happening—sadness, joy, surprise, fear. We are not meant to cover our faces, as is done is some cultures. Modesty is not about hiding. It is about the freedom to express the truest essence of your soul. It could be that an overemphasis on the external attributes will actually prevent others from seeing the inner soul. (Consider this if you're looking for a soul mate.) Feeling beautiful and looking your best is a wonderful experience, but if it's *only* about the body, if it's only about attracting attention from the outside, the inner experience will be overlooked, and that's where the richest treasures are.

Reflections in Sarah's Mirror: Nobility

Let's start with what nobility from a Jewish perspective is *not*. It is not haughty. It is not a feeling of being "better than" others. Nobility is something that is inherited. We have inherited the nobility of our matriarchs and patriarchs. As Jews, our nobility is not about ruling over others. It is about the goodness, integrity, generosity, and selflessness of service.

It is about rising up to become our best selves!

As we learned, Sarah's name means "princess." She was considered a royal matriarch of the Hebrew nation. Her mission was to build the nation. What was she building, exactly? It certainly was not about gathering a large number of followers. God made it clear that the Jewish nation would never be large in proportion to the peoples of the world. The total world population of Jews is *a fraction of a percent.* Jews who live in predominantly Jewish neighborhoods may forget just how tiny a minority we are in the world.

So what was Sarah's mission, which we carry on today? The Jewish mission is to be light bearers. That is the service. Standing in nobility means rising up in the face of darkness. Nobility means standing up for what is righteous. Nobility is courageously serving, stepping forward in large and small ways to build the nation. It means clinging to what is good, just, and moral. How do we know what is good or just or moral? The Torah is a brilliant source whose true richness is only revealed through in-depth study. If you are a Jewish woman, you have concepts of morality in your bones. You may take it for granted that all people must know what is right and moral. There are movements today about taking pride in yourself or your group. Nobility is not about pride. It is focused on a bigger picture of service.

The nobility you carry in your soul is a gift, and it is also a responsibility to see the bigger picture. It is a kind of power. Genuine nobility expressed with modesty and humility is all about service. It is a positive force. It enables you to set an example, uplifting those in your sphere of influence, if they are paying attention. (You may be very surprised who is watching!)

Sarah had miraculous signs take place in her tent confirming her mission, but she still needed to speak up to keep her son safe in his home. It could not have been easy for Sarah to tell her beloved husband to send away his oldest son. She could not stay silent when action needed to be taken. What Sarah teaches us about speaking out is that the power of speech must be used for a noble purpose. This wasn't about her wanting to get her way and ranting or throwing her weight around. Asking for Yishmael to leave was about protecting her son Yitzchak's well-being. Protecting her son was about setting a course for the nation that would descend from him. Difficult as it must have been, this was about a higher calling. We know it was an extraordinary circumstance because God told Avraham, "Listen to her voice."

So how do you know when it's the right time to find your voice and *use* it? It is not about letting off steam. It is not about wanting your way for your own sense of being right. Your truest voice comes from the mission of the soul. Not that every conversation is lofty. What if "you are what you say"? What if your words are so influential that through them you are shaping the world around you? How would you wield that power? Speaking up might be about setting boundaries, as Sarah needed to do in her home, or uplifting others, as Sarah did when she taught the women who came to be in her circle of influence. Being a teacher or an influencer requires finding your voice, your style, and your innermost vision and purpose.

If you wish to combine finding your voice with the energy of nobility, one question to ask yourself is, "Am I using my voice to serve?" Do you use your voice for service, to speak to God, to heal the hurt places within yourself and others? Do you use your voice to express love, to build your world, to set boundaries that keep you or others safe? I bless you, my dear reader, that you may find and know your voice. May you have the tone, wisdom, and courage to speak out when something must to be said so that others can hear what you have to say.

Rivka
Loving-Kindness in Action

The Story of Rivka

After Sarah died, Avraham knew it was time to put forth the effort needed to fulfill God's promise to build a nation through him and Sarah.[1] It was time to find a wife for their son Yitzchak. Avraham called his right-hand man, his servant Eliezer, to leave Canaan (the original name for what became the Land of Israel) and travel to Haran, where Avraham was raised, to find a soul mate, a bride, for Yitzchak. This would be the first arranged marriage mentioned in the Bible. But it was not a forced marriage, as you'll see. It was a marriage so full of love that people still use Yitzchak and Rivka (Rebecca) as models for a joy-filled, loving union based on mutual respect and awe.

Eliezer made an oath with Avraham regarding this mission. He was concerned about finding the right woman and whether she would agree to return with him. Avraham told Eliezer that he would not be asked to bring a woman back against her will, but made him promise not to take Yitzchak to Haran. He reassured him that there would be divine assistance, that God would send an angel to make sure the mission would be successful. Avraham also emphasized the importance of the connection to the land that God promised

---

1.   Rivka's story can be found in Genesis, chapter 24, 25:20–26:11, and chapter 27.

Avraham and his descendants. Avraham did not want Yitzchak to lose the spiritual elevation he had achieved from the experience of the trial of the Akeidah, when he was bound on an altar as a sacrifice to God (see the chapter on Sarah).

As Eliezer traveled with his entourage of camels and other manifestations of Avraham's wealth, he prayed to find the right woman. When he arrived in the city of Haran, he settled his camels near the well. In a time of no running water, can you imagine the public well? This was the place where everyone in town went. It was a place full of activity. The shepherds came with their flocks, and every household sent someone to collect water for drinking, cooking, and cleaning. It was bustling and busy. Eliezer arrived at evening time, when the daughters of the city would come to draw from the well. Here Eliezer could observe the way they behaved, and their natures were revealed. Eliezer asked God for a clear sign: a woman who would greet him with great *chesed* (kindness)—and who, when he asked her to share her water with him, would offer to give him *and his camels* water. That is a lot of work for a young girl to fetch that much water—one thirsty camel could drink up to thirty gallons of water in fifteen minutes.

Even while Eliezer was still in his prayer, the girl destined to be one of the mothers of our nation entered the scene.

"Let me sip a little bit from your jug," Eliezer requested from the young girl.

"Drink, my master," she said, and she quickly lowered her jug from her shoulder and offered Eliezer to drink. When he was satisfied—just as he prayed for—she said, "I will also give water to your camels until they have finished drinking." It's said that the waters in the well rose up to fill her water vessel.[2]

Right away Eliezer realized she was the destined match for Yitzchak. He gave Rivka the gifts from Avraham: a gold nose ring and two bracelets. He asked her whose daughter she was. Lo and behold, she was from the very family that Avraham intended—the

2.   Rashi, Genesis 24:17.

family of Nahor, Avraham's brother. He asked if there would be room with her family for him that night; Rivka assured him that there was room for more than one night and plenty of straw for the camels too. Eliezer bowed to God in gratitude for providing the match and guiding him to find her.

Rivka ran to her mother's tent (husbands and wives had separate tents in those days) and told her what happened. Of course, the whole household heard, and while her father, Betuel, remained in the background, Lavan (Laban), her older brother, ran to get involved. We'll see more clearly in the next chapter (about Rachel and Leah) that Lavan was a conniving man. Some sages believe that Lavan ran to welcome Eliezer out of greed after he saw the generous gifts that were given to Rivka.[3] Lavan welcomed Eliezer and invited him to their home. They settled in, the camels were fed, and food was served to the guests, but Eliezer would not eat until he spoke first about his mission. He recounted the events up until that moment: his oath to Avraham, his prayer, finding Rivka, learning that her family and Avraham were related, the gifts, and thanking God for the guidance. Then, straightforwardly, he asked them to tell him what their intentions were.

Lavan and Betuel answered that it was all from God, that Rivka should be a wife for Yitzchak. More gifts were given to Rivka—silver and gold and clothing. They ate and drank in celebration of the agreement. The next morning Eliezer got up ready to leave with Rivka. But her brother and mother thought she should stay with them for a longer time and come at a later date.

A Child Bride?

We may think their request was logical, since Rivka was quite young. Some sources say she was twelve or thirteen;[4] others say she was only three years old![5] Why take her from her family at such a young

3.   Midrash, *Genesis Rabbah* 60:7.
4.   Talmud, *Yevamot* 61b
5.   Rashi, Genesis 25:20.

age? This is something that is hard for us with the sensibilities of our generation to understand, so it's important that we dig deeper.

The Torah text says that Rivka was a "virgin that no man had known." *Why* the Torah gave such a detail is important to our story. In that generation and culture, most young girls were sexually molested (in addition, Betuel, with the status of a king, took every virgin before her wedding night, and there was pressure from his subjects to take his own daughter[6]). Unfortunately, there are cultures in the world today where it is still the norm for little girls (and boys) to be abused sexually, and though it's not "officially" accepted in Western culture, sexual abuse is epidemic. For this reason, to this day Jewish law prohibits *yichud* or the private "seclusion" of males and females. Beginning at the age of three, a female is not to be left alone with a man who is not her immediate family (there are many nuances, but that topic is not for this book). For boys, this prohibition begins at age nine.

When Eliezer wanted to take Rivka away from her home, he wanted to get her out of the immoral environment she was in; the idea was to keep her safe. She would be raised and grow up in the home of Avraham himself, the master of *chesed*, whose behavior continues to be a model for our nation.

Eliezer was persistent in wanting to take Rivka right away. So Rivka's mother and brother suggested they ask the girl what she wanted. Rivka's family asked her if she wanted to go immediately, and she readily expressed her desire for this arrangement. Rivka had heard storytellers who brought tales of her relative Avraham. His kindness might have sounded fantastic and large —large enough for her to choose kindheartedness as a quality for herself. Maybe it would be more accurate to say that these stories awoke the kindness and compassion that was her inborn nature.

---

6. See Midrash, *Yalkut Shimoni*, Chayei Sarah, remez 109, cited in Rabbi Ari Kahn, *Echoes of Eden*, Parshat Toldot 5770 (November 14, 2009), http://arikahn.blogspot.co.il/2009/11/parshat-toldot-5770-echoes-of-eden.html.

Rivka's family gave their permission and blessing for their daughter to go. They understood where she was going and what her potential was, to be the mother of a great and mighty nation. Rivka, along with her handmaidens, returned to Canaan with Eliezer.

In the evening, as they traveled and came closer to Avraham's home, they came to a field where Yitzchak had gone out to pray. He lifted his eyes and saw them coming. Rivka, on her camel, raised her eyes and saw Yitzchak. The text here gives us a clue that when Yitzchak and Rivka "raised" their eyes, it may not refer only to their physical eyes. They were seeing in a spiritual way. They saw more than the external image, they perceived on a soul level. Rivka saw the air of holiness surrounding Yitzchak. The text says she "fell from her camel." (Was it a quick dismount? Did she fall off as if stumbling?) Some sages interpret that she wanted to meet him on the same level, not "from above" as if superior.[7]

She asked Eliezer, "Who is that man walking in the field to-ward us?" Avraham's servant answered, "He is my master." When she heard it was Yitzchak, she covered herself in modesty with a veil (and from this comes the tradition of a bride wearing a veil[8]). Yitzchak brought Rivka to his mother's tent.

Rivka was young, but her true nature was already revealed. We cannot compare what it was like to be a child at that time with what it is to be a child today, although perhaps we can find some hints about how a child's nature can be revealed even at a young age.

When my neighbor's daughter was very young and tender, she would visit me and always very sweetly offered to help me do whatever I happened to be working on. She was so eager to please. I saw her express compassion in ways that I never would have thought a child so young could even feel. When this nature is fos-tered, it ripens into the beautiful, caring qualities that we women

---

7.   Midrash, *Genesis Rabbah* 60:15; Ramban, Genesis 24:64.
8.   See Rabbi Maurice Lamm, "The Veiling Ceremony (Bedeken)," https://www.chabad.org/library/article_cdo/aid/313719/jewish/The-Veiling-Ceremony-Bedeken.htm.

use to nurture others. The truth is, this quality can be seen in lots of little girls.

Another similar story is one my father told me about when he was a little boy in New York in about 1920. One day he sat on a park bench swinging his feet back and forth. Each time his feet came under him they clicked on the wooden slats beneath him. An old man sitting on the same bench snapped at my father to stop swinging his feet. My father decided in that moment that he would never be a mean old man, that he would be nice. And indeed he was. Even years after his passing, when I meet people who knew him, they always share a story of his kindness. A young child can certainly be aware of his or her surroundings and make a decision of a direction to take in life or a quality to take on.

In today's lifestyle and framework, our children are often put in front of a TV to watch a giant purple dinosaur dance or little round space men babble. They're given cell phones and iPads to teethe on. The treasures of their tenderness are often overlooked in the busy hustle and bustle of moving from one activity to the next.

Not that long ago (perhaps this applied to your great-grand-mother?), it was common for a girl to marry at twelve. Consider what is happening in the minds, bodies, and hearts of twelve- or thirteen-year-old girls. Their bodies are transforming into the bodies of women, and they are physically ready to bear children. Their hearts can beat a little faster around a certain boy. Today girls are exposed to apps on their smartphones for "hooking up," and adolescent participation includes twelve- or thirteen-year-olds. This is going on without the benefit of emotional commitment or love. In context we can see that the marriages of our grandmothers were not only for childbearing and certainly not arrangements for legalizing rape (as can be seen even today in some cultures where underage girls are wed to much older men). In the Jewish tradition, the wife is a *partner* for building a family. The significance and im-portance of the matriarchy is real and true. It is not just essential; it is crucial in the formation of the family and the nation. You'll read more about that later in this chapter.

It's important that we see Rivka in the perspective of her time. She was not in a high-tech world, getting lost in electronic devices for hours at a time. She was present in the reality of her life, moment by moment. When she agreed to go with Eliezer to be Yitzchak's wife, she understood what she was choosing.

The Signs Return

The Torah tells us that Yitzchak married Rivka, and he loved her. It was an "arranged" marriage—*and he loved her.* This was spelled out for all eternity, for all to see and know and understand about their relationship. The lesson is also that the truest love cannot be understood before marriage.

The text goes on to tell us that the legacy of Sarah would be continued through Rivka. When Sarah was alive, her Shabbat candles stayed lit for the entire week, her bread stayed fresh the whole week, and there was a divine cloud of God's presence that rested on her tent. These three signs disappeared when Sarah died. They returned when Rivka moved into her tent.[9]

The Torah tells us that when Rivka restored the divine signs to Sarah's tent, "Yitzchak was comforted after his mother." Yitzchak knew that Rivka had the qualities and spirituality necessary to continue the lineage that would build the nation that God had promised. One idea we might consider as guidance from this is that *love must be based on goodness.* Having shared values of goodness (decency, kindness, honesty, integrity, and the like) is a strong foundation for marriage, in our times as well as theirs. Yitzchak and Rivka are one of the truest examples of a loving relationship. The honor and respect they had for each other and the nuances that are revealed through the study of these short passages give us a foundation for a successful marriage today.

---

9. Midrash, *Yalkut Shimoni* 109:12.

Twenty Years of Infertility

Rivka and Yitzchak endured twenty years of barrenness. If you or someone you know has felt the disappointment of infertility, you appreciate how painful and difficult this is. Our sages teach us that when we face hardship, the Infinite wants our prayers. It can be a confusing concept because we know that the God Who Is, Was, and Always Will Be does not *need* anything. In our generation we can easily get a perspective on not just how tiny a human being is on this earth, but that this great planet itself is nothing more than a speck of dust in the whole universe. So how could the Creator of all that we know and all that we will never know need my prayers or your prayers or even the prayers of the prophetess and matriarch Rivka?

Prayer is required because it is an intimate connection with the Divine that raises consciousness and insight, *for us*. It's not as if we are going to tell God about something He hadn't considered before, so prayer is not about convincing God to change His mind. Prayer is like the fire of the silversmith, which purifies the silver, bringing it into its most beautiful potential. Prayer is the fire that changes *us*. If we are changed, the world is changed to some degree, too. If we are changed, our thoughts are changed and so is the direction of our actions.

In one line, the Torah tells us that Yitzchak prayed abundantly for Rivka, and she also prayed to conceive. The Hebrew word used (*vayetar*) gives the picture that this was deep prayer. Why did they both pray only for Rivka? In our generation we know that fertility issues can also come from the men. God had already promised that the nation would come from Yitzchak. Now Yitzchak was praying that Rivka would be his partner in this. Remember what they saw in each other the first time they met. A love so profound, a love that is rooted in a significant spiritual mission, grows. Rivka was worthy to be a mother of the nation. And Rivka conceived.

The Struggle

Rivka conceived twins, but her challenges weren't over. She felt a struggle and agitation within her womb. When she passed a house of study, she felt a pulling, and when she passed a place of idolatry, she also felt a pulling. She wanted to know what was happening, so she prayed to God. Rivka received a prophesy from God which the sages reveal came through a prophet called Shem. God said to her that she was carrying two separate nations, and while the power would go from one to the other, eventually the older would serve the younger.

It is important that the prophecy was given *to her*. She understood that this was for her to know, but not for her husband. She knew the destiny of her sons.

The struggle between good and evil was being played out from the beginning of Rivka's pregnancy. It was clear from the prophecy that these two babies who eventually become two nations would not be mighty at the same time, that when one fell the other would rise. This is something history has demonstrated repeatedly. One nation teaching morality and the other acting in barbaric ways cannot coexist. The two nations represented by Rivka's sons were Yisrael (Israel—meaning the nation of Israel, the people—not to be confused with the tiny State of Israel, which today is the homeland of the nation) and Edom, also called Rome (as in the ancient Roman Empire). The ancient Roman Coliseum that stands today in Italy is a testament to the sadistic cruelty of an empire in which it was considered sport to pit men against each other to fight to the death, or for people imprisoned for their religious beliefs to be torn apart by hungry lions, all in front of a jovial, cheering hoard. Edom was the father of Amalek, the name associated with the most evil force in the world that barbarically works to destroy the Jewish nation. (An example of the work of Amalek is how, at the end of WWII even as the Nazis ran away in defeat, they continued to murder Jews.)

As we will see, there was a dramatic contrast between Rivka's two sons, between good and evil. A more recent set of dramatically different brothers was the Goerings, Albert and Hermann. Hermann Goering was a top Nazi working directly with Hitler toward genocide. Recently, documents were unearthed that show his brother Albert worked to save Jews from humiliation and death.[10]

When Rivka's pregnancy came to full term, twin brothers were born. The first was born red and hairy. He was named Esav (Esau). (The name of the nation that came from him, Edom, comes from the same root as the word for "red" in Hebrew). The second baby boy emerged grasping his brother's heel, so he was named Yaakov (Jacob), which comes from the same root as the word *heel* (because he was holding on to his twin's heel, and he would bring godliness into the lowest parts of society).

The boys grew up. Esav clearly had a more material nature. He was described as a hunter and trapper, a "man of the field." Yaakov was a wholesome man of a spiritual nature who "dwells in tents," meaning that he sat and studied Torah.

The Birthright

As Yaakov and Esav grew into young men, their struggle continued. The struggle between these brothers, though a story about men in Torah, is important for gaining insight into the choices Rivka made to ensure that Yaakov received the blessings that would help him build the nation. Throughout history and across cultures, there is a theme of the firstborn being in a unique position. In royal families, it's the firstborn who will take the throne. While the firstborn has a special status in Judaism, it's not necessarily the firstborn who takes the position of leadership. Yitzchak had a vision for his twin sons. He thought there could be a partnership, and they could work together; they could complement each other. Yaakov would lead in spirituality; Esav would be the material benefactor (this kind of

---

10. See Zoe Brennan, "The Goering Who Saved Jews: While Hermann Masterminded the Final Solution His Brother Albert Rescued Gestapo Victims," *Daily Mail*, April 9, 2010, http://www.dailymail.co.uk/news/article-1264738/The-Goering-saved-Jews-A-new-book-reveals-Hermann-masterminded-Final-Solution-brother-Albert-rescued-Gestapo-victims.html.

relationship does eventually manifest within the twelve tribes). The problem was that Esav expressed his material nature in evil ways. There are many stories in the Midrash that paint a clear picture of Esav as an adulterer and murderer.[11] Clearly, he did not have the ethics that would be necessary, nor did he relate to women in a way that was fitting. He did honor his father. However, even in this respect there was deception. (For example, Esav would ask his father questions that made him appear to be scrupulous in his spiritual actions.[12])

Yitzchak loved Esav and looked for reasons he could love him. We should remember that Yitzchak had been through the Akeidah, the remarkable experience of being bound for sacrifice, and yet God making it clear that human sacrifice would never be a part of our spiritual way. In a sense, he ascended to those great spiritual heights and never descended. Of all the patriarchs, he was the only one who never left the Land of Israel. So his inner vision was elevated in an extraordinary way.

Rivka was given clear information from the highest Source that Esav would not take on the mantle of leadership of this nation. He proved himself unworthy of leadership when he sold his birthright to Yaakov for a dish of lentil stew.

Esav came in from the field one day and saw his brother cooking a pot of red lentil stew. Esav said to Yaakov, "Pour that red stuff into me, I'm exhausted." (Another reason for the name of his nation, Edom, meaning "red.") But Yaakov didn't give it freely. He struck a deal to trade the meal for the birthright. Esav tossed the position away as unimportant: *Look, I'm going to die anyway, so what use is a birthright?*

Why wouldn't Yaakov just give his own brother a serving of stew? Why did he want to make a deal for the birthright? It was clear that Esav did not want anything to do with spirituality and was not interested in holding up his end of the partnership. Yaakov

---

11.   Kli Yakar, Genesis 25:27; Talmud, *Bava Batra* 16b.
12.   Rashi, Genesis 25:27.

knew his brother's nature made him unfit to be the father of the nation that was promised to Avraham.

Esav gobbled the stew and left, rejecting his birthright. (Knowing this story will help us understand more about the beginning of Leah's story in the next chapter.) Rivka's role in our history ensured Yaakov would be the father and leader of the Jewish nation, and she accomplished this masterfully without damage to Yitzchak's relationship to Esav, as you'll soon see.

Famine in the Land

There was another famine in the land of Canaan. During the previous famine, God had told Avraham and Sarah to go to Egypt to find food. This time God appeared to Yitzchak and told him to stay in the land promised to him and his descendants. God went on to say that Yitzchak's descendants will be "like the stars in the heavens" and that "all the nations of the earth will bless themselves by your descendants." From this we learn that the Jewish people are meant to bring light to all nations.

Yitzchak and Rivka traveled to the region of Gerar, which was within the Land of Israel. When the men asked about his wife, he realized that they might kill him to take the beautiful Rivka, so, as his father did, he said that his wife was his sister.

But Avimelech, the king of the Philistines, was snooping around and peeping in their window! He was coveting Rivka, and he was suspicious because he had experience from the similar incident with Avraham and Sarah.

He was watching Yitzchak and Rivka and saw them "jesting." The Hebrew word the text uses comes from the root "to laugh." Was this the kind of intimate play that really reveals something so much deeper? We all know what it's like to be with a young couple in love. There's a kind of playfulness they share. They make eyes at each other. They giggle. They have a very intimate way of whispering to each other. They may not even be physically touching, but there's clearly something intimate between them. Yitzchak and Rivka's many years together had not diminished their affections—the opposite. Perhaps it was precisely their shared devotion and purpose that served to increase their intimacy and affection.

By this time, Esav had married. His behavior had always been immoral. He had a reputation for chasing married women. He married at the age of forty with the idea that he was emulating his father. It was only an act, since he did not have the same intentions as his father.[13] Esav married two women, who came from a culture of idolatry and continued its practice.[14] Why did he marry two women? It was a custom among men from before the flood (in the story of Noah's Ark) to marry one beautiful woman for pleasure and the other wife for childbearing.[15] This way of thinking is about seeing women as objects and actually was one of the contributing reasons for the flood. His choice was a disappointment to his father and mother.

Blessing of the Firstborn: A Difficult Deception

The time came for Yitzchak to pass on the mission of building the nation. He had a vision that his sons could work together. The Torah also tells us that "his eyes were dim." Although Yitzchak had in fact become blind in his old age, as we saw above, this is not just about physical eyes, it's about seeing the spiritual. God had made it clear to Rivka back when she was pregnant which of her sons would take on the yoke of being the next patriarch.

Yitzchak called Esav to give him the blessing that would give him dominion in the material world. His idea was that this power would be used to support the spiritual side represented by Yaakov. Rivka knew both from the prophecy and through Esav's depraved behavior—his treatment of women, his choice regarding wives, and his having tossed aside the birthright—that he had no intention of

---

13.   Midrash, *Genesis Rabbah* 65:1.
14.   Genesis 34:25–26; Midrash, *Tanchuma*, Toldot 8.
15.   Rabbi Ari Kahn, "Na'ama," Parshat Noach 5770 (October 19, 2009), http://arikahn. blogspot.co.il/2009/10/parshat-noach-5770.html.

participating in this divine work. Rivka knew what she had to do to protect the line that would bring light into the world. She could not let a force known to be evil step up and take a power that it should not have.

In this dramatic passage of the Jewish nation's story, Yitzchak, who could not see (he could not see with his physical eyes, and his spiritual eyes only looked for the potential of good), called to his elder son Esav, who was a hunter, and asked him to bring him delicacies of fresh game. Rivka overheard, and when Esav went to the field to hunt game, she knew the time had come to act. She told her younger son, Yaakov, what his father had said to Esav. With the prophecy and insights she possessed, she orchestrated that Yaakov would get this blessing, since she knew that Esav would not carry any portion of the weight of the nation. You may wonder why she was so concerned about a blessing—it's just words, after all. But there is great power in the spoken word. With speech, the world was created. (We see this in Genesis, where for example in 1:3, "God said, 'Let there be light.' And there was light.") With speech, lives can be saved or lives can be lost. The blessing or the prayer of a simple Jew has great power. The blessing of a patriarch or matriarch carries with it even greater consequence. Rivka knew what had to be done.

Rivka instructed Yaakov to "listen to my voice" and bring young goats. She would prepare the food his father loved, "Then bring it to your father and he will eat so that he will bless you before his death."

Yaakov was not sure about this plan. He reminded Rivka that Esav was hairy, while he was smooth-skinned. He was afraid his father would realize their deception, and he would wind up cursed instead of blessed. Rivka said if that were so, she would take the curse on herself, and she insisted that he listen to her. He went to get the young goats as his mother instructed. Rivka took some of Esav's clean clothes, and Yaakov put them on. She covered his smooth arms and neck with goatskin. Then she gave Yaakov the delicacies she had prepared. So Yaakov went to his father, posing as Esav.

"Father," he said.

"I'm here, who are you, my son?"

"It is me, Esav, your firstborn," Yaakov said. "I did as you told me. Get up, please, and sit and eat so you can bless me."

Yitzchak questioned, "How were you able to find [game] so quickly, my son?"

"Because your God set it up for me."

Yitzchak said to Yaakov, "Come close, if you please, so I can feel you, my son. Are you my son Esav or not?" (Why is he not sure which son it was? Because since when does Esav talk about God? But from Yitzchak's point of view, maybe he's hopeful that his son is rising.)

Yaakov came close to his father, who felt him.

"The voice is Yaakov's voice, but the hands are Esav's hands," Yitzchak observed. Yitzchak ate the food and drank the wine that his son had brought him, and then he said, "Come close and kiss me, my son."

He came close and kissed him. Here an interesting thing happens. Yitzchak smelled the scent of his son's clothes and blessed him—he said, "See the scent of my son is like the scent of a field that God blessed." It's said that Yitzchak smelled the fragrance of the Garden of Eden.[16] From this fragrance, he believed that his son Esav was really on track, as was his highest hope. He gave a blessing (the first of three altogether) to Yaakov, thinking it was Esav.

"And may the Almighty give you from the dew of the heavens and from the richness of the earth, plentiful grain and wine. Nations will serve you and regimes will prostrate themselves to you; be noble to your kinsmen, and your mother's sons will prostrate themselves to you; cursed are those who curse you and blessed are those who bless you."

Shortly after Yaakov left, Esav came in from his hunt, bringing his father the requested delicacies. He said, "Get up, father, and eat of your son's game so that your soul will bless me."

---

16. Rashi, Genesis 27:27.

Yitzchak asked, "Who are you?"

"I am your son, your firstborn, Esav!"

Yitzchak trembled. In an instant of prophecy, he perceived the darkness of Esav completely. "Who…where is the one that hunted game and brought it to me when you had not yet come? And I blessed him, so he will be blessed!"

When Esav heard his father's words, he screamed out a great and bitter cry. Did he realize what he had lost? Was there regret? Was it just anger or jealousy?

"Bless me, too, Father!"

"Your brother came and with cunning took your blessing."

Esav said, "Is it because his name was Yaakov that he outwitted me these two times? He took my birthright and now he took my blessing. Haven't you saved a blessing for me?" Esav blamed Yaakov for taking the birthright, ignoring that he himself gave it up.

Yitzchak told Esav that it was too late; his brother would be master over him and the material world. Esav still wanted a blessing from his father, "Have you only one blessing, Father? Bless me, too, Father!" Esav lifted his voice and wept.

So Yitzchak answered (with the second blessing), "Here from the fatness (riches) of the earth will be your dwelling and of the dew of the heavens from above. By your sword you will live, but your brother you will serve. Yet it will be that when you are aggrieved, you may throw off his yoke from your neck." What does this mean? That there will never be coexistence between the two: when one is in power, the other will be subservient, and it can switch. When one is up, the other will be down. Historically, we've seen this pattern repeated.

This story of the apparent deception is a difficult one. In Jewish teachings, the values of truth and integrity are paramount. One of the Ten Commandments is "Do not bear false witness."[17] There are

---

17. For a detailed essay on deception in Judaism and when it is permitted, read Aryeh Citron, "Telling the Truth…and When It Is Permissible to Be Less Than Honest," https://www.chabad.org/library/article_cdo/aid/1049008/jewish/Telling-the-Truth-and-When-it-is-Permissible-to-be-Less-than-Honest.htm.

laws governing the way to do business; it's even spelled out that the weights used in commerce must be calibrated and accurate. The Torah clearly says not to accept false reports, not to partner with the wicked to be a corrupt witness, not to allow yourself to be bribed, and to distance yourself from lying speech.[18] There is a teaching that when a soul passes from this world to the World to Come and stands before the Eternal in judgment, one of the questions it will be asked is "Were you honest in business?"[19] Yet we know that this is not a world of black and white. There are times when not telling the truth is actually the high road.

When is it okay to blur the lines?

- **To protect someone's feelings.** Your friend asks you how you like her new dress, haircut, painting, car, or whatever else. She paid a lot of money for it, or put energy into making it; she *loves* it. What good does it do to hurt her feelings and tell her you think it's awful? It would do no good and likely cause pain.

- **To protect someone's privacy (including your own).** If someone asks you how so-and-so is doing and you know that so-and-so is a wreck, it doesn't mean you gossip and tell intimate details that are not yours to share. "I don't know" is a great response. Some people just say "Thank God," which doesn't really give information but is a way of saying "It's all for the good."

- **For peacemaking.** Helping to make peace between people is a noble thing to do. One example we're taught is that Aharon, the High Priest, would go to one party in an argument and say the other side confided in him that he or she wanted to make peace. Then he would go to the other side and say the same.[20] He was a known and beloved peacemaker. Especially important is peace within marriage,

18. Exodus 23:1–13.
19. Talmud, *Shabbat* 31a.
20. Bartenura, *Pirkei Avot* 1:12.

so encouraging couples to find peace (and not stoking a fire) is very noble. Another example is not to tell parents every detail of what their child did wrong. It's not about compromising a child's care or education, but some things don't need to be said if they could damage a relationship between a parent and child.

More Guidance from the Matriarch: Run from the Hatred

Esav hated his brother because of the blessing he got from his father. He actually wished his father's death would come, so that he could take revenge on his brother. You have to give one thing to Esav: he did honor his mother and father. It's the one right thing he did with vigor. He would not murder his brother while his father was still alive.

A common misconception about these blessings is that Yaakov stole the blessing to continue the nation. Be very clear, the blessing that Yitzchak gave his son Yaakov when he thought he was blessing Esav was only to succeed materially, so that they could form a partnership. That was the ideal in Yitzchak's vision. But the battle of good and evil was strong, and that partnership could not happen. The blessing that Yitzchak actually gave to Esav was also for the abundance of the world (not the Land of Israel) and that it would come naturally (not supernaturally or with divine intervention).

Now, when Rivka heard what Esav had said about killing his brother, she warned Yaakov. She told him again to listen to her voice and to run to her brother's home in Haran until Esav's anger cooled off. This story seems to emphasize the relationship between the father Yitzchak and the elder son Esav, on one hand, and the relationship between the mother Rivka and the younger son Yaakov on the other hand. Rivka knew what the outcome would be, but that didn't mean that she didn't love Esav. The next thing she said revealed that Rivka loved both of her sons, the elder and the younger. As she instructed Yaakov to leave, she added, "Why should I be bereaved of both of you on the same day?"

The Third Blessing

Rivka did not want to tell her husband that Yaakov was in danger of being killed by their son Esav. Instead, she gave him the idea that Yaakov needed to go to another place to find a wife.

Yitzchak called his son Yaakov and instructed him not to take a wife from the Canaanite women, but rather to go to his grandfather Betuel's house and to take a wife from the daughters of his uncle Lavan. Then Yitzchak gave Yaakov the Abrahamic blessing, the blessing that was always intended for him, to continue the legacy that was promised to Avraham, that passed to Yitzchak, and now to Yaakov: "May El Shaddai (God) bless you, make you fruitful and make you numerous, and may you be a congregation of peoples. May He grant you the blessing of Avraham to you and to your descendants with you, that you may possess the land of your sojourns which God gave to Avraham." Yitzchak sent his son Yaakov out to continue his journey to marry and build the nation.

Here is something powerful and maybe even life changing. In the extreme situation that Esav wanted to kill his brother, it would seem natural that parents would discuss details of such import about their children with each other. There are whole meetings about children at schools and files full of information over far more minor issues. Yet sometimes giving negative information can be harmful. It may rob the child of a chance to grow into something better, because people are always expecting the worst from them. Some sources criticize Yitzchak and Rivka for not parenting their son Esav according to his needs. But here we see that Rivka is preserving the loving relationship between Yitzchak and Esav, not giving the father a reason to distance himself from his son in anger. Rivka told Yaakov that Esav wanted to kill him so he could take clear action to be safe. What could Yitzchak, old and blind, have done to make things different in any case?

How can we apply such kindness in our lives today, in the way we talk about others, or more importantly, do *not* talk about others? One measure to consider is that if there is some action that can be done to prevent danger or to intervene in a helpful way, then telling something you know about another is worth doing. If not, let it rest. Preserve relationships and keep doors open for the opportunity to rise.

Rivka's Gift: Kindness

What is extraordinary about Rivka is revealed by taking a closer look at her circumstances in life, how she was raised and the environment she lived in. People who were completely self-serving raised her. We learn from a midrash that when Rivka's family hosted Eliezer, her father Betuel tried to poison Eliezer's food so they could steal the wealth Eliezer brought. The angel Gavriel came and switched the plates of food, and Betuel (Rivka's father) was poisoned instead.[21] (This could explain why he suddenly disappears from the story.) Why would Betuel deserve to be poisoned? As noted earlier, another midrash says that Betuel was in a position of kingship and took all virgins for himself before their wedding night. In fact, his name could be translated as "god of the virgins." The people of the region wanted Betuel to take Rivka sexually, since he also took their daughters.[22]

Are you getting the picture of the times, and of this family in particular? And even still, it was a family that had some kind of positive character traits that would make Avraham want a bride for his son from this community. And we think the West was wild! Even in all of the depravity, Rivka emerged as a woman of kindness. She qualified to be one of the mothers of the nation.

Rivka and Yitzchak balanced and complemented each other. They each developed the inner quality of the other. Yitzchak took after his mother Sarah, embodying the quality of *gevurah* (strength). The quality needed for balance and to build the nation with Yitzchak would be *chesed* (loving-kindness), and the woman who would be

---

21. Midrash, *Yalkut Shimoni* 109:5; Baal Haturim and Rabbenu Bachya, Genesis 24:33; Chizkuni, Genesis 24:53; Daat Zekenim and Ikar Siftei Chachamim, Genesis 24:55.
22. Midrash, *Yalkut Shimoni* 109:5.

the next mother of the nation would need to naturally exemplify that character trait. *Chesed* is giving beyond what is required or obligated.

You may see that about your own nature, that you have a personality strength which, when developed, can accomplish great things in whatever you do. Then there's the other side of the coin, which is developing the characteristics that you need for balance. For example, someone who is very kind also needs to know how to set boundaries. Someone who is very disciplined and strong needs to develop the quality of kindness, so that the strength doesn't turn into cruelty. Too much of a good thing can do damage if it's not in balance.

So what is kindness? It's giving beyond what is necessary. Rivka not only gave water to a thirsty stranger, she drew water for all his camels. It's one thing to host someone for a night in your home. It's something else to make that guest feel welcomed and cared for. It's one thing to feed your children dinner every night; it's something else when they understand that you are happy to see them. Giving is good; giving with kindness is greater good.

What is the power of a simple smile? There is a teaching from Rabbi Yochanan that says, "Better is the one who shows the white of his teeth to his friend than the one who gives him milk to drink."[23] The white of your teeth is your smile. You have likely felt the power of both giving and receiving a smile at just the right time. I recently heard a story on the news of a little boy whose parents both died by the time he was six years old. He was tired of seeing so many sad people, so he came up with a project: to give little toys to people and make them smile. This six-year-old boy's goal was to make thirty-three thousand people smile. With the help of his aunt, he has far exceeded that number![24] How can we be inspired to share a smile or a kind word?

---

23. Talmud, *Ketubot* 111b.
24. CBS Evening News, "After Losing Parents, Six-Year-Old Boy Seeks Smiles," August 7, 2015, https://www.youtube.com/watch?v=OCPc2RlMTII.

What if your focus for your community, neighbors, and family came from this place of kindness? It's easy to go on autopilot: cutting vegetables—*again,* doing laundry—*again,* cleaning the kitchen—*again...* How do you do things like this with kindness? Rabbi Zelig Pliskin suggests asking questions to evoke shifts in your thinking or attitude. This can be transformative. Rabbi Pliskin gives examples such as, "How can I transform and elevate the meaning that I am giving to this action? How can I do what I'm about to do in an elevated way? Who will this benefit?"

A focus on kindness infuses meaning into seemingly mundane actions and adds reasons to be grateful. This is the truest alchemy of life, transforming straw into gold. It is a foundational quality of the Jewish nation. It doesn't mean always saying yes. It does generally mean going past your comfort zone, so even when you're saying no, you can say it thoughtfully. It's about awareness and consideration of the other.

Reflections in Rivka's Mirror: The Silence of Power

There are two kinds of silence. There is silence that is a result of not finding your voice. That is a feeling of being gagged, not being able to speak, or not being allowed to speak. Most of us have experienced that at one time or another. Sarah teaches us it is important to find your voice. Rivka also told her son to "listen to her voice." She had her voice, too. So from the place of knowing your voice, we find the *silence of power.* It is *not* being silent because you don't know what to say or because you don't feel you can say it. This is *not* the silence of being a doormat. The silence of power is the silence of directing inner power. People can mistake being gracious for being weak or think that running from a conflict is a sign of weakness. In the martial arts—the art of fighting—students are taught to avoid fights. It is better to run away from many situations on the street. Imagine a black belt who has the capacity to mortally hurt his opponent being challenged at a bar by a drunkard. It is higher and more honorable for that martial artist to run away from that situation than to prove the extent of his power.

That Rivka never spoke to her husband Yitzchak about the terrible deeds of his son Esav is so hard to understand. We count on our husbands to be our partners in raising our children. Parents are often quick to tell a spouse the news, behaviors, and problems of their children, but Rivka's silence brings us another option and perspective. Important to note is that Rivka loved and respected her husband. She was not silent out of fear. In fact, perhaps it was her reverence for her husband, her deep respect, that allowed her to let go and give Yitzchak the space to develop his relationship with his son.

One of the popular teachings for parents is to give children the chance to rise to the expectations of vision that their parents have for them. If you expect your children to be good and take action for the good, they will rise to that. Conversely, they may sink to lower visions and disappointments. Is it possible that by being silent about the dark side of Esav, Rivka was both giving Esav the space to rise, and in such a loving way, nurturing the flow of love from father to son? We know that our great-great Uncle Esav did some pretty evil things, but Yitzchak and Rivka's love for him never faltered or failed, even when Rivka knew the blessing intended for Esav would never be fulfilled by him and that it had to go to Yaakov. What a striking example for us to choose carefully what we share about our own children and to whom.

This idea of holding in silence (even with those closest with you) is that it is not a silence of discomfort or not having something to talk about. Yitzchak and Rivka had such a loving relationship that it was noted in more than one place in the Torah. How much richer might a relationship be if it does not include complaining, blaming, or conversations about others?

How else can silence be a powerful tool for building and healing? When someone needs to talk, just listening with a loving heart can relieve pain. "Active listening" is a technique in psychology. Holding in silence when someone is grieving is an act of great love and caring. Silence can give someone the space to explore or examine, or find his or her own answers from within.

Rachel and Leah
Unity, Prayers, and Tears

The Story of Rachel and Leah

The story of our mothers Rachel and Leah begins after Yaakov leaves his parents' home.[1] Yaakov fled for his life when his twin brother, Esav, threatened to kill him for receiving a blessing that was originally intended for himself (see chapter on Rivka). Esav did receive a different blessing from their father, Yitzchak. But it was Yaakov who was given *the* blessing to continue the nation, and this blessing had always been intended for him. Esav would never have risen to the spiritual level necessary to carry out this blessing.

The time came for Yaakov to seek his soul mate and life partner, the woman with whom he would fulfill his mission. As if it was not intense enough to receive a blessing of such magnitude, and to have to run from his twin brother who wanted to murder him, Yaakov had a vision. As he was leaving the Holy Land, he had a mystical dream of a heavenly ladder—Jacob's Ladder. He saw angels ascending and descending it. In this place he experienced God. "I am the Eternal, the God of your father Avraham and the God of Yitzchak. The land on which you are lying I will give to you and to your descendants. And your descendants will be as the dust of the earth, and will spread seaward (westward), and to the east, and to

---

1. The story of Rachel and Leah can be found in Genesis 29:1–35:29.

78

the north, and to the desert (south); and all the families of the earth will bless themselves by you and your descendants. Behold! I am with you. I will guard you wherever you go, and I will return you to this soil. I will not leave you, and I will do all that I have spoken to you." (Now you know why Israel is called "the Promised Land.")

With this intense, transcendent experience and the promises from God, Yaakov made his own promises to tithe—give a portion of his income—to God. Yaakov continued his journey to find a wife and partner to fulfill this godly vision.

Yaakov came to a well. (Wells are a theme.) The water below the ground represents the blessing of what is hidden. Water is symbolic of kindness[2] and also of Torah itself.[3] Our part is that we have to go to the well; our effort matters.

At the well, Yaakov saw shepherds. He asked about his uncle's family, and lo and behold, Rachel (his uncle's daughter) approached with her flock. She was a shepherdess. Yaakov saw Rachel, kissed her, and wept. This passage holds some mystery. At first glance, people may see something romantic. But romance falls short in explaining what was happening between Yaakov and Rachel. It's not surprising to know that a man who just received a promise directly from the Creator also experienced a vision with this kiss. It was clear to Yaakov that Rachel was his soul mate. It was clear that he loved her and she loved him. They both knew that they would marry. That kiss contained a vision of the eternal connection and the earthly outcome.

Rachel ran to tell her father, Lavan, about Yaakov's arrival. Lavan went out to greet Yaakov. (Cue the low, ominous soundtrack.) Lavan was not a trustworthy character, though he made a welcoming show. Perhaps Lavan expected the same rich entourage that his sister Rivka had received when Eliezer came to find a bride for Yitzchak. But Yaakov, fleeing his brother, came with nothing. Yaakov stayed with his uncle Lavan and started working for him.

---

2. *Zohar* 2:175b.
3. Talmud, *Bava Kama* 17a.

Suddenly, the Torah describes for us the two sisters: "Leah's eyes were soft, and Rachel was beautiful of form and beautiful of appearance." A deeper look into that one sentence teaches a lot about our mothers Rachel and Leah. Leah represents what is concealed, hidden: prayer. There is a depth we cannot understand or see fully. Rachel represents what is revealed, more visible to the eye on a basic level: action.[4]

With the help of commentaries and Midrash, we can go deeper to learn that Leah's eyes were soft because she cried. Holy, salty, glistening water poured from the eyes of Leah. It is written she cried so much that her eyelashes fell out.[5] Why did Leah cry? For Leah, each tear was a prayer. The people in her world talked and gossiped, and even without magazines or Internet, news spread. Twin boys had been born to Rivka: Esav and Yaakov. Two girls were born to Lavan: Leah and Rachel. The talk was something like, *oh, well then, of course Leah will marry Esav and Rachel will marry Yaakov.* The four matriarchs (Sarah, Rivka, Rachel, and Leah) were prophetesses. Leah knew that there was truth to the possibility that Esav could be meant for her. Leah inquired about Esav. Who was this man whom people assumed she should marry? Esav did not rise to his potential. He spurned his birthright and tossed away the responsibilities of the firstborn. He was licentious. He seduced married women. He treated women as objects. When Leah learned of Esav's base, immoral character, she wept. Leah cried at the thought of winding up with the likes of him, and she prayed for God to change the situation.[6] God heard her prayers.

Things are about to get complicated.

After a month, Lavan asked Yaakov what his wages should be. Yaakov responded, "I will work for you for seven years for Rachel, your younger daughter." Of course, Lavan knew that Rachel was his younger daughter, but Yaakov was making the terms of the contract

---

4.   Arizal, *Sefer Etz Chaim* 25:5.
5.   Talmud, *Bava Batra* 123a.
6.   Rashi, Genesis 29:17.

very clear. Yaakov knew Lavan's nature and realized it was possible he would be tricked, or Lavan would twist things. The terms were agreed upon.

Why seven years? One thought is that Yaakov used that time to refine himself spiritually, to become the man who would father this nation. Yaakov knew that the consciousness of a man and a woman at the moment of conception impacts the soul that comes through into this world. Seven years passed, and the time came to marry.

A feast was prepared. Lavan gathered all the local people for the wedding. Our Midrashic sources say that Yaakov suspected that Lavan might switch his daughters.[7] To prepare for that deception, Yaakov made up signs that Rachel could give from beneath the wedding veils, so Yaakov would be assured that it was really Rachel.

A switch is exactly what happened. Lavan substituted Leah beneath the bridal veils. This would be the answer to Leah's prayers! But what about the love between Yaakov and Rachel? Of course, there is so much more than meets the eye. Here is where one of the deepest acts of self-sacrifice enters into this story. Rachel would not allow for the public humiliation of her sister. In a single moment of profound compassion, Rachel gave Leah the signs so that when Leah was standing under the wedding canopy, she would not be revealed and humiliated in public (before people who, by the way, all knew what was happening! Were they hoping for a show of drama?). There is one source that says Rachel gave the signs to Leah in a way that was so subtle that Leah did not know she was being given signs, so that it would all seem natural to Leah![8] Rachel not only saved her sister from humiliation in front of the community, but it is possible she hid the fact that Yaakov expected *her*, Rachel, under those veils! Rachel knew that she should have been standing with Yaakov. Such was the sacrifice of love from Rachel for her sister Leah.

Hidden beneath the wedding veils, Leah married Yaakov, the man Rachel loved.

---

7.   Midrash, *Genesis Rabbah* 70:17.
8.   *Minchat Yom Tov* on the Talmud, *Bava Batra* 120.

It was nighttime.

All was dark. (There were no streetlights to stream in the windows.)

The marriage was consummated.

The morning light revealed to Yaakov that his bride was Leah.

The Midrash fleshes out Yaakov's reaction to Leah when he saw her in the morning.[9] He confronted her deception. She pointed out to him that he was also a deceiver. Here are two of the most righteous people in our ancestry, who were both guided by their parents (who happened to be brother and sister) through deception. Yaakov did what his mother told him to do, to receive the blessing intended for his brother, and Leah did what her father told her to do, to marry Yaakov. We know that Rivka had the future nation's best interest in mind. Lavan, on the other hand, had only his own best interests in mind.

At this point, Yaakov could have backed out of the deal. It would have been reasonable to march over to Lavan and call out his trickery and demand it be corrected. The terms were crystal clear. But Yaakov did not call off his marriage to Leah. There was a spark of knowledge that his being with Leah was actually orchestrated from the heavens *for a reason*. And since he had been intimate with Leah, there was also the possibility of a conception—which did happen. Whether through Leah's prayers or (as explained in the chapter on Rivka) acquiring the birthright of the firstborn, on a mystical level, Yaakov got the status of soul mate with Leah, the elder of the two sisters. Yaakov was actually meant to be with Leah.[10]

Still, Yaakov did confront Lavan over the deception. Lavan kept his cool and answered that it wasn't the local custom to allow the younger daughter to marry first. He offered a new agreement: seven more years of work for Rachel. After the week of wedding festivities with Leah ended, Yaakov married Rachel, and his second

9.   Midrash, *Genesis Rabbah* 70:19.
10. Rabbi Ari D. Kahn, "Yaakov—or Yisrael?" in *Echoes of Eden: Sefer Bereishit* (Jerusalem: Gefen, 2011), 213–28.

term of work began. At the time of their marriages, Lavan gave each of his daughters a maidservant (more on this soon): Zilpah for Leah and Bilhah for Rachel.

Next the Torah tells us, "God saw that Leah was hated, so He opened her womb." What does that mean, "He opened her womb"? The Torah is revealing that Leah was actually barren. All our four matriarchs were afflicted with barrenness. Their desire to conceive was so strong, and conception did not happen without hardship. Leah's hardship was compounded because Leah "was hated," so God opened her womb to conceive. And what does it mean, that she was hated? The Torah does not say that Yaakov hated Leah. In fact, Yaakov did love Leah, but he loved Rachel *more*. Some commentaries suggest that perhaps it's relative; perhaps it's in Leah's own eyes, that she sees herself as hated.[11] This is a source of such deep pain. Rachel's suffering was also deep. She remained barren while her sister conceived and gave birth.

Through their faith and trust with the complexities of their lives, our mothers Rachel and Leah gave us the strength to have patience and faith through the mysteries, complications, and anguishes of life.

Twelve Tribes, One Vibe

Leah bore a son and named him Reuven (Reuben). That literally means "See, a son!" She declared that God saw her humiliation, and now that a son was born to them, her husband might love her. Why humiliation? Because of the deception of their wedding night. This conception made it clear that they were destined soul mates. Leah conceived again and called her second son Shimon (Simon), because God "heard" (the root of that name means "to hear") that she was hated and gave her another son. She conceived again and bore a third son. He was named Levi ("one who accompanies")—in hopes that her husband's heart would become attached to hers. She

---

11.   Rabbenu Bachya, Or Hachaim, and Radak, Bereishit 29:30–31.

called her fourth son Yehuda (Judah), in gratitude to and praise of the Creator. Leah was the first in the Torah to declare her gratitude. Yehuda would father the kings of Israel. In fact, the word *Jew—Yehudi* in Hebrew—comes from the name Yehuda. The word *Jew* itself means "grateful." We are the grateful ones.

Leah yearned for Yaakov's love—the very thing her sister had. At the same time, Rachel was still barren and longed for children—like her sister had. The Torah tells us Rachel became jealous of her sister Leah. While we understand that jealousy is not a positive trait, the commentaries teach us that Rachel's was the only kind of jealousy that is positive—a jealousy that causes a yearning to rise to a higher level. Rachel saw her sister's goodness and knew that was why she merited those sons.[12] Rachel knew the story of Yitzchak praying for Rivka to conceive, so she went to her husband Yaakov and said to him, "Give me children; if not, I am dead." Yaakov snapped back at her that it was God Who withheld the fruit of her belly.

The Handmaids: Bilhah and Zilpah

Each of the matriarchs had a degree of prophecy, and it was known that there would be twelve tribes from twelve sons.[13] Now Leah had her portion. Wait, what? If Leah had four sons, how does that add up? Two sisters creating twelve tribes equal six sons per woman. At this point a proper introduction to Bilhah and Zilpah is in order. Rachel and Leah's maidservants were also sisters. They were daughters of their father Lavan's concubines. Bilhah and Zilpah also gave birth to sons who would be leaders of the tribes of Israel.

Rachel gave Bilhah to Yaakov to have children in her name. Remember when Sarah brought Hagar to Avraham? Hagar did not work with Sarah in partnership. But here our story takes a different turn. Bilhah—and also later Zilpah, Leah's handmaid—rose to the unique chance to participate in building this nation. Bilhah was

---

12. Midrash, *Genesis Rabbah* 71:6.
13. Yaakov's prophecy. Midrash, *Genesis Rabbah* 68:11 and 70:18.

with Yaakov and bore a son. Rachel named him Dan, from the word meaning "to judge," because "God judged me and also heard my voice." Bilhah had a second son, Naftali, whose name hints at the sacred twists in life. When Leah saw that she had stopped giving birth, she also gave her handmaid, Zilpah, to Yaakov to have more children. Zilpah bore a son, and Leah named him Gad for the "good fortune" that had come. There was a second son from Zilpah, and Leah named him Asher, which means "happy" or "fortunate."

Why four women to give birth to twelve sons? In the deeper spiritual and mystical teachings, we are taught that the natures of the father and mother—and even their very thoughts at the time of conception—come into play as souls are chosen from the heavens to come through them into the world.[14] While Avraham and Yitzchak both fathered sons who were *not* part of the Jewish people, all of Yaakov's sons were leaders of the twelve tribes. Each of the four women who brought these twelve souls into the world represents different energies and aspects of the nation, more than could be contained in one woman.

This is a difficult part of the story for us to comprehend. It's hard enough that Yaakov took two wives, sisters no less, but he also had children with his wives' maids, who were another set of sisters. The laws of the Torah given to the Jewish people at Mount Sinai expressly forbid marrying sisters, but at this point in the story, those laws had not yet been revealed.

Chances are that the idea of polygamy is completely foreign and disdainful to you. In general, multiple wives were discouraged in Jewish culture, though it was sometimes done. In some Middle Eastern and African Jewish communities, families with multiple wives and mothers existed not that long ago. Perhaps you might be able to imagine that there were times when a woman would be safer, more protected, and better able to survive as a second wife rather than being single. There are still cultures in the world today where single women are exceptionally vulnerable. There is a Jewish

---

14. *Tanya*, Likutei Amarim, chapter 2.

woman I know whose family came from Morocco. Her father had two wives, and this woman is the daughter of the first wife, but she shared with me how beloved the second wife is to the entire family. Not all Jewish homes with more than one wife had such an idyllic story. Just as some marriages today are filled with love and respect while others are bitter or abusive, the same is true of the stories of our not so distant history. Learning about the women of our nation who lived in different times and places requires an open heart and mind.

The story of Rachel and Leah together with Bilhah and Zilpah, while complicated, is full of loving self-sacrifice. We honor Bilhah and Zilpah as mothers of the tribes, but they are not considered matriarchs of our nation. Their personal sacrifices were made in order to create something greater that would benefit not just the tribes of Israel but also the world. The idea of self-sacrifice is not in vogue today. The buzz in our Western world and generation is more about what *I'm* entitled to, or what *I* have to say. How will this affect *me*? The very concept of sacrifice is foreign and unfamiliar. Self-sacrifice means there is something greater than my own self—giving up something of myself for a greater good has value. Of course, we understand that concept to some degree. We understand it's necessary in a marriage or as a parent. We might understand that we sometimes trade our life's energy and time for work; we sacrifice to earn that paycheck and support our families. If you've ever donated blood, you've sacrificed something for someone else's good. But what if you had to really push past your comfort zone and give up something that's really uncomfortable for you to give up? It could be time, energy, or money.

In our generation we don't have handmaids to give to our husbands to conceive with, but we do have the complexities of adoption, surrogacy, egg and sperm donation, in vitro fertilization, and who knows what the future will bring. What if you knew you could give birth to a child and know that he or she would carry out an important mission and bring light to the world and all mankind, but for this to happen you wouldn't get the credit? Could you do it? Would you want to invest your DNA and love to participate in this monumental mission without the acclaim? Maybe you would be happier without the attention. Maybe you would never agree. In general, we don't like the idea of surrendering to something else. Perhaps we feel acquiescence is a loss of influence in a world where perceived power is king. Maybe it comes from the idea of not wanting to be seen as lower or devalued or weak. It goes against our independent grain. But what if there's a healthy—even lofty—aspect to acceptance of this kind of mission? Surrender can be negative (think "giving up"), but surrender can also mean bonding, merging. Most people can probably relate to both kinds of surrender, the negative and also the positive. Can you see it in nature? Parent-child relationships? How about team sports? Does a team player lose power or credit because there is a captain or a coach?

We are standing on the shoulders of Rachel, Leah, Bilhah, and Zilpah. The idea is that we will rise to meet our challenges. We have different challenges in our generation than they did. Perhaps our ancestral mothers would cringe or weep if they saw the challenges of our times.

The Exchange

One evening, Rachel saw Leah's oldest son, Reuven, bringing his mother a plant called *dudaim*, which were known to increase fertility.[15] We're not exactly sure what these were, but they are often translated as mandrakes; others say they were some kind of violet or jasmine.[16] Rachel, who still had no children, asked for some of them. Leah (who hadn't conceived in a while) asked, isn't it enough that you took my husband, you also want my son's *dudaim*?

Some people see Rachel's request and Leah's answer as coming from places of pain and maybe even antagonism: Leah from her perspective as the unfavored wife and Rachel from her barrenness.

15. Or Hachaim, Genesis 30:15.
16. Rashi, Genesis 30:14.

Or maybe, as Rabbi Samson Raphael Hirsch's insights explain, it was a lively, perhaps even playful exchange. These were sisters who intimately shared their whole lives. Leah's reaction, that Rachel took her husband, may also hint at the interpretation mentioned earlier, that Rachel gave Leah signs for the wedding night in such a subtle way that Leah never even knew she was being given secret signals.

This is one of the hardest conversations for some of us to wrap our hearts around. Rachel and Leah were two sisters who were so close, so cherished, and they loved each other so deeply. They were on the same mission. Rachel responded to Leah, "Then he will lie with you tonight in exchange for your son's *dudaim*." Yaakov was supposed to be with Rachel that night, but she traded that union away to her sister for the *dudaim*. Herein lies a lesson on marital relations. Rachel made the herbs more important than the actual union with her husband. Leah made that union a priority and met Yaakov on his way in from the field, saying, "Come to me; for I have surely hired you with my son's *dudaim*." He lay with her that night. The Torah tells us that the Almighty heard Leah's prayers. She conceived, and a fifth son was born. His name was Issachar. Her sixth son was Zevulun (Zebulon). Interwoven in the story of Rachel and Leah are their trials, their goodness, their pain, and their love.

More Sisterly Love and Compassion

At this point, there were ten sons. Leah gave birth to six, and Bilhah and Zilpah each had two. There were to be twelve sons, each the father of one of the tribes, and Rachel had not given birth yet. Leah was pregnant again. She knew that if she gave birth to another son, it would take away from Rachel's portion. Her compassion that her sister would birth a solid portion of the tribes was so deep. According to Rashi (who is perhaps the greatest commentator), Leah prayed that the fetus be changed into a girl![17]

Leah gave birth to a daughter, Dina.

---

17. Rashi, Genesis 30:21, citing Talmud, *Berachot* 60a.

"The Almighty heard Rachel and opened her womb." It may seem as though the *dudaim's* properties for fertility helped Rachel conceive, but the clear point is made in Torah that God *heard* Rachel; it was her prayers that were answered. Oh, the power of prayers. The action we take is our effort, our part in the partnership with our Creator. In a way the actions we choose, the effort we put into our lives, is also our prayer. How Rachel longed for a baby. How compassionate and generous she was. At last she conceived. She called her son Yosef (Joseph), which means "to increase." His very name was her prayer for another son.

Time to Leave

Meanwhile, Yaakov worked for Lavan with his flocks. Yaakov tried to negotiate a fair wage, and with every negotiation, Lavan tried to change the deal to his own advantage. But divine intervention worked in Yaakov's favor. This episode, written about in detail, tells that the two made an agreement about which color of sheep Yaakov would receive from the flocks, and miraculously the majority of the lambs were born that color. Lavan would change the terms and get upset when his cheating did not succeed. God directed Yaakov, "Return to the land of your fathers, to your homeland, and I will be with you." He went to Rachel and Leah, who consented to the journey. They packed up to leave. Rachel stole her father's idols in the hopes he would not continue his idolatry. When Yaakov and his family left, they did not tell Lavan. Lavan, unwilling to lose his worker, began to chase them. God spoke to Lavan through a dream and warned him not to try to bribe Yaakov to come back. Still, Lavan pursued and confronted Yaakov. Lavan accused Yaakov of cheating and said he could easily harm Yaakov but that God had warned him not to. Then he said he would have sent the family off with music and celebration, had they left openly. Finally, he asked him, "Why did you steal my gods?"

Yaakov told Lavan the truth about why he left; he was afraid Lavan would take back his daughters by force. Yaakov then said that whoever had taken Lavan's idols would not live. If only he had not spoken so quickly. We know how powerful spoken words are, especially the words of those who stand in greatness. Yaakov did not know that his beloved Rachel had taken the idols or that his words would be a curse upon her. He gave Lavan permission to search everything. When Lavan came to Rachel—who had hidden the idols in the saddlebag of her camel—she asked for pardon for not rising out of respect, giving as an excuse that she was menstruating! Yaakov and Lavan had it out and finished up with an agreement, a covenant before God. They built a monument and broke bread.

Their journey continued with a deeply significant episode. Remember that Esav, Yaakov's brother, meant to murder him. Yaakov, in an effort to reconcile, sent word to Esav that he was returning with his family. His messengers were angels.[18] The angels returned and let him know that Esav was advancing with an army of four hundred men. Yaakov split his entourage into two camps, so that if one should be brought down, the other would survive. He prayed to God.

Yaakov made a second effort to make peace. He sent gifts to Esav: hundreds of goats and sheep, camels, bulls, and donkeys. He sent servants with the herds in waves, and each bore the message that this gift was a tribute. Then he sent his family off to safety with all their possessions.

Yaakov, alone at this point, now faced one of the defining moments in the birth of our nation. He wrestled with an angel—but not just any angel. It was the guiding and guardian angel of the nation that would emerge from Esav. They wrestled all through the night. Yaakov's faith was so strong that the angel could not triumph over him, but it did injure him, on his thigh. At daybreak the angel asked Yaakov to release him. We're told this angel needed to join a daily gathering of all angels to sing the heavenly songs of praise.[19] Yaakov said he would only release the angel in exchange for a blessing. The

18.   Rashi, Genesis 32:4.
19.   Talmud, *Chulin* 91b.

angel blessed him by changing his name to Yisrael (Israel). Now you know why we are called the children or nation of Israel. One interpretation of the meaning of the name Yisrael is to be victorious over man and angels. Another is to struggle with God.

Knowing that the very name Yisrael/Israel contains a struggle with God, doesn't it make sense to you that you carry a piece of that struggle within you, as you struggle to understand your personal mission? Each one of us can tap into the reality that we can overcome our trials. Our mission is in our name! A third meaning of the name Yisrael is "straight to God." We are a nation that has a faithful relationship with the Eternal. Although the angel said the name Yaakov would be replaced by the name Yisrael, we still call our patriarch by the name Yaakov, also. Each name represents a different aspect of his divine mission. (Mystically, his name represents the balance of strength and kindness into the beauty of spiritual integration of heaven and earth.)

After the struggle with the angel, Yaakov saw Esav coming with his army. They met. Esav saw Yaakov's power and invited him to join forces. Yaakov graciously declined, of course. They went their separate ways, though their descendants would clash, and still do. Yaakov and his family settled in Canaan, the Promised Land.

Dina

A difficult chapter of this story is about Leah's daughter, Dina. As they passed near the city of Shechem (still on the map of modern-day Israel), Dina was kidnapped and raped by the prince of Shechem (who shared the name of the city). The prince wanted to take Dina for a wife. His father, King Hamor (which in Hebrew means "donkey" or "severe"), went to Yaakov to negotiate for Dina as a wife for his son. He invited Yaakov to join with them, to intermarry, live together, trade and do business together.

Dina's brothers were outraged by the violation and took matters into their own hands. With a plan in mind, they led them on by telling them all the men of their nation must be circumcised before they could intermarry. King Hamor and Shechem went back to their people, giving a grand speech about how the two people would become one, and *that the people of Shechem would gain all the cattle and riches of Yaakov's family*. The pitch to their people was telling.

With greed for Yaakov's wealth, the men of Shechem all got circumcised. On the third day, when the pain from the circumcision was the greatest, Shimon and Levi, two of Yaakov's sons, went into Shechem and killed all the men. Yaakov, well aware that the Israelites could easily be attacked, reprimanded them. Shimon and Levi answered as Dina's protectors: "Should he treat our sister like a whore?"

Was it right for Shimon and Levi to do what they did? Was it right for Yaakov to do nothing? Was he considering the options of how to deal with the rape of his daughter? Could there have been another outcome here?

Rachel Bears a Second Son

Rachel, in the meantime, had become pregnant again. As mentioned above, Leah bore a daughter, Dina, so that Rachel could have the twelfth son. As they continued their journey, Rachel went into labor. She died in that childbirth, bringing the leader of the twelfth tribe into this world. (Remember, Yaakov had inadvertently cursed her over the matter of the idols.) As her soul was leaving her body, she called this son Ben Oni, "son of my grieving," but Yaakov named him Binyamin (Benjamin). Rachel was buried on the side of the road.

Rachel Weeps for her Children

Why was Rachel buried next to the road? Avraham and Sarah, Yitzchak and Rivka, and later Yaakov and Leah would all be buried in the same cave, Me'arat Hamachpelah. Why not Rachel? It was known through prophecy that the Jewish nation would be exiled from their land.[20] Twice our Temple in Jerusalem was destroyed, and we were exiled. The first exile lasted seventy years, and then the Temple was rebuilt. It was destroyed the second time nearly two thousand years ago. Although we have returned to the land, and the prophecies are being fulfilled about the ingathering of the exiles, we are still considered to be in the second exile because the Temple hasn't been rebuilt. Rachel, or "Mama Rachel" as some affectionately call her, is still there, by the side of the road, to comfort her children. Jews have gone to her gravesite for the past two thousand years to pray, and still do so today, in the hopes that her soul will intervene on our behalf to have our prayers answered. In particular, women go to her grave to pray when they want to find a husband or conceive.

During Operation Cast Lead, a military confrontation in Gaza (December 2008–January 2009), a strange thing happened. Israeli soldiers were about to go into a building in Gaza when a woman dressed in all black came out of the building and told them, in Arabic, to go away, that it was not safe there. They weren't sure about her, but proceeded to the next building on their list. The same woman came out of the next building (had she come through the tunnels?) and told them this building was also not safe. They wondered how this old woman could have known where they were going, and how she could possibly have managed to get there before them. It happened a third time. They asked her who she was. She told them she was Mama Rachel. It was later confirmed that the three buildings were booby-trapped.[21]

---

20. Ramban, Genesis 48:7.

21. For the details of this story, see Hillel Fendel, "Chief Rabbi Confirms Gaza Miracle Story," *Israel National News*, January 20, 2009, http://www.israelnationalnews.com/News/News.aspx/129532. While this story is considered a legend by some, after the war I shared this miracle story with my neighbor, who responded, "I know! My son's friend was one of the soldiers who was in the unit this happened to and told me about it."

Rachel's Gift: Holy Tears

Precious crying—*bechiyah*—tears pouring from the innermost recesses of the soul, stream through the gates of Heaven to change worlds: both inner, private ones and outer, public ones. It is said that the gates of Heaven are always open to tears.[22]

Rachel and Leah teach us the power of tears. Yet we are also cautioned to use our tears wisely. What are wise or worthy tears, and what are wasted tears? There is not a clear black and white answer. There is not one specific way to value tears. If you listen to a baby cry, sometimes you can hear that the tears are not serious, and other times they are the tears that make you rush to scoop them up for comfort. Perhaps the most profound thing about tears is the way they influence, change, and refine us. Our tears and our prayers open our hearts as we reach toward that intimate place of connecting with our Creator, and we are changed. Our tears and prayers change *us*. How honestly can we know the difference between wallowing in misery—being stuck—and reaching inside ourselves or heavenward, connecting? Tears at a commercial that was written to manipulate your emotions are not the holy tears that storm the gates of Heaven. Yet, if you find your eyes and nose are dripping and your throat is tight, there is likely a connection to something deeper; you may be able to turn within and tap into hidden places to channel those tears for meaningful prayer. Following are several stories to illustrate different kinds of crying.

An illustration of using and transforming tears comes from a story of a man called Rabbi Baruch Ber Levovitz of Kamenitz. When he was a young boy, his father reprimanded him with a smack. The child started to cry. Then, surprising his father, he ran to grab his prayer book and began to pray. He was asked why he did that. The boy answered that he didn't want to waste the tears.

Then there is the story told of the mother of one of the greatest Mishnaic sages of our nation, Rabbi Shimon bar Yochai, also

---

22. Talmud, *Bava Metzia* 59a.

known as the Rashbi.[23] His grave is the site of perhaps the largest gathering of Jews in our generation. Every year on the anniversary of his death, hundreds of thousands gather for bonfires and dance and prayer. (In the Jewish world, the date of someone's passing is more commemorated than a birth date because that's the day you can celebrate or honor all that an individual accomplished.) Rabbi Shimon's parents, Yochai and Sarah, were together for some years without becoming parents. Sarah wept and prayed, did acts of loving-kindness, and gave charity in order to beseech Heaven to grant her a child. On Rosh Hashanah, the Jewish New Year, the Day of Judgment, Sarah's husband Yochai had a dream. He dreamt that there was a forest of trees, some blossoming, thriving, and bearing fruit. Yochai was leaning on a dried tree without any leaves at all. He saw a figure who was pouring water from a vessel onto some of the trees. When the figure came to the tree where Yochai stood, he pulled out a small flask and poured its contents onto the ground where his tree stood. The tree blossomed and grew fruit! Yochai felt great joy and woke with a song from the Psalms on his lips: "He seats the barren woman of the house as a happy mother of children. Halleluyah!"[24]

He told his wife the dream and understood this meant that they would have a child. But he didn't understand what that little flask was. They went to the great sage Rabbi Akiva, who told them that Yochai's interpretation was correct and that his wife's destiny was to be childless, but because of her heartfelt, prayerful tears, her fate was changed. It was those precious tears that were collected into the flask that watered the tree and made it bloom.

There is a midrash that says that all the heartfelt tears of the Jews are collected in a reservoir and will be used to build the third Temple and usher in an era of true and permanent world peace. The idea of a third Temple and the era of peace for the entire world is not just a dream; it's a prophecy. Our sources say that this era

---

23. Written in *Nachlat Avot* by Moshe Shmuel of Zvehill.
24. Psalms 113:9.

of true peace will come to be reality in the merit of the good and virtuous women. That includes you, my dear reader.

Our matriarch Rachel sets the bar for us to use our tears for the good, for connection. The mystery of our tears can be used for transforming pain into light. The deepest of tears come from the place of the soul reaching out (or in) to the Source for the comfort of connection and the truest peace. It's a raw moment of connection, no hiding who you are as you stand (or crumble) in that most intimate and private place; there, the One Who gives you each breath awaits you.

Leah's Gift: The Secret to Happiness

Leah is the first one in the Torah to express gratitude, which she does by naming her fourth son Yehuda, the root of which means "grateful." The word *Jew* comes from the name Yehuda, so it's in the fabric of our name to be grateful. Nothing will change your life for the better as powerfully as gratitude. What is gratitude? It's looking for the good from every angle and understanding that the good you see in your life is a gift. Since there is a Creator of the world, and that Creator is infinite, it follows that there is nothing outside that Creator. All is divine. This world is all by design. So every tiny detail in your life is a gift, from your automatic breath and heartbeat to the smile the stranger shared that lifted your spirits. You are a conduit for the Divine, since you are a divine creation. The art that you create, the love you give your children, the sunset you enjoy—all are gifts. Recognizing this opens the channels for *more!*

How joyful would your life be if you lived in an attitude of gratitude? The only way you'll know for sure is to up the ante and step more fully into the concept. Deepening gratitude is a lifetime process. Gratitude is actually its own reward; it builds and opens you.

This concept includes being grateful for the challenges and trials we are given. As you discover the stories and hardships of the women in Tanach, you can easily see, just as you see in your own life, there is no such thing as being in this world without hardships and sufferings. We see from the stories of our women, and hopefully you can see it also in your own world, that trials bring you to growth. You become better. You get stronger. You understand what matters. Getting to a place of being able to say "thank you," even for the difficulties or for what you *don't* have, can be a life-changing paradigm shift. What we're avoiding here is the sense of entitlement. We are releasing assumptions that we're "supposed" to wake up and have everything working or falling into place.

There is a short declaration of gratitude we're taught to say first thing upon rising after sleep (see the mini-guide of Spiritual Pathways at the back of the book). In this blessing we remind ourselves that the Eternal One has faith and believes in *us.* By giving us another day, He's giving us the message that we can accomplish what we need to; we can bring or be a light in the world and make a difference by being here.

You might need to purposefully cultivate your imagination with some of the hard stuff of life. One thing that might help is thinking about the ways that you were told "no" as a child. Today you understand how fortunate it was that your parents didn't give you everything you wanted. Parents "made" you go to school, and now you can read. A kid only wants to eat sugary sweets, but parents limit sweets and present healthy food to grow on. There are certainly painful experiences in life. A man I know actually expressed his gratitude that his mother was taken by cancer! Not that he wished her harm, God forbid, but because it gave him the chance to take time to connect with her at the end.

Gratitude does not necessarily or automatically take away pain or grief in those hardest of trials. When three Israeli boys were kidnapped and murdered by terrorists in 2014, the grief of Jews and Israel swelled to international proportions, and the families were surrounded with massive love and support. Even in their unfathomable loss, they expressed their gratitude. It was a gift to them to know they were not alone in their grief and bereavement.

The way you get good at anything—riding a bike, playing an instrument, speaking a new language—is by practicing. It's the same with gratitude. By being grateful, you'll become more grateful. One of the most powerful yet simple techniques to expand your gratitude is to sit at the end of each day and list ten things you are grateful for *that you have never said thank you for before.* How do you do that? You look for the minutiae; the smallest of details count! Say, think, or write, "I'm grateful for..." and fill in that blank. We want to be grateful for our kids, grandkids, spouses, friends, pets, and so on, but can you find the thing that happened *today* that was unique to this day?

Thanks for that delicious piece of watermelon at lunch.

I'm grateful for the visit I had with my friend Susan.

I'm thankful for the online class today.

I'm grateful for stumbling upon that passage in a book that answered a question I've had for years!

Thanks for the ride to the doctor.

Or the kind nurse.

Or my favorite magazine in the waiting room.

No detail is too small to acknowledge. Gratitude leads to happiness. We're taught in the wisdom of the sages that happiness with your portion makes you rich! In the body of wisdom called *Pirkei Avot* (Ethics of the Fathers), we can find the timeless teaching of Ben Zoma: "Who is rich? The one who is happy with his portion."[25]

It is a lifetime of seeking to find what brings value to life and how to overcome hardships in every stage. It's clear that gratitude is one of the single most powerful keys to a good life. Expressing gratitude, out loud or in writing, is even more powerful. Say thank you to the people in your life, to the angels who guide you and whisper in your ears, and of course, to the One Who created the people, angels, and all the other creatures and gifts in your world.

---

25. Mishnah, *Pirkei Avot* 4:1.

Reflections in Rachel's Mirror: Sisterhood Unity

If we seek world peace, we need to begin by being in peace inside ourselves and with those around us. It's important for women to rise up and foster unity within the family, within the community, and with each other. Rachel teaches us this in the most profound ways. Here are some tips for promoting peace in relationships with others.

Transform jealousy. Getting past jealousy is a significant piece of the relationship puzzle. Rachel teaches us that the only kind of jealousy that will serve is the jealousy of seeing the brilliant good in your sisters and desiring that for yourself. Framing your perspective in this way will help you grow and elevate your life on many levels. So what do you do with the jealousy that bubbles up in you about another woman's intellect, clothes, looks, wealth, relationships, and so forth? We're always on the lookout for a shift in thinking or perceiving. In place of jealousy, we can say, "Seeing the good others have must mean that my own good is very close at hand!" This simple shift in the thought process and self-talk can transform jealousy into sincere happiness! Be creative in the way your good can come to you. The good that will come to you will not look the same as someone else's. Remember that in any case, what you see is not really the whole picture for anyone else's life. So that leads into the next tool.

Develop a good eye: look for the good. Building the good in relationships has to do with looking for the good within the other. It's not about false flattery, but honest compliments. Focusing on the positive builds kindness within you and can boost the character of others. None of us knows the battles that are raging in another. No one knows another's trials in life. Giving the benefit of the doubt in situations that feel irritating or even hurtful will bring you to a place of peace. If you really have the courage to grow in relationships, know that everyone and every situation comes into our lives to *reflect* something. Doing the sometimes-difficult inner work of considering what is there for you to see about yourself is transformative. When you admire someone, remember he or she is also reflecting your good and your potential!

This call is for you to rise. How else to keep peace in your relationships? Be the one to rise. Imagine that you get a message from God to you personally, letting you know that tomorrow you will be tested and that He'll be watching you. When someone gives you a sour face (or fill in the blank), you won't be pulled into responding in kind; it's just a test, remember? You will rise to the challenge.

Bless. It's easy to stand in sisterhood and unity when things are going well, but when they are not, what can you do? Changing the way you feel toward another brings peace within and is often reflected in changes in the people around you. When people are not so nice, it's often because they are in pain. When people are in pain, what they need is a blessing. This simple technique is a power tool in a quantum way! How do you bless? You just start, even if you don't feel sincere. The other person does not need to hear this blessing for it to work, though it has been used to defuse uncomfortable situations. Say, "May you be blessed..." and fill in the blank. Use your heart, your intuition, and your imagination. Someone cuts you off in traffic? Bless them to get home to their family safely. The amazing thing about blessing others is that what you bless others with is actually a blessing for yourself! Your own upset will be transformed. You can bless people with prosperity or peace; you can bless them with health or comfort, or all of the above. The more you practice blessing others, the easier it gets. It's a form of prayer. If our words have great power, use them to build blessings and peace. Bless those you love, too. Don't wait for upset to invoke your blessings in this world. Blessing those you love is like a kiss to the spirit. Phrases as simple as "have a great day" or "drive safely" or "enjoy" are blessings. Experiment with blessing others with your words to tap into the healing and building properties of this tool.

Reflections in Leah's Mirror: Weaving Struggles into Gold

Leah's suffering began with the vision that Esav might become her mate. Then she suffered in a marriage in which, although she was loved, she was not the favored wife. There has always been much suffering in the world, much greater than Leah endured, but here Leah gives us an important key to dealing with the suffering in our lives. Unfortunately, there is no easy or simple answer for the millennia-old question of why there is suffering in this world.

Touching into this most complicated question begins with the simplest answer, the least satisfying of all, which no man or woman will ever fully grasp: there is a bigger picture. We cannot know from our limited human perspective what that is.

Each of us is a soul, created for a divine mission and purpose. We do not have access to the "whole picture" of the soul or its journey—why the soul is here in this earthly experience. From a broader, heavenly perspective, there is purpose and meaning to each and every breath we take. We think we can understand some of it, but then we have the hardest of times, loss, change, upheaval, or pain, and it can feel as if life is crashing in on us.

When one grain of sand enters the shell of an oyster, it secretes a substance to coat the offending source of pain. It coats and coats and coats until the surface is smooth: a pearl is created. From pain and hurt, a beautiful gem is created. We know how annoying a small pebble that slipped into our shoe can feel; now imagine that this delicate creature is subjected to sharp pain against its tender flesh. Yet its natural reaction to this pain is to create something beautiful.

This life, though full of pleasures and delights to be sure, is also full of pains and disappointments. We live with an illusion of what we think life "should" be, and then we are *dis*illusioned and disappointed as we see that life does not fit our expectations.

Yet, from the spiritual perspective of Torah, *everything* that we experience has meaning and purpose. Every life experience holds rich gifts for us to cash in on if we stay awake and aware, or conscious, to what we are experiencing. Each trial or pain comes with a gift of its own—an insight, deeper compassion or understanding or wisdom, and it is our job to find the pearl and treasure it.

It is at this point that our personal power comes in. We may not be able to control what happens around us, and most likely we truly can't control most of what goes on in and around our lives. What we can control is the way in which we receive our life experiences, and we have a choice about the "outflow"—the actions and reactions we choose as a response to what shows up in life.

Our choices are what build us, and our choices are how we build ourselves. So what can you do when you experience some degree of suffering? Start with compassion for yourself and others, and add a dose of trust in the Creator that even what looks like a difficulty is ultimately for the good.

One simple example of this is the story of a Jewish girl born in Brooklyn, New York, in 1922. She grew up speaking only Yiddish. When she entered school, she learned English, and because she felt that she always struggled with English, she put all her effort into strengthening what she felt was her weakness. She became an English professor and taught English as a Second Language (ESL). This woman, my own mother, was able to help countless students who passed through the doors of her college campus learning center.

Another example is from the 1890s when many Jewish immigrants came to the United States from eastern Europe. Immigrants who had a lung disease (at the time called consumption, now known as tuberculosis) were sent to Denver, Colorado, where, they were told, the dry air would be better for them. Many of them died in the streets. A charitable woman worked to build a place where poor sick people could get treated. National Jewish Health, the hospital that was born and evolved from that time, is now the leading respiratory hospital in the United States.[26]

---

26. "History of National Jewish Health," https://www.nationaljewish.org/about/history.

There are many kinds of personal suffering, and you also know that suffering is on a spectrum. Only you know what you personally are suffering, or where it is on the spectrum.

Here are some tools to help transform your perspective from pain to GOLD:

G=Gratitude. Being grateful means having the understanding that every detail we have in our lives is a gift: our senses, our possessions, our relationships, all the good, and even what looks bad. The things that don't seem to be what we want are there to teach, guide, or prepare us as we move forward on this journey of life. Gratitude opens the channels to seeing the good even in the difficulties.

O=Optimism. You choose your attitude. Orient your attitude in the direction of joy. There was a sage called Nachum Ish Gamzu. *Gam zu* in Hebrew means "also this." No matter what pain or suffering befell Nachum Ish Gamzu, he always responded, "Also *this* is for the good."[27] We may not see the good now, but that just means we don't see it *yet*. A popular quote has it that "A pessimist sees the difficulty in every opportunity, and an optimist sees the opportunity in every difficulty." You may not be able to control what comes in to you, but you do control what you do with every experience.

L=Let go. You don't need to carry things that will not serve you. You know what that means: grudges, hurt feelings, or upsets. You may feel you are justified. You may feel that letting go lets the one who did wrong off the hook. What you're really doing when you let go is releasing what hurts *you*. Imagine a toddler with a big, full, saggy diaper. The diaper has served its purpose, but it is time to let it go. Get clean. It's about elegantly eliminating what isn't working in your life. Let go of the thoughts that bring you down. What about the nasty email that so-and-so sent you? Delete! Don't allow the thief called pettiness to steal your joy. Replace the negative thoughts with thoughts that lift your spirits. Change your posture.

27. Talmud, *Taanit* 21a.

Imagine wearing a royal crown, and smile in the knowledge of who you are at your best. Letting go with a blessing is a brilliant practice.

D=Divine direction. Include a higher power. You already have a higher perspective than a child. You no longer cry about the same things because you've grown. Knowing there is a perspective that is higher still, no matter where we find ourselves, opens the door for trusting that there is a bigger picture and that there is more to the story than you know at this time. The most potent way to transform yourself so that you create a different life experience for yourself is to pray. (See "Reflections in Chana's Mirror" for more about prayer.) Prayer taps into higher places and opens intuition and the whisperings of the divine spark that always glows within you. You're not in this life alone.

Miriam
Righteous Rebellion and Unity Dance

The Story of Miriam

If you want to break through stereotypes about age, study the prophetess Miriam.[1] She demonstrated how a woman could impact reality in spite of her age. You are never too young or too old to make a difference. Miriam models for us how to courageously step forward to do what's right, how to joyfully dance and bless, and how *everyone* falls and can rise again.

We are a tribal nation, and people are identified with names that describe what they do, their mission, or what they are like. The name Miriam has two meanings. The first is "bitterness" or more literally, "bitter sea," from the Hebrew *mar* (bitter) and *yam* (sea), because she was born at a bitter time of oppression and slavery in Egypt.[2] The second is "rebellious," from the Hebrew *meri*, because she rebelled against that very oppression and slavery.

When we first meet Miriam in the Torah, she is five years old, working as a midwife with her mother, Yocheved. The Torah mentions two midwives working among the Jewish slaves in Egypt: Shifra and Puah. We are taught that these midwives are Yocheved and Miriam.[3] As we have seen, some biblical characters have more than one name. In her work as a midwife, Yocheved was called Shifra, which means "to beautify," because she would clean

---

1. The first part of Miriam's story is told in Exodus 1:15–3:9 and Exodus 15:20.
2. Rashi, Song of Songs 2:13.
3. Midrash, *Exodus Rabbah* 1:13.

and dress the babies after they were born. Miriam was called Puah because she made sweet sounds and cooed to the babies to comfort them.

We can easily imagine a five-year-old cooing to a newborn, but how can we imagine a five-year-old as a midwife? What would it have been like to allow children to grow up participating in life, instead of parking them in front of some screen! While it is rare, there are families today that allow young girls to be a part of the birth of their younger siblings. If children are raised to be sensitive, they will feel empathy for those around them. In large families, older children are called quite naturally to take care of the younger siblings. How natural it was in ancient times for a child to follow and learn from a parent. This was what Miriam did.

A Murderous Plan

At such a tender age, Miriam was called to stand before Pharaoh along with her mother, Yocheved. When we read stories of ancient times, we sometimes imagine the people to be like the cartoons that illustrate a children's book. Yet here, it's important to know that Pharaoh was a formidable man. Think of Saddam Hussein or Pol Pot: evil, powerful, and fearsome. Pharaoh hanged his baker because he found a fly in the bread! This is a sickening hint to the nature of Pharaoh. He was not a cartoon character. (Keep in mind this is the new pharaoh who did not know Joseph,[4] not the father of Hagar whom we met in the chapter on Sarah.)

Pharaoh gave an order to the midwives to murder all the male babies of the Children of Israel. He wanted Yocheved and Miriam to lie to the women, to murder the newborn boys and tell the mothers that they died in childbirth. Of course, the Hebrew midwives would defy this command. They knew that they could be executed for defying Pharaoh, but they chose to be true and accountable to God.

---

4.   "Now there arose a new king over Egypt, who knew not Joseph" (Exodus 1:8).

In previous generations, when human sacrifice was a norm, the Jews had the ethic not to take part in this murderous custom. There are 613 commandments in the Torah, and "Do not murder" made the top ten—it's one of the Ten Commandments, which were given even before the full Torah. While this sounds pretty obvious to you—you have this ethic in your blood and bones—the value of life is not revered across all faiths or cultures. Tragically, in China where one baby to a couple was the legal limit, it was possible to find buckets of water in some birthing rooms, to drown babies of the "wrong" gender; other baby girls were deserted and abandoned.[5] Known primarily in Muslim culture, "honor killing" is an acceptable act of murder by the father or brother of a woman who is accused of bringing shame to the family name.[6] In ancient Rome, a fight to the death was sport. The Aztecs and the Incas had a constant flow of human sacrificial blood from atop their pyramids. There are people in recent world history, as well as the present day, who murder in massive numbers for money and power.

Righteous Rebellion

What about the young Miriam, who faced a murderous and powerful man who commanded her to murder? Could fear for her life justify the murder of newborn babies? According to Jewish law, saving a life is so important that we are actually obligated to transgress or break almost any Torah law for this reason. (The exceptions are idolatry, murder, and sexual immorality, which we must not transgress even if our lives depend on it.) It actually becomes a mitzvah to break the law in order to save a life. This concept is called *pikuach nefesh* (literally, preserving life). One example is that, although Jewish law says a body should be buried whole, Jews may

---

5. Winter Wall, "China's Infanticide Epidemic," *Human Rights and Human Welfare Topical Research Digest: Human Rights in China* (2009): 202–10, https://www.du.edu/korbel/hrhw/researchdigest/china/InfanticideChina.pdf.

6. Phyllis Chesler, "Worldwide Trends in Honor Killings," *Middle East Quarterly* 17 (spring 2010), https://www.meforum.org/articles/2010/worldwide-trends-in-honor-killings.

donate bone marrow or a kidney to save a life. That is a beautiful thing. Similarly, many people observe Shabbat by refraining from using electronics or driving. However, if someone's life is in danger, calling an ambulance or driving someone to the hospital is paramount. The Talmud teaches us, "Whoever destroys a soul, it is considered as if he destroyed an entire world. And whoever saves a life, it is considered as if he saved an entire world."[7]

For Yocheved and Miriam (Shifra and Puah), fear for their own lives could not compel them to break God's laws. They did not follow Pharaoh's orders. The midwives were called to Pharaoh again, and he asked them why they let the boys live. The midwives told Pharaoh the Hebrew women, unlike the Egyptians, gave birth before the midwives could arrive. Yocheved and Miriam were rewarded for their fear of God. (See "Reflections in Miriam's Mirror" to explore this concept.)

Prophecy and Determination

When his plan to use the Hebrew midwives to murder babies didn't work, Pharaoh decreed the death of Hebrew baby boys by drowning. Yocheved's husband, Amram, was the leader of the Jewish people at that dark time of bitter slavery in Egypt. He thought it would be better to stop having babies than to submit to the evil decree of drowning the infant boys. So Amram separated from (divorced) his wife Yocheved. Many Israelites followed his lead, and couples separated.[8]

Miriam, the daughter of Amram and Yocheved, was gifted with prophecy. This young girl of five years old approached her father and told him that his decree was also against the girls, since if couples separated, no girls could be born either. She also revealed to him the prophecy she received that he and her mother would give birth to a child who would be the redeemer of the Jewish nation. He

---

7.   Mishnah, *Sanhedrin* 4:5.
8.   Midrash, *Exodus Rabbah* 1:13.

listened. He heard. He remarried his wife. Once again, the people followed his lead and remarried. Moshe was born.

The Egyptians (not unlike the Nazis) kept track of things and knew when a Jewish woman was pregnant.[9] They would wait for the due date. If the baby was a boy, they would take him and drown him. Moshe was born prematurely, so he was spared this fate. His mother nursed him for three months until she could not continue to hide him. She made a basket and smeared it with clay and pitch so that it would float. She placed the infant Moshe inside it and put it to float on the Nile River. His loving big sister Miriam followed the basket. She waited, hidden in the bushes, to watch over the fate of her brother.

Enter the daughter of Pharaoh, Princess Batya. She was bathing in the river; her handmaidens were on the shore. She saw the basket and sent a maidservant to bring it to her. When she opened the basket, she saw the crying infant. She figured out that it was one of the Hebrew babies, but she took pity on him.

Miriam approached Princess Batya and offered to bring a wet nurse. Batya agreed. Miriam brought her mother Yocheved. This is how Moshe was given back to his own mother, who nursed him until he was weaned. Then he was given to Batya to live in the palace with his adoptive mother. We know sociologically how strong a mother's influence is with her child in the youngest, formative years. This story anchors and demonstrates the strength and importance of that bond. Moshe always knew where he came from.

What an amazing story for Jewish girls to grow up with, to be taught that a young girl could impact the future of her entire nation. It doesn't matter how young you are. There is not an age that a girl or young woman has to reach in order to be qualified to make a positive impact on the world. You don't have to be old enough to vote, you don't have to have a degree. You don't have to wait to bring light into your family's home or make the world a

---

9.   Talmud, *Sotah* 12a; Ibn Ezra, Exodus 2:2.

better place. *You are never too young to make a difference. You make a difference right now.*

Beauty in the Bitterness:
Where the Copper Mirrors Fit In

Moshe was saved, but in the meantime, the brutal conditions of the Hebrew slaves continued. And it was harsh. Infants were cemented into brick walls.[10] Pharaoh even bathed in the blood of Jewish babies.[11] Humiliated, beaten, and exhausted, the men dropped in the fields at the end of their day of work, finished. The women rose up in those harshest of conditions. They would not allow themselves to feel defeat. The Hebrew women, slaves in Egypt, used mirrors of copper to beautify themselves.[12]

We know what it is to put ourselves in the best frame possible. We know which outfits in our closets look the best and make us feel the prettiest, or the way we wear our hair, or position the scarf that is just the right color to set off our eyes, or skin, or that helps us feel that glow. A woman can look in the mirror and focus on her flaws or wrinkles or weight, or she can look in the mirror and focus on the soul level, bringing out the most beautiful and glowing aspect of all, her soul essence. Tapping into the truth of the godly soul brings balance and confidence. From that place, we take action, and we do what we do with conviction.

The women beautified themselves using their copper mirrors and went to the fields to their husbands. Taking their men to private places for intimate connections, they would see to it that even in those severe conditions, the nation would survive. They had faith that there was a purpose, that there was meaning. Like the matriarchs, the women of that generation knew they were building something important for the future of the nation. They knew that

---

10. Rashi, *Sanhedrin* 101b.
11. Rashi, Exodus 2:23; Midrash, *Exodus Rabbah* 1:34.
12. Rashi, Exodus 38:8.

the harshness and slavery they were enduring would end. They persevered.

Miriam was the inspirer, the teacher, and the motivator of that generation of women. She was a prophetess. She knew the slavery would end, and she shared that with the women—women whose faithfulness to that truth was strong. It was so strong, in fact, that they actually made tambourines and other instruments of music and celebration to use during their anticipated redemption from the Egyptian slavery. Pretty bold move at the time, don't you think? They knew without a doubt that they would be leaving that life. It's a scary thing to give up all that is familiar, and by that generation, Egyptian life was all they knew. Yet these women were not only willing to go way beyond what was familiar, they even prepared themselves to go with joy, song, and dance. They prepared themselves for the celebration they knew they would surely experience. *That* is faith: something deeper than hope.

Exodus

God sent Moshe and his brother Aharon as His human emissaries, to tell Pharaoh to release the Jews.[13] Pharaoh would not let go of his slaves. It's an epic story. Only after God sent ten miraculous, hard-to-wrap-your-brain-around, dramatic plagues to descend upon Egypt did Pharaoh finally agree to let the Hebrews leave. Astoundingly, we are taught that only one in five of the Jews in Egypt had the courage to leave. Four out of every five Hebrews stayed and perished![14] If you are a Jew today, you are descended from ancestors who were full of a kind of faith that the English language has no word to describe.

The Exodus, leaving the slavery of Egypt, was more than letting go of an external bondage. The Exodus was not just about what that new nation was leaving; it was also rooted in what the nation was walking toward.

---

13. The story of the Jews' exodus from Egypt is told in Exodus, chapters 3–15.
14. Midrash, *Mechilta d'Rabbi Yishmael* 13:18; Rashi, Exodus 10:22.

Song of the Sea

As the multitudes of Hebrew slaves were leaving, Pharaoh changed his mind. He called his army, loaded his chariots, and chased after them. Imagine modern-day military tanks chasing after people who are traveling by foot. The Hebrews reached the sea, and the Egyptian army was upon them. They cried out. One brave soul had the faith to step off the shore and plunge into the water.[15] The water rose to his nose, and the miracle happened: the sea split. It was an open miracle, a great miracle! The nation crossed in safety—the Hebrews walked on dry land. The Midrash paints the dramatic picture for us that there were twelve lanes, one for each of the twelve tribes—each bordered by walls of water.[16] As they stepped out of the sea, the Egyptian soldiers embarked onto the dry sea floor, but the sea closed on them. The chariots were submerged. The water churned. The warhorses and the soldiers all drowned. Pharaoh alone was the sole survivor. Why was Pharaoh the only survivor? He would bear witness to the power of God.

Safely back on shore, the nation broke into a mystical song. It was not a song that they practiced. It was not a song that was already known. It was a spontaneous song that everyone just knew in the moment when they connected with the heavens as one people. The men sang from a deep place, and the women—with Miriam in the lead—played those drums and tambourines that they had always known they would use. They danced!

What was that faith that had the slave women certain that redemption would come, and that they would have need of instruments with which to celebrate? That was the inspiration of Miriam and the knowing of the women of that generation. These were the women who took their copper mirrors to beautify themselves, in spite of the brutality of Egypt. These were the women who knew that even in the face of the most painful of life circumstances—such as having their infant sons torn from their breasts and drowned—it

---

15. Nachshon ben Aminadav, prince of Judah. Talmud, *Sotah* 37a.
16. Midrash, *Tehillim Rabbah* 136:5; Rashi, Psalms 136:13.

was still worth it to build families. These women cast their eyes to look through their oceans of tears, toward a future that would be bright and full. These worn and beaten women, who faced anguish that cannot be described and still made instruments for celebration, were our mothers. These women reach into our very bones, so that when we think of them, we can tap into and feel their strength and determination.

But wait, there's something more for you to know! When I ask women to picture Miriam leading the Jewish women in song and dance by the sea, I ask how old they see her in their mind's eye. Perhaps as you were reading her story, you had an image in your own mind? How old did she look in your imagination?

The Torah tells us that Moshe was eighty years old the first time he stood before Pharaoh to ask for the release of his nation.[17] Miriam was his older sister. It was a process that took time: many months, at least. So that would put Miriam in her late eighties, maybe closer to ninety years old!

The lesson is of course: just as you are never too young to make a difference, *you are never too old to have an impact* on your family, your community, your nation, and even the world. You're never "retired" from contributing to life, you're never used up. Never. Miriam teaches us you are never too young or too old to make a difference. That means that wherever you are in your life right now, in this very minute, what you do matters, and your contribution to your family, your community, your nation, and the world makes a difference.

National Revelation in the Desert

This next portion of the story is critical to the nation as a whole, not just to the women.[18] After witnessing miracles and wonders, Bnei Yisrael (the Children of Israel) were in the Sinai Desert. In an astounding and unique experience, a defining moment for our nation, God spoke to the Jews at Mount Sinai. The first of the Ten

---

17. Exodus 7:7.
18. See Exodus, chapters 19–20.

Commandments was given directly by God to the Jewish people. Unlike any other spiritual path or major world religion, the Eternal spoke to the entire nation all at once. This was a *national* revelation. The Midrash tells us that the souls of all who were present were literally blown out of their bodies (the whole nation died!) when they heard God speak.[19] God restored the souls to the bodies. The second commandment was given, and it happened again: the souls were blown out of their bodies. That intense level of spirituality is unfathomable to us today. Because of the intensity of dying and being brought back, the Jews asked Moshe to receive and then transmit the Torah that the Eternal would give the nation. We're told that at this point, because of his direct connection to God, Moshe glowed so brightly that he had to keep his face hidden to protect the eyes of the people.[20] It's bewildering to consider this because we are attracted to that spiritual light, and at the same time it can be overwhelming.

As the nation wandered in the desert, they received manna from Heaven for their nourishment.[21] It is described as a delicious white substance with a dough-like texture that can taste like nearly any other food.[22] They gathered the heavenly portion they would need each day, and it was fresh for that day. Any amount that was kept for more than that day became inedible. There was one weekly exception: on Fridays they would take a double portion, one for that day, and the extra portion would stay fresh for Shabbat. Today, millennia later, we begin our Shabbat meals with two loaves of braided challah bread in order to remember the double portion we received in the desert.[23]

For drink, the nation was provided sweet water that came from Miriam's well.[24] When you picture a well, what do you imagine? Do

19. Midrash, *Exodus Rabbah* 29:4.
20. Exodus 34:29–35.
21. Exodus 16:4.
22. Midrash, *Exodus Rabbah* 25:3.
23. Talmud, *Shabbat* 117b.
24. Exodus 17; Talmud, *Taanit* 9a; Mishnah, *Pirkei Avot* 5:6.

you see a quaint, small stone structure with a bucket and a rope? Miriam's well is said to have been a rock that traveled with them in the desert as they walked.[25] Keep in mind that somehow Miriam's well would have to provide for the approximately three million Jews who left Egypt. You can only imagine what it would be like if even fifty people had to wait in line to fetch water to drink after walking in the desert. That's a lot of water, and an extraordinary open miracle, explicit in a way that anyone could see. When they stopped, it was a place from which whole rivers sprang forth, twelve rivers to be exact, so that each tribe would be supplied.[26]

Wells have meaningful symbolism throughout the Torah. They repeatedly come up as a place where couples have met and covenants or contracts have been sealed. A well is a place of mystery. Water comes from below and rises up, but only after digging for it. It takes effort on our part to dig, and then the water rises up. Might it symbolize the meeting of earthly efforts and heavenly assistance? In Judaism, water is connected to kindness, and also to Torah itself (see the chapter on Rachel and Leah).

Also in the story of Miriam, the well is significant. It's said that Miriam's well still exists at the bottom of the Sea of Galilee (known as the Kinneret in Hebrew) in northern Israel.[27] We're told it will spring forth rivers again at the time of redemption, when the world shifts to true peace, and evil is no more.[28]

A Difficult Lesson

There is another time when Miriam appeared in the Torah to teach us an important lesson.[29] If any part of you thinks that the Torah is about romantic stories and that our heroines are flawless, this part of Miriam's story is one of the hardest to bear and integrate. Yet, it may be one of the most powerful lessons for refining and

25. Rashi on the Talmud, *Taanit* 9a, *Pesachim* 54a, *Shabbat* 35a; Tosefta, *Sukkah* 3:3.
26. Rashi, Psalms 78:16.
27. Midrash, *Leviticus Rabbah* 22:4; Jerusalem Talmud, *Kilayim* 9:3 (43a).
28. Midrash, *Pirkei d'Rabbi Eliezer* 51:10–13; Maharal, *Netzach Yisrael*, chapter 54.
29. This part of Miriam's story is in Numbers 12:1–15 and 20:1.

strengthening human relations and also our own humble journey of self-improvement.

In the midst of the era of the birth of the Jewish nation and in the presence of Moshe, Miriam spoke to her brother Aharon, the High Priest.[30] She questioned something about their brother Moshe's relationship with his wife. Miriam learned that Moshe had to separate from having sexual relations with his wife in order to be ready in any moment to talk with God. Miriam was concerned. Now, if we review the history of Miriam's life experiences, we can see a kind of replay of what happened when she was a little girl. Her father separated from her mother, and the nation followed suit. What would happen now? God also spoke to Miriam and Aharon—they were also prophets—but they had not been told to separate from their spouses. Maybe something was wrong? Miriam spoke to Aharon about it.

That was not okay. She should have seen the uniqueness of Moshe's relationship with God. At the very least, she could have spoken directly with Moshe—he was, after all, clearly receiving direct divine guidance. Immediately, God reprimanded her and punished Miriam with a skin affliction called *tzara'at, Tzara'at* is often mistakenly translated as "leprosy." There is no accurate translation for this word: that's why the Hebrew word is always used in Torah study. *Tzara'at* is a kind of skin eruption that could also appear on clothing, or even on the wall of a dwelling place.[31] *Tzara'at* was caused by speaking *lashon hara*, which translates literally as "evil tongue," and can be anywhere on the spectrum from seemingly innocuous gossip to the worst slander or libel.

In that time, in the desert, the nation got instant feedback about the way they used their speech. Once people were afflicted with *tzara'at*, they would be in a kind of quarantine. They would separate from society for a week. Just as their words may have

---

30. Rashi, Numbers 12:1.
31. Leviticus, chapters 13–14.

caused others to be pushed away, they would now understand what it is like to be estranged from the community.

What was a private transgression would be publicly visible. Why? Because what we do in private actually does affect the whole community. Think about a guy in a boat who decides to drill a hole in the wall of his cabin so he can see outside. It could cause the whole boat to sink and endanger everyone. This is how powerful our speech is.

The concept goes the other way, too. When a person repairs relationships or does healing work or acts of kindness in private, that also affects the whole, but in a positive way. You can probably see painful or helpful ways in which this concept works in your own family or community.

We know that Miriam was a prophetess; she was a leader. We know she was such a good woman: sincere, spiritually elevated, and loyal. Yet she was punished for talking about her brother Moshe, with whom she had a very close relationship.

Here's the difficult lesson: *We're not meant to talk about each other!* It seems so crazy that we are being taught to draw a line and not talk about others when relationships are such a huge part of our collective reality. We can easily relate to Miriam and understand her position based on her life experience. We know she loved her brother Moshe. She tended to him as an infant. She waited in the bushes and followed him. There's no stretch of the imagination that would lead anyone to think she meant her brother harm in any way. Still, her speech caused him harm. If you dent another person's car, even if you didn't mean to, and you're sorry, and they forgive you, you still have to repair the damage. There's a price to pay.

Right then, in the heat of the moment, Moshe prayed that Miriam's *tzara'at* be healed. It was, but she would still have to be isolated for the prescribed seven days. The entire nation would wait for her before they would continue their desert journey and move camp.

Each one of us is accountable, in accordance with the level we're on. If you think about parenting children, you understand there is a different expectation of a two-year-old than of an eight-year-old. You have a different expectation of a mature adult than you have of a thirteen-year-old. So too, if someone is a leader, their accountability is more significant. Miriam was at such a high level and so up close to what was happening that there had to be a consequence for speaking about her brother. Her pain is a lesson with a precious gift for us. If that kind of nuance in care about speech matters, how careful should we be about our own speech?

Perhaps this is such a painful lesson because, sadly, so many of us fall short in the area of speech. This lesson serves as a clear reminder of the gravity of gossip and the importance of increasing our sensitivity in the area of gossip and speech. It is a basic human desire to talk about others. Refining our speech is an extraordinary opportunity to rise up, as we master this desire that can so hurt others. We can tap into our strengths to repair relationships and build others up, no matter what level we are on. *Being mindful of our speech, and how it builds up or tears down another, is a critical piece to the Jewish spiritual journey.*

Miriam's Gift: Guard Your Speech

Why all this attention to speech? The world was created with speech. Since we each contain a spark of the Divine, we have power to create our reality, affecting others and ourselves with our speech. Words have great power. Every one of us has experienced being hurt by words. Hopefully they have lifted us as well. Refining speech to eliminate talking about others is guaranteed to be life changing. It's so easy and natural to talk about other people. We're around people all day. Our lives are made up of relationships, so it's normal to talk about what we're involved in. There are whole magazines that report about others, exposing people's personal or intimate lives as "news." But Judaism has perspective on talking about others. Again, the Hebrew term, *lashon hara,* tells us more than the English. The best English word we have for *lashon hara* is "gossip." This conjures images of spreading lies about someone. *Lashon hara* is even more explicit about the issue, though. *Lashon hara* means simply talking about someone else, even when what's said is *true.* There is a separate term (*rechilut* or "slander") for spreading lies, which is a severe offense.

King Solomon, known as the wisest of all men,[32] wrote in Proverbs, "Death and life are in the power of the tongue."[33] The Talmud gives us more about that: a person's tongue is more powerful than a sword. A sword can only kill someone who is nearby: a tongue can cause the death of someone who is far away. When someone withdraws a sword to kill, he can change his mind, returning the sword to its sheath. Once words have left your lips, the damage is done. Killing doesn't only mean a physical death. Words have the power to harm someone's reputation or ability to earn an income, or damage a relationship, and this damage can be devastating.

Judaism is a path of refining relationships: relationship to God, relationship to others, and relationship to self. We're taught that before Yom Kippur we must make amends with the people in our lives. Yom Kippur is the holiest day of the Jewish year. It's the day we are supposed to stand humbly before our Creator and take account of our actions, both intentional and unintentional. We correct and repair what we can through prayer, yet we are taught that before we show up to the synagogue to ask God's forgiveness, we must go to the people we hurt—even if we didn't mean to hurt them—and repair those relationships. Dear reader, you are a good person. You bring light to this world. There is no question that you do your best, and that you don't want to hurt anyone. When you fine-tune the words you choose, you increase the good you do, and you decrease possible harm.

---

32. I Kings 5:11.
33. Proverbs 18:21.

Experiment with these ideas to see for yourself that life can be improved by making changes in your speech habits. Make small changes to get started. (Note: Learning to be careful not to harm others through speech is powerful, and it also does not negate that there are real issues that must be spoken about. If you or someone else is in danger on any level—of physical abuse or self-harm, emotional abuse, and even financial loss—do not keep silent. Ask for help.)

Points to Ponder about Speech

Speaking about someone in a way that seems neutral, or even in a way that seems positive, could actually be harmful. Things that are said with no ill intention can cause harm just the same. Words taken out of context or newsy items shared without permission can lead to hard feelings. Someone could feel left out in a situation, and misunderstanding could damage friendships.

Conscious silence *will* improve relationships. It's so natural to talk about the people we are closest with or spend the most time around. Not talking about people will improve relationships. You have to try this to believe it. Holding your tongue instead of complaining about another will bring positive changes.

Blowing off steam is overrated. Everyone has relationships that are difficult or strained. People need to process their thoughts and feelings, it's true. At the same time, consider that the more you talk about a difficult situation, the more you may actually be stoking the fire and increasing the resentment. (Therapy may be an exception, since it is confidential and in theory you are processing your own experience and feelings). Experiment with just holding off on talking about a troublesome situation. The negative feelings may just dissipate with some time. If you find that you really need to talk about a stressful relationship, try talking with someone who doesn't know the other person so that no harm will come of it. Choose carefully whom you talk with. You know who will help you diffuse emotional turmoil the best.

People don't need "a taste of their own medicine." Have you ever been hurt by someone who said something thoughtless or acted sternly to you, or who gave you the cold shoulder? As tempting as it may be to give it back so he or she can see what it feels like, don't do it. It never works. People never see that you're just giving back what you were given. If it hurt you, it's likely to hurt someone else in turn, who will never connect the message you thought you were trying to give.

What you say about others is a reflection of you. Speaking negatively about others reflects poorly on the speaker. In psychology, it's called "spontaneous trait transference." That means that when someone is accusing another of negative traits, the listener will perceive the traits spoken about in the speaker!

You will be happier. Our thoughts and actions (in this case, speech) impact our feelings. Finding fault in others or discouraging speech brings people down. On the other hand, when you are looking to the positive, you will feel more positive. One woman shared with me that she imagines that angels are cheering for her when she succeeds in not speaking about someone else.

How to Avoid Lashon Hara

So how do you graciously get out of speaking or listening to *lashon hara*? Here's a short list of ideas (see also the chapter "Spiritual Pathways" at the end of the book for more on this):

- ❧ Judge others favorably by giving the benefit of the doubt; it is very likely there is more to the situation than you know. You have no idea what it is like to be in another's position.
- ❧ Walk away when the people you're with start gossiping.
- ❧ Change the subject: graciously bring up another topic to talk about or ask questions that will change the direction of the conversation.
- ❧ Be honest and share that you're working on this aspect of self-growth.

- ❧ Smile and let the speakers know you'll also cut off the conversations of anyone who wants to gossip about them, too!

- ❧ If the person who is speaking clearly needs to blow off some steam, be aware that it's an out-of-balance perspective, so while nurturing the person in pain, you don't have to believe all he or she is saying.

Reflections in Miriam's Mirror: Reverent Awe

When Yocheved and Miriam defied Pharaoh's order to kill the baby boys, they were referred to as "God fearing." Some people don't relate to that term and find the concept to be a big turn-off. Maybe that's because, deep down in our bones, we know and want to feel that God is really about love. It's in our souls to know that God loves us, even when we don't consciously know it. Still, in Judaism, the concept of being God fearing comes up, so let's have a deeper look.

In Hebrew, there are two words for fear. One is *pachad*, which is the word you'd use to say you're afraid of snakes, or spiders, or bad guys. The other is *yirah,* which comes from the root "to see," and that is the word that's used when speaking of God—*yirat Shamayim*—literally, "awe of Heaven." Awe isn't really a good translation, either, as it's overused and doesn't quite express the power involved.

Think of fire. While we can use it for cooking and heat, we know it can be deadly and destructive. If you've ever witnessed the speed at which a fire can spread, you know. It is an awesome power, and we have all been taught not to play with fire. That is true of all the elements; they can be so beautiful, and also deadly if not handled or approached with respect for the laws of nature. The Torah teaches us that nature is a *servant* of God. Whole civilizations worshipped the sun. Sun in Hebrew is *shemesh,* which comes from the root word for "service." The sun is in service to its

Creator. Hopefully, we can gain an inkling of the power of God by considering the power of even a fraction of His creations!

We are accountable for everything we do. You know that the choices you make have consequences. You make a choice, and you reap the benefit or pay the price. It's a bit like "what goes around comes around" on a great, cosmic scale, and over all incarnations. Judaism contains teachings about what is called *gilgul neshamot,* the cycle of the soul or reincarnation. (For more on the Jewish approach to the topic of reincarnation, see "Reflections in Ruth's Mirror"). There is no separating or hiding from God. You can fool yourself for a while, but in the end, when we face the truth before the heavenly court, there will be an accounting. Our teachings assure us that the justice of God is happening way beyond what we can see or account for.[34]

A woman may know for a fact that she can steal and not get caught, yet she does not steal, because she knows that there is another, more powerful force watching her, and the glowing spark of the Infinite that resides within, her godly conscience, is accountable to a higher force: God.

God fearing means that you know there's a God and that what you do matters—positive or negative—even if no one else knows or sees. God fearing means you understand that for each action, positive or negative, there is a heavenly accounting; everything is recorded,[35] *with love.* It doesn't mean that God will be angry. Even though we hear about the anger of God in biblical teachings, that "anger" is a metaphor; it's spoken about in that way to help our limited minds to understand the direction the Eternal is guiding us toward: just and moral action. The highest way to serve God is through love, not from fear,[36] and also not because of the reward.[37] A metaphor to describe what this might look like is that of a husband and wife who would like to please each other out of love. In a

---

34. Jeremiah 9:23. Psalms 33:4–5.
35. Mishnah, *Pirkei Avot* 2:1.
36. Talmud, *Sotah* 31a.
37. Mishnah, *Pirkei Avot* 1:3.

loving marriage, spouses try to be pleasing by avoiding actions they know are likely to be upsetting. Another approach is to increase the effort to do the things that will develop the relationship and deepen the intimacy.

Earlier, we used the metaphor of someone not paying attention while driving and rear-ending the car in front of her. She can be so sorry. Her apology can be accepted. But she still has to pay for the damage. In Hebrew, repairing the damage we've done is called *tikkun*. Sometimes, we have to do a *tikkun* for something we have long forgotten about. Trust in God's accounting and know that any *tikkun* is, ultimately, for your highest good, even if you can't see that in the moment. Not only is it for your highest good, but also all accounting is kept with love to help you grow into the best version of you.

Tziporah
Swift Action

The Story of Tziporah

Tziporah, who came from the nation of Midian, became the wife of Moshe.[1] Moshe was called the most modest or humble of men,[2] yet he was the greatest leader the Jewish nation has known. They say that soul mates are two halves of the same soul. What does that teach us about his wife Tziporah, his soul mate?

It is said that the letters of the Torah are black fire, and that the space between the letters is white fire.[3] The black, inked letters seem to get all the attention, yet there would be no black letters if there were not a white contrast. Tziporah's character and story are revealed in the black fire, but also in the white fire. Her regal story can ignite quiet strength within every woman.

Tziporah was the daughter of Yitro (Jethro) the high priest of Midian, who served idols! Yitro was in a position of power. Not only was he high priest, he was an advisor to the Egyptian pharaoh. Imagine such a powerful leader, and imagine how his children would have been raised. They would have wanted for nothing. They would be pampered. They would have guards.

---

1. The story of Tziporah can be found in Exodus 3:21 and 4:24–27.
2. Numbers 12:3.
3. Rashi, Song of Songs 5:11; Midrash, *Tanchuma* 1:1:1.

But Yitro turned his back on idolatry to face the truth of one God. Something stirred inside him.[4] Was it that he witnessed God in the world? Was he ultimately repulsed by the cruelties he saw in the ways of the leaders of idolatry all throughout the world and its history? Imagine any spiritual leader today standing in front of his or her followers and saying to them in all seriousness and sincerity, "You know, I've been searching for the deepest truth, and I've found another path, significant and true, that you should all know about. This whole thing we've been doing is bogus, but I've found the real thing!" Could you imagine the reaction? It wouldn't be just a shake-up for the congregants. It would be chaotic.

When Yitro proclaimed the truth he saw, he was rejected by his people, whose whole lives were invested in the status quo. Idolatry serves those in power. After all, no idol communicates; its founders and those in power project and design what will be said. Yitro fell from the graces of popularity and power. He was taunted, rejected, and outcast. And, of course, so were his daughters. So they built a new life of godliness.

What an incredible life change: from being in the limelight one day, popular, adored, and indulged, to the next day being on the outside. Still, Yitro and his family gained the dignity and nobility of knowing the truth about God and living that truth.

There are Jewish converts today who were once leaders in their non-Jewish worlds. They sought the truth, and it led them to a life of Torah and Judaism. They attest to the attacks that came as a result of converting, including the ever-present threat of eternal hell expressed by some other faiths for not adhering to their ways. (Judaism does not require conversion of all mankind, but rather righteous behavior.)

Compare Tziporah's life to the life of Moshe. He was born the child of a slave. As an infant, he was hidden in a basket on the waters of the Nile, the very place where Jewish newborn baby boys were drowned by Egyptian officers. Plucked from the river as a gift

---

4.   Midrash, *Exodus Rabbah* 1:32.

from the "god of the Nile," Moshe was adopted by the daughter of
Pharaoh and raised in the home of the mighty pharaoh as a "prince
of Egypt." He was raised as the grandson of the powerful, idolatrous pharaoh (see also the chapter on Miriam). Could we possibly
fathom how his every whim was met? Yet, when he saw his people,
the Children of Israel, being tortured, he acted to strike down an
Egyptian.[5] He understood what was right and where his loyalties
were. He ran away from his life of wealth for the life of truth. He ran
away from Egypt and became a simple shepherd. Moshe rejected
unfathomable treasures and power in favor of identifying with his
people. He heard the voice of God through a mystical bush that
burned but was not consumed,[6] and he spoke with God.

We can see how Tziporah's early life was the training ground
that would prepare her to become the wife of a leader of a new and
godly nation. From a life of power and plenty, she also experienced
the conviction to hold on to truth no matter what.

When Moshe knew it was time to find a wife, he went to a well.
Our Midrash fleshes out that Moshe knew our patriarchs Yitzchak
and Yaakov's matches had been found by wells, so he went to the
well in Midian.[7] The daughters of Yitro arrived at the well early to
water their sheep before the other shepherds came. Some sources
say they came early to avoid the mocking and insults that came
as a result of their family rejecting idolatry.[8] Moshe, still dressed
as an Egyptian, offered them help in getting their flocks watered.

The daughters told their father about the man who had helped
them. Yitro sent them back to bring Moshe home. There is a most
wondrous story in the Midrash of a sapphire staff and its role in
Moshe becoming Tziporah's husband.[9] (This story is far older than
a similar one you may have heard, of King Arthur and the sword in

5. Exodus 2:11–12.
6. Exodus 3:2.
7. Midrash, *Exodus Rabbah* 1:32.
8. Ramban, Exodus 2:16.
9. Nissan Mindel. "Tzipporah: The Wonderful Staff," http://www.chabad.org/library/
   article_cdo/aid/111923/jewish/Tzipporah.htm.

the stone.) The sapphire staff came from the Garden of Eden.[10] It was given to Adam and was passed through the generations until it came to Yosef, who had it in Egypt, when he was Pharaoh's second-in-command. Yitro received the staff when he was Pharaoh's advisor. When he left Egypt, he set it in his garden, and it embedded into the earth. When suitors would come for his daughter, he asked them to simply get the staff. No one could budge it, until Moshe touched it and it became his staff. While not every midrash is literal, this story gives us a sense of transcendence. We encounter the stories of Moshe and his staff throughout his meetings with Pharaoh and the Exodus from Egypt—one of the most meaningful, mystical, and significant historic events in the history of the Jewish nation.

Moshe and Tziporah married. Their first son was named Gershom, which means "stranger there," because Moshe was a stranger in a strange land. Then Moshe the shepherd was called by the Eternal to take on a mission. Standing before a bush that was burning with fire but not consumed by it, Moshe was told he was to stand before Pharaoh and represent God with a message to release the Hebrew slaves: "Let my people go." Moshe was chosen to become the leader of the Hebrew nation for the momentous Exodus out of slavery in Egypt, into the covenant of Torah and freedom in the Land of Israel. Interestingly, Moshe tried to turn God down.[11] He didn't want the job. Finally, God put an end to Moshe's excuses by telling him that his brother Aharon would help with the mission.[12]

Moshe went out to meet Aharon and travel to Egypt to fulfill his task. (Moshe and Aharon were from the priestly tribe of Levi, who were not enslaved while in Egypt, so they could move freely.[13]) He was on his way to literally save an entire nation, to redeem them out of slavery and into freedom. The Torah relates that he had two sons, Gershom and a newborn.

---

10. Midrash, *Yalkut Shimoni* 173:3.
11. Exodus 3:11, 4:1, 4:10, 4:13.
12. Exodus 4:14–16.
13. Midrash, *Tanchuma*, Va'era 6; *Tanchuma Buber*, Va'era 4.

Because they were traveling, Moshe did not circumcise his new baby son. Circumcision is a surgery, after all, and in the extraordinary circumstance of traveling, they were exempt from the commandment to circumcise their son on the eighth day, with the understanding that it could jeopardize the baby's health. As mentioned earlier in the chapter on Miriam, nearly every commandment can be broken if the purpose is *pikuach nefesh* (preserving life).

When they came to an inn just outside of Egypt, they stopped to rest.[14] Moshe went to check in to the inn. But what was required was his attention to the covenant of his people with God. He needed to circumcise his son at the first possible moment. As we learned from the story of Miriam, people are judged according to who they are and the spiritual level they are on. Moshe lost sight of his spiritual priorities in that moment by not performing the covenantal circumcision of his son at the first opportunity.

A serpent appeared and began to swallow Moshe. Some say it was an angel in the shape of a serpent.[15] This would have been his end. When Tziporah saw that her husband was being swallowed, she knew it was because her son had yet to be circumcised. She had the presence of mind to understand what needed to be done. She did not hesitate. She did not roll her eyes or heave a heavy sigh. She moved. Right away. Without delay. Swift action. Not after they settled in, but in that very moment, Tziporah took a flint and circumcised her son.[16] Some things are of such spiritual significance that we cannot overestimate their importance and their impact—whether we understand them fully or not.

Tziporah's swift action to do what needed to be done saved the situation and rescued Moshe, the redeemer of the nation. Her intervention not only saved her husband but impacted the entire nation, because Moshe would be able to continue on the journey to get the Israelites out of Egyptian slavery.

---

14. Rashi, Exodus 4:24.
15. Exodus 4:24; Talmud, *Nedarim* 32a; Midrash, *Exodus Rabbah* 5:5.
16. Exodus 4:25.

Tziporah's Gift: Ready Enthusiasm

This character trait Tziporah displays, of acting without hesitation, with eager, positive readiness, is called *zerizut*. It may be translated as alacrity. In a world where people are in such a rush to go here or there, or are pushing for the mundane, this character trait is worth investigating and applying to our lives. The quality of *zerizut* is a significant attribute in our teachings on personal development. Alacrity is the idea that when something needs to be done, you do it, without hesitation, with clarity, purpose, and even joy. It is the opposite of procrastination.

There is opportunity in every moment. We make choices about what we want, what we like, where we want to go, and so on. The key to swift action is to think about how your actions reflect your values. How might you increase your focus on the areas that matter, that light up the world? This could be helping someone in need, donating money to a charity, starting or increasing your soul connection through prayer, or opening your home to a guest. There are areas that we're taught make a big difference—not only to the receiver, but also to us as givers—such as helping a bride and bridegroom feel happy and special on their wedding day and launching them into their life together, or attending a funeral and escorting the deceased to his or her final resting place. Alacrity means acting with a full heart and knowing, as Tziporah knew, that our actions make a difference. This is true even if no mortal knows what we are doing; the Eternal always sees and knows.

Life can feel like a heavy load, but with each person doing what he or she can with joy, we can transform and lighten the load for all. The doing is not about overdoing. It's about stretching a little past your comfort zone. Think about limbering up your muscles. Stretching doesn't feel so comfortable, but with consistency, it actually feels good. When you have felt what it's like to be limber, you never want to be stiff again. So too with the actions we take. We want to be limber and ready. You already know how good it feels to give. What if you could increase the good you do in life with joyful intention? Just a bit. Baby steps. Each of the little bits adds up over time in significant ways. Our *mitzvot* (plural of mitzvah) are the garments of our souls. When we ascend to the heavenly realms as we leave this world behind, we wear the "clothes" of the beautiful deeds we have done in this world. The good deeds we do are the only thing we take with us to the next world. Swift action to do what we can do is true, eternal, indelible beauty.

Reflections in Tziporah's Mirror: Quiet Greatness

We have seen that women play very significant and diverse roles in our history, and while there are few words written about Tziporah, her greatness is apparent and without question. *Quiet does not mean insignificant.*

Tziporah took action. All the rest of her life that is not written about in the Torah is hidden to us only because it is not relevant for us, in our generation. Many are the Jewish women who have contributed to the building of this nation through their quiet yet significant and purposeful actions. The women mentioned in our biblical texts lived full lives, and however much we can know about them, even more is unseen. The Jews are a nation built from generations of women and men who were living, giving, and sacrificing, with conviction. Our matriarchs didn't need fanfare. They didn't need to be "liked." They did what was right.

It's impossible for us to know and comprehend the stories of all Jewish women. We know some of the stories of some of their lives, who they were, what they stood for, and what they accomplished. One question we might ask ourselves is how we weigh the importance of our mothers' and grandmothers' accomplishments. Greatness does not require press coverage. Greatness is not reflected by fame, the size of a bank account, or in the flash of clothing. For every woman written about in this book, there are many thousands who followed in her footsteps. There were other women who have sacrificed and celebrated to build this nation as selflessly as the women in this book. Among those women are your ancestors, your grandmothers and great-grandmothers. They did so boldly, rebelliously, with quiet determination, committed with purpose and meaning. Our nation exists today—outliving some of the grandest, most powerful conquering empires of the world—because our mothers and fathers understood something deep and real about holding on to a life of Torah values.

Tziporah means "bird." If each of the women in the Tanach lives within us, then what is Tziporah like within you? Are you the beautiful but fierce hummingbird who, though small, will defend her territory and dive-bomb those who are hundreds of times larger than she? Are you like the swan in the story of the ugly duckling, who thinks she is less-than but then discovers her grace and majesty as she matures? Are you the robin who fills the world with song, the owl who symbolizes wisdom, or the flamingo who fills the world with vibrant color?

Most of all, are you willing to take your place within this nation? It is the unity of every individual that makes the nation whole and complete. Every contribution and every soul matters. It's not just the obvious main-stage women and men making the boldest of contributions who light up the world. There is untold light in whispering a sincere prayer, lovingly changing a diaper, saying a kind word, or learning Torah that enriches you—as you're doing right now!

Rachav
Persistent and Inspired

The Story of Rachav

As a young girl of ten years[1] in Jericho, Rachav (Rahab) heard the buzz about the Children of Israel leaving Egypt with wonders and miracles.[2] She heard that the Red Sea split open, allowing the Jews to cross safely while it swallowed the massive Egyptian army who pursued them. It was at that tender age that Rachav understood that the God of Israel was true. She made the decision then to join the Jews when they arrived in the land that God promised them.

For the forty years after Rachav heard about the Exodus, the Jews wandered in the desert. They went through trials, tribulations, and plagues. They gave in to idolatry. They received the manna from Heaven and their water from the miraculous well of Miriam. They took comfort in the clouds of glory that surrounded and protected the nation of Israel in its travels by day, and were warmed by a great pillar of fire that guided them by night.

Meanwhile, Rachav went about her life and waited for the Jews to arrive. When the time came for the Jews to enter the land, Rachav was ready.

---

1. Rashi, Joshua 2:11; Talmud, *Zevachim* 116b.
2. The story of Rachav can be found in the Book of Joshua, chapters 2 and 6.

Rachav is said to be one of the four most beautiful women of the Tanach.[3] A striking facet of her story is Rachav's profession. When Rachav heard about and committed to being part of the nation of the Children of Israel, she was a prostitute, a harlot. And not just any harlot; she ran an elite and famous inn that attracted the highest of nobility. (She wasn't in Sinai to receive the Torah, so did not know its teachings yet.)

As the Israelites were approaching the Land of Israel, two Hebrew men, Calev (Caleb) and Pinchas (Phinehas), were sent in to scout the situation within Jericho.[4] They were honest, loyal, and true—they truly lived according to the highest teachings of God and Torah. Their reputation preceded them. So how could they travel in a way that would be discreet and hidden? A brothel could be the perfect cover.

Rachav knew what was going to happen when the Children of Israel arrived. Anyone who wanted to live in peace with the Jews would be allowed to stay, and anyone who did not would be conquered and expelled. The world could see God's hand revealed in the life and travels of the Children of Israel.

When the king's army came looking for the Jewish scouts, Rachav hid Calev and Pinchas under stalks of flax on the roof of her brothel. She told the pursuing enemy soldiers that the Jewish scouts had in fact been there, but that they had left. She told them to hurry to the gate of the city to chase after them before the gate closed for the night.

She told Calev and Pinchas that when the people of Jericho heard of the Exodus and that God promised the land to the Jewish people, they were afraid.[5] Rachav made a deal with them. She would protect and help them. In return, she asked for protection for herself and all those in her house when the Jews would enter the city. The sign was set: Rachav had a red rope that was used as a ladder for

---

3.   Talmud, *Megillah* 15a.
4.   Rashi, Joshua 2:4; Midrash, *Tanchuma* 4:4:1.
5.   Joshua 2:9–11.

some of her clients to come and go discreetly. That red rope would be wrapped around the building to mark it, so that when the Jews took siege of the city, Rachav and her family would be protected.

And that is what happened. Rachav's place was secured under Jewish rule.

Oh, and by the way, were you doing the math?

Just in case you didn't notice, Rachav was fifty years old when the Jews arrived. Still, she is called one of the most beautiful women of the Tanach! After forty years of waiting and yearning, Rachav converted and became a Jew. Rachav married none other than Yehoshua (Joshua), the man to whom Moshe passed the leadership of the nation.[6]

As we have seen, in the Tanach, a name reveals something about the nature of a person. *Rachav* is the Hebrew word for "wide" or "broad." To some, Rachav's name conjures the image of a full-figured woman. More deeply, Rachav is remembered for having a broad, open heart. In learning about character traits, we can see that even the most wonderful of traits, such as having wide acceptance of people, can become negative if it is taken too far out of balance. The trait of loving-kindness can even become dangerous; loving without boundaries can look like promiscuity.

Rachav's legacy to her nation was as broad as her heart. Her daughters married into the priestly tribe of the Kohanim.[7] Her sons became prophets, as did her descendant Chulda the prophetess.[8]

Rachav was beautiful on every level—even in more mature years, and even with a past that was the opposite of what she grew into. We learn from her: *Who you were and what you have done in the past is not as important as who you are becoming and the direction you are heading.*

---

6. Midrash, *Ecclesiastes Rabbah* 8:10.
7. Midrash, *Numbers Rabbah* 8:9.
8. Talmud, *Megillah* 14b.

Rachav's Gift: The Truth about Faith

Rachav waited forty years, from the time the Children of Israel left Egypt and the sea split, until they finally arrived in the land of Canaan. She wasn't hoping for it; she was waiting for it. She knew that if the same force that took the Jews out of Egypt and split the sea also said that the Children of Israel would come, they would be there.

This is not blind faith. This is knowing—a certainty that this world is not by chance, but created intentionally. No one can possibly know what God will do (unless God makes the promise through prophecy). What we can know with certainty is that what God does is for the highest good. This is not an easy mindset to slip into. It is an ongoing process of deepening, and the opportunity for inner deepening is infinite. The Hebrew word for this kind of relationship with God is *emunah* (usually translated as "faith"). You could also think of it as faithfulness. We are faithful to our covenant, to our union with God. In our songs and prayers, God is also called our beloved.

Having *emunah* doesn't mean surrendering your decisions. To the contrary, your free will to make choices is your dance with the Divine. *Emunah* is a place of being and knowing you're in a relationship that is working for your good—even if it doesn't seem that way sometimes. God is above and beyond the logic of the human mind.

There's a classic story of Chinese origin of a farmer who had one son. They had one horse. One day, the door to the stable was left open, and their horse ran away. The villagers were sympathetic. "Oh, such a shame," they said. The farmer answered, "Good, bad, who knows?" Sometime later, the horse came back with a bunch of wild mares following him. The villagers said, "What good fortune!" Again the farmer answered, "Good, bad, who knows?" Then, while working with one of the new horses, the farmer's son was thrown off and broke his leg. "What terrible misfortune," the villagers cried. But the farmer replied again, "Good, bad, who knows?" The very next day, draft officers came to take all the eligible young men to war. Because the farmer's son was injured, they left him behind.

In any situation, what appears to be not so good can actually be for the best. What feels like it is great could work out to be disappointing.

In Jewish thought all that happens is ultimately for the good, even the disappointments. We may never understand or be able to explain the way this world works, but there is a foundation of *emunah* that everything that happens is all for the good on a soul level. This world is beyond human understanding. If we could understand things from a godly point of view, we would be God. That doesn't mean we just accept things the way they are and do nothing. If there is injustice in the world, we are to do what we can to create justice. Where there is hunger, we are to feed. When we find a lost item, we are to return it to its owner. When someone is hurting, we are to bring healing. The Torah is a system that teaches us the values and morals we need to partner with our Creator in repairing and building. We do the best we can, keeping in mind that we are not God, so we can never fix it all. At the same time, we are to do our portion.

Sometimes in hindsight, we are given a glimpse into the spiritual workings of this world. There is a story within a story that is told of two young people who wanted to understand suffering in the world. They went to their teacher, their rabbi, and asked him to explain. The rabbi told them to talk to a certain blind man. Sitting with the blind man, the students asked him how it was that he could accept his suffering without complaints or feeling sorry for himself. He told them the following story.

"Once there was a couple who gave birth to a child who was born with no hands. They were so upset, so angry, that they stormed into the study of their rabbi, saying, 'What kind of a God brings an infant into the world without hands?' The rabbi invited the couple to sit with him as he shared a story.

"'There lived a very great man. He had it all and was good, generous, and charitable. It happened one day that he reacted angrily to one of his servants, by slapping him. When it was time for this soul to stand in the heavenly court before God to be judged, he was told that he would have to return to the world to correct the mistake he made by slapping his employee. The soul did not want to go back to the earthly realm, but this was the decree. So the soul pleaded with God, "Please, *please*, if I must return, please help me so that I will never smack or hurt anyone when I'm back in that world."

"'And so,' the rabbi continued, 'the soul came back in a body with no hands.'"

We cannot know all there is to know about any situation. Whatever you can see, it is never the whole story. From God's perspective, the view is over lifetimes.

The comfort of *emunah* is the understanding, the certainty that everything that happens has a purpose and is ultimately for the good. Holding on to this part of your inheritance as a Jew lightens the load of this world. The result of claiming *emunah* as a quality for yourself means that you have more peace. You still take action where you can, but you know that ultimately, God's got His creation covered. The Jewish nation endured hundreds of years of slavery with the certainty that there would be another chapter. The story wasn't over.

To illustrate how to apply this, imagine that there are two pipelines in your life. One is what comes in, and one is what goes out. You cannot always control what comes in, but you have free choice about what goes out. What comes in—your life experiences—is out of your control. What you experience in life is custom made to grow you. The test could be to endure or it could be to make a change. *The only thing you can truly choose or control is how you react or respond.* What goes out—your thoughts, speech, and actions—is within your control. That doesn't mean it's easy, but it is about growth. If you need to learn a lesson, that particular test will keep coming up until you change. If you change who you are, the world around you will change, too.

Emunah is a way to draw closer to the source of spirituality. *Emunah* is a way to deepen your relationship with the Eternal.

Reflections in Rachav's Mirror: Onward and Upward

While Rachav waited for the Israelites, she knew what she would do when they arrived. Even as she worked her brothel, she knew she would leave it behind to be with this new nation. The Israelites came into the land, and Rachav did as she had planned. She became a part of the nation. Once she had the chance to learn more about this nation and to learn what the Torah teaches, she let go of her past. She released the life she had lived and stepped into godliness. With the guidance of the Torah, she forged a path of righteousness and became the mother of prophets.

It's a very tempting trap to see your mistakes or vices and just resign to being in a place of limitations or narrowness. Rachav opened the way and exemplified that no matter what mistakes we've made, no matter how far off course we've traveled, any one of us is absolutely capable of rising. *Don't spend your time berating yourself for mistakes made or cursing the rungs of the ladder that brought you to where you are.* Rachav didn't wallow in disdain for her former life. Instead, she put her energy into contributing to the nation by building a family and raising her children to make big contributions in their own right.

Rachav teaches us to focus and refocus, looking in the direction we want to go. Your past is not as important as what you make of the moment right now. You can make a choice over and over in each new moment to leave the past in the past and to rise and grow. Judaism has a concept called *teshuvah*; it literally means "return." The idea is to return to the truth of your soul's mission and journey. What does that mean?

When you fall, get up.

If you break something, repair it.
If you lose your way, wake up and get back on track.

Release the mistakes of the past. Move forward in your life with renewed joy.

Devorah and Ya'el
More Than Warrior Women

The Story of Devorah and Ya'el

Devorah (Deborah) was a prophetess and a judge.[1] She rose to lead the nation in war against a military attack. Following Devorah's victory, Ya'el would strike the final blow of defeat against the enemy. Then Devorah sang. The Song of Devorah is one of the ten biblical songs.

During the times of the Judges (approximately 1106 BCE),[2] when Devorah lived, the nation of Israel mostly lived a good life, a life of tranquility and plenty. But there were periods, as we were warned there would be, when life would become too comfortable, and the nation would get distracted. In times of comfort, people can slip into taking things for granted. The Jewish people would forget their foundation as a nation bound to God and slip into idolatry.

"They chose new gods, then war came to their gates." So sang Devorah.

The trap of success can lead to ego and to people thinking their prosperity comes from their own power and not from the blessings of the Creator. In the Torah, God is clear: if we, the Jewish nation,

---

1. The story of Devorah can be found in the Book of Judges, chapters 4–5.
2. Rabbi Ken Spiro, History Crash Course #68, "Timeline: From Abraham to the State of Israel," http://www.aish.com/jl/h/cc/48964541.html.

keep our agreements, and if we stay on our national mission, we will be blessed. If we turn our backs on the promise, we will suffer curses. One of the metaphors we use to describe our relationship with God is that of a lover. There is intimacy on every level in that relationship, and when one partner is unfaithful, the relationship can tear apart. For a Jew, idolatry is likened to adultery! If we do not stay faithful to our beloved, the curses are clear. But these curses, as painful as they feel, are actually a blessing to remind us of who we are and to help us get back on track.

The idea of a curse as a blessing might sound like a paradox at first, but if you think about it, you may even see how something that seemed negative in your own life worked out in the end. Something that seemed terrible turned out to open doors to something wonderful. Those who were teased in childhood can develop compassion as adults. When efforts in one area fail, in relationships, studies, work, and so on, it can cause a change in direction toward a path that is more fulfilling. It's possible that failed efforts can create even more strength to accomplish the original goal in a way that wasn't previously imagined.

During the time of the Judges when the Jews became idolatrous, the activated curse came in the form of an enemy. It was a pattern that happened many times in the era of the Judges: first tranquility, then the Jews got too comfortable, next, the distraction or seduction into idolatry, and then, *bam!* An enemy rose up against the Jewish nation. What a wake-up call! You'd think they would get the idea after the same pattern happened time and again, but there were long periods of tranquility, so the people could easily lose track of the feedback.

Whenever we felt the oppression of an enemy, the nation would remember and cry out to God. When the nation cried out in unity and turned their backs to idolatry, they returned to face the mysterious Eternal with renewed commitment to the ways of our people. Then the attacking enemy would be defeated. This was the pattern.

Devorah's Palm Tree

Devorah was an arbitrator of disputes (called a *shofet* in Hebrew), with tremendous knowledge of Torah laws. Devorah worked under a tree that was called *tomer Devorah*, Devorah's palm. She worked out in the open, where everything she did or said could be seen by the people. There was no room for accusations of misconduct in her court.[3] She was above doubt in her integrity in the way she handled all disputes that came before her.

Interestingly, *tomer Devorah* was not named for Devorah the Judge. It was named for Rivka's nursemaid and may have actually been an oak tree.[4] (There is one sentence in the Torah about Devorah the nursemaid's burial under that tree.[5]) Why are the two Devorahs juxtaposed at the beginning of our story? Devorah the prophetess stands out as a leader, a woman of power and influence. Devorah the nursemaid seems hardly noticeable—yet she is *notable*—her role was that of nurturer. It's not accidental that these two Devorahs are contrasted. Even with the hundreds of years that lay between their lives, Devorah the Judge was influenced by the qualities of compassion and understanding of a nursemaid.[6]

Devorah's introduction in the Book of Judges makes it clear: she was a prophetess, a wife, and a judge—in that order. The first connection means she was getting direct messages from God, which is not to be confused with intuition. She was known for her fire. She was the wife of a general, a man named Barak or "lightning," who is also called Lapidot, meaning "torches" or "wicks." Devorah made wicks for the lights of the Menorah that stood in the Sanctuary and sent her husband to deliver them.[7] (If you ever visit Jerusalem, you can see a replica of that Menorah near the Western Wall in the Old City.) In this way her husband, the military leader of that

---

3.   Talmud, *Megillah* 14a.
4.   Daat Zekenim, Genesis 35:8.
5.   Genesis 35:8.
6.   Rabbi David Silverberg, "Devorah the Nursemaid and Devorah the Prophetess," http://www.hatanakh.com/en/content/devorah-nursemaid-and-devorah-prophetess.
7.   Rashi, Judges 4:4.

generation, who was not known for being a great scholar, would be influenced by the spirituality of Torah.

The Women Stand Up

In Devorah's generation, a king rose up to attack Israel: his name was Yavin. Devorah called Barak and told him to gather ten thousand men to strike against the forces of Yavin's fearsome army, which was under the command of General Sisera. The Book of Judges records that Sisera had nine hundred iron chariots (think nine hundred military tanks). You know how heavy a small cast iron pan is. Can you imagine how many warhorses it would take to pull just one iron chariot a great distance into war? How many foot soldiers would accompany each chariot? Nine hundred iron chariots against the Jewish soldiers—really farmers, shepherds, or fishermen—on foot. You wouldn't think the Jews stood much of a chance.

Barak gathered the Jewish army from the tribes of Naftali and Zevulun. Before they even made the first move, Devorah the prophetess declared their victory. Why? She knew that the nation had returned to God, and that their spiritual return, their *teshuvah*, was real and sincere. She knew that God was with them and would deliver them from the enemy. Devorah assured Barak that God's hand would guarantee the Jews' victory and told him to go. But Barak wanted the merit of the prophetess to ensure their victory, so he said, "If you go with me, I will go; but if you do not go with me, I will not go."

Devorah answered, "I will go with you, but the journey you're taking will not be for your honor. The Lord will give Sisera over to the hand of a woman." Devorah went with Barak, who was in command of ten thousand men. When the war went into full swing, Sisera took his nine hundred iron chariots to meet the impromptu Jewish army and attack the nation of Israel. Fear came into the hearts of Sisera's army, and though they retreated, every last soldier was killed. They were defeated.

In the recent history of the modern State of Israel, there are similar miraculous stories of the few fighting the many. Our victory and survival continue to be uncanny and miraculous. During Israel's War of Independence, five trained military armies attacked the new nation, which was comprised of farmers and Holocaust survivors. The Jews were victorious. In the Yom Kippur War, the Syrian forces entered Israel with great might, and it looked like it could end in Israel's defeat. It didn't. The sheer numbers and firepower of the Syrian army made it seem impossible that the Syrian tanks would retreat. Credit is given to the hand of God giving victory to the Jews, both in ancient times, and by many in modern times.

In the time of the Judges, Yavin's army was defeated. Sisera, the mighty general, jumped off his chariot to escape on foot.

Enter Ya'el.

Hever and Ya'el

Ya'el was the wife of a man named Hever. They were part of a community connected to Israel through the lineage of Tziporah's father Yitro (Moshe's father-in-law). They lived somewhat apart from the rest of the nation. Hever made himself friendly with King Yavin. A king is not open to getting friendly with just anybody off the street who wants to hang out. Hever was a kind of diplomat and powerful in his own right. Yavin and Sisera thought Hever was alienated from the Jewish nation; in truth, he remained loyal to them.

As Sisera fled the battlefield, he saw Hever's wife, Ya'el. A friendly face, a refuge! Ya'el told him not to be afraid and invited him into her tent, her home. Sisera came into her tent, and she covered him with a blanket. Sisera asked for a drink of water. She gave him milk instead, because of its soothing and relaxing properties. Sisera asked Ya'el to stand guard and not to tell anyone he was there.

He felt safe. Once he was in a deep sleep, she took a hammer and a tent peg, and in a striking act of courage, she drove the peg through Sisera's temple and into the ground, killing him. As

Devorah prophesied, a woman gave the final blow that defeated the enemy's attack on the Jewish nation.

Barak pursued Sisera. Ya'el came out to meet him and to show him the man he was seeking—the dead general. Yavin, the king of Canaan, was conquered. The land was returned to tranquility. Some say that what Ya'el did for the nation was greater even than the matriarchs' contribution.[8]

Shameless and Vulgar

As Devorah's song came to a close, she gave us a glimpse at another kind of woman, Sisera's mother. First, she described Sisera's mother watching through the window, worried about her son returning from battle. That would be common for any mother whose beloved son has gone to war. The answer that she got from the women around her, the answer that was intended to comfort her, was sick and tells us volumes about their culture. Their "comforting" thoughts were that their men were looting good stuff and enjoying the sport of molesting and assaulting the women they found. It is a repulsive thought. This kind of attitude is the antithesis of Jewish values. Devorah is giving us a glimpse into the training and focus of those who want to destroy Israel.

More on the Song of Devorah

The entire nation sang at the splitting of the sea (see the chapter on Miriam). Devorah and Barak sang what we call Devorah's Song. The Hebrew word for "song" is the same word used for "poem." The same word is used for King David's psalms. Song. Poem. It makes sense that the same word is used for both meanings, if you think about it. Today, young people have something they call a poetry slam. It's the recitation of a poem that is packed with emotion and heavily rhythmical, almost like a rap song. King David's psalms

---

8.   Talmud, *Nazir* 23b. See Rashi.

and the songs of the Torah are the original, celestial, transcendent, mystical, and eternal slam poetry.

Devorah's song finishes with a blessing: "So perish all your enemies, Eternal One; and they that love Him be as the sun when it goes forth in its might." The story of Devorah is ancient, but the message to hold fast to our faithfulness and to rise when we need to rise is relevant still.

Devorah's Gift: Sing Your Song

Devorah sang. She sang praises. She sang a challenge of holding the fearful accountable. She sang the timeless story of the time. The psalmist (King David) sang, "My heart is steadfast, O God; I will sing. I will sing praises, even with my glory."[9]

Are you singing the song you came here to sing?

Every instrument in an orchestra has a different sound. Together, the instruments give the music texture and contrast; the sounds blend to make a symphony. Every soul has her mission. Just as every instrument in an orchestra makes its contribution, you are an important and unique part of the music of life in this world. Living the truth of your soul is the song you have to sing. Grandioso, glee, or grave, no matter the dynamics or where you are in development, your song is a gift to all of creation.

With the way this world is set up, we don't receive a letter to tell us exactly what our mission is. That is the adventure and gift of free will. Every day, every moment, we choose how to be, who to be. It's not actually about the career you choose; whether you're a judge or a mother (or both), it's about the way you walk your walk. The way you relate to yourself and your world is a foundation for singing your song with joy. It's so easy for women to doubt or undervalue what we do. If we have a natural talent, we can sometimes slip into the notion that the talent is of little value. "Well, I'm just [a mom, a nurse, clerk, teacher, fill in the blank]; that's so easy, but

---

9.   Psalms 108:2.

that [neurosurgeon, rocket scientist, celebrity, fill in the blank] has much more value."

If your voice is high, you are a soprano. If your voice has a lower pitch, you are an alto. All voices are needed to complete the harmony. There is no part that is too small; as each contribution influences the next, one sets a foundation for another, or one inspires another. The way we affect, move, or touch each other is not about age or social status; it is about courage, it is about honesty; it is the way we shine, be it privately or publicly. It is about a small act of kindness or generosity of spirit, or being a role model of persistence.

We have two inner voices, one that is intuitive and light filled, and the other that brings thoughts of fear and self-doubt. Don't let that tricky voice of fear and self-doubt get a hold on you. Be careful: it can be disguised as logic, realism, and even humility.

It takes courage to sing the song you are here to sing, and action to build the way you want to be in the world. Embrace your strengths, nurture your nature, and gratefully, courageously sing the song you came into this world to sing. How do you sing your song? How do you walk confidently in your mission? Here are some ideas to consider:

- There is a pulse and rhythm to life. If things aren't as harmonious as you know they can be, wait. Be compassionate with yourself.
- Feel the cadence and give yourself permission to enter the song from right where you are.
- Speak to yourself with the kindness with which you would speak to others.
- Seek and surround yourself with support and encouragement.
- Nurture your strengths and the strengths of your support network. Remind each other of the goodness and light that you bring to the world. Brainstorm about the actions that will best serve each of you.

✺ Ask for heavenly assistance. The song in you is the spark of your soul. That spark is magnificently divine and has a natural connection with All That Is.

Ya'el's Gift: Conquering the Darkness of Assimilation

Perhaps we can imagine what kind of a life Ya'el had as the wife of a dignitary. What we know about her is that she had the courage to step forward to take down the great warrior Sisera, a seasoned military leader. Ya'el struck the final blow against an enemy of Israel. Sisera set out to conquer the nation, and in the end he was crushed.

What does Ya'el teach us? What doors does her story open for us in this generation? If Ya'el conquered that which threatened to destroy the Jewish nation, perhaps we should consider what threatens the Jews today. What is the biggest threat to the Jewish nation above all else at this time in history? Certainly, anti-Semitism is alive and well today around the world. There are countries where anti-Semitism in the form of violence and vandalism has grown so drastically that Jewish citizens have left in great numbers, such as Venezuela and France. A quick Internet search will reveal the hate crimes against Jews around the world. It's not a secret that openly Jewish students on university campuses throughout the United States are threatened. We know that the Jewish State of Israel faces constant attack. Yet the biggest threat to the Jewish nation today is not even physical. It is the quiet spiritual threat of assimilation.

Dramatically, some rabbis have likened assimilation today to a holocaust. Assimilation is abandoning the customs, teachings, and sometimes even the values of Torah, and adopting the ideologies and lifestyle of popular society. For the Jewish nation, assimilation has meant many Jews have lost any connection to their spiritual heritage. There are Jews who do not know they are Jews (according to Jewish law, Jewish status is passed from a Jewish woman to her children, so any child of a Jewish woman is a full Jew). Assimilation is the sometimes intentional, sometimes unknowing disconnection from the essential teachings and mission of Torah. Jews today are assimilating in astounding numbers.

One familiar story to many is the story of Chanukah.[10] The Assyrian Greeks took control of the Beit Hamikdash over two thousand years ago. Unlike more modern attacks on the Jewish nation (such as pogroms or the Holocaust), when Jews were murdered just for being Jewish, in the story of Chanukah the goal wasn't to murder Jews. The goal of the Hellenists was to destroy Judaism by making the practice illegal and forcing conversion. If a Jew would not abandon his Jewish life, then he would be murdered, often through torture. Ancient Greek culture revered beauty over all. Judaism calls for justice and goodness, the teachings that God gave us through the Torah. A revolt took place, and miraculously, the small Jewish army took back the Temple. (The Temple was not just a place of worship; it was a place where God's presence was revealed to all, and a place of open miracles. It would later be destroyed again by the Romans and has not been rebuilt since.)

The primary symbol of Chanukah is the *chanukiah,* a candelabra with nine branches (also called a Chanukah menorah or simply menorah by many). Why is it the symbol of Chanukah? As the victorious Jews returned to do the service of God in the Temple, they wanted to light the Temple's Menorah (which had seven branches). They needed olive oil that had been sanctified and found only one small cruse that could be used—enough for just one day. Miraculously, that oil lasted eight days, exactly the time it would take to make more oil (this is the simple version of why we celebrate Chanukah for eight nights). The menorah is a symbol of light. The fuel for the Temple Menorah was olive oil. Olive oil is also symbolic for us in that it does not mix with water; it will always rise and maintain its own identity.

If you know you are a Jew today, you are descended from the Jews who fought to preserve Torah. You come from generations of

---

10.   Rabbi Ken Spiro, History Crash Course #29, "Revolt of the Maccabees," http://www.aish.com/h/c/t/h/48942121.html.

Jews who held tight to this legacy—the commitment to live as a Jew—rather than convert or assimilate.

Of the Jews who immigrated out of eastern Europe in the late 1800s, many left behind their commitment to a Torah way of life, seeking a life of comfort in new lands. Others were influenced by the intellectual ideas that religion was archaic and out of date. It has been more than seven decades since the Holocaust and the devastating loss of life during WWII. You might even be able to trace back the journeys of your families over these decades. Some of those who survived or who ran away from oppression or destruction believed that hiding their Jewishness was a key to survival, and in turn hid it from their children. The idea of ending anti-Semitism by assimilating has never worked. Historically some of the worst persecutions have come in places where Jews were most comfortable and assimilated.[11]

There are Jews from Europe whose families may not even be aware that they are considered Jewish according to halachah (Jewish law). There are stories of adult children whose mothers lay on their deathbeds and did not want to die without telling their children the truth about who they were.[12]

The statistics in the United States and Europe of Jewish assimilation are staggering. Jews make up less than 0.2 percent of the world's population. That is only *a fifth of a percent* of people alive today! Though it's easy to lose perspective if we live in a community with many other Jews, our numbers are actually very small. So when Jews walk away from such a small nation, when they assimilate, it has an impact. But so what? What's the big deal about being a Jew? What's wrong with just being a "good human being"? What's the difference? What does it matter if children are brought up with knowledge and understanding of what it is to live

---

11. Rabbi Ken Spiro, "Assimilation and Anti-Semitism," https://www.simpletore-member.com/media/a/26-ke806nn-28/.

12. Follow this link for one of the more famous stories of a man finding out he was actually a Jew: Chana Weisberg, "My Father and the Priest," http://www.aish.com/sp/so/48901842.html.

as a Jew? If you have learned the stories of the matriarchs thus far, you know that they purposefully built their families to become a nation that would bring godly morals and values into the world. This was not about building a nation for ego's sake, not for wealth, and not for fame. Today we are on the same mission. The purpose of building a Jewish family is to be a part of a chain that is meant to bring light into the world, for the whole world.

It is traditional for the *chanukiah* to be placed in the window—so its light will be available for the entire world. What is the light of Torah that we bring to the world? Fair courts of justice, honesty in business, social services such as charity and feeding the poor, peace in the home (marriage and children), and so much more, all based on the teachings given to us in the form of the Torah.

Ya'el inspires us to step up and to do our part. After what must have been incredible conquest and triumph on the battlefield, Ya'el, one woman, took the final blow to establish victory for the Jews.

Now, in our generation when the threat to our nation is assimilation, so many Jews have been cut off from their deeply spiritual and infinitely joyful inheritance. Each one of us has the ability to step up to add our own individual divine sparks to a light that can be uplifting and healing to the world.

What might this look like, this shining of the divine spark within you? While each human has his or her own expression of godliness, as Jews we have rituals that express our spirituality and connection to God. (Check out the last chapter of this book, called "Spiritual Pathways.")

Judaism does not focus on the idea of eternal hell. It's not about burning if you don't believe a certain way, but there is certainly accountability, and the "burn" a soul might feel in the next world is that of embarrassment when it realizes how far off course it went in life. Judaism does have a concept that no soul will be lost! So the idea is not to walk the walk because of a threat of eternal damnation. The idea is to walk the walk because doing so brings light into the world for all. Sometimes that does take some self-sacrifice. It's not always about what makes you "happy," it's about doing what needs to be done with the understanding that what you do serves the whole—and doing it with the joy you generate. There's no question that you know the fulfillment and joy you've felt when you have been of service to others. It doesn't always come with fanfare or even gratitude. In the big picture, over a lifetime, the most meaningful contributions stem from living in a way that positively impacts your family and community.

Conquering the darkness of assimilation will look different for each of us. It may be celebrating Jewish holidays with your small children. It may be contributing financially to a Jewish institute or an organization on college campuses. It could be taking a class or teaching a class. It is simply allowing the spark within to ignite and sharing that light.

Reflections in Devorah and Ya'el's Mirrors: A Woman's Strength

In recent decades, women's rights have been in the spotlight. Standing strong against injustices and supporting opportunities for growth or advancement are still important topics for women across the world, whether in education, work, or home life. Such topics stir up conversations about the roles of men and women. Confusion abounds about what is masculine and what is feminine. Is masculinity stronger than femininity? There are certainly spectrums of possibility for both men and women. And yet, some people contend that there are no differences between male and female.

Male and female bodies are different structurally, chemically, and hormonally. According to some Jewish teachings, each part of the body reflects something in the spiritual realms. So, the physical differences reflect the nature of our spiritual differences. These differences are not for better or worse, not for good or bad, not higher or lower, not important or irrelevant, and certainly not worthy or unworthy. So what is the man's role in life and what is the woman's role? Can it even be clear-cut?

This is not about seeing women as shallow, froufrou objects, nor is it about seeing men as brutish, grunting cavemen. This is not about justifying oppression or abuse of women or men. Torah teachings on the roles of men and women are about honoring the strengths of women and the strengths of men, and allowing every precious soul to strive to live up to his or her potential.

The Torah does not try to be "politically correct." Societies and cultures the world over and all throughout time have adopted different trends or popular notions about how to treat women. Arguably, women throughout most of human history have been objectified. Women are often portrayed and perceived as sources either of procreation or sexual pleasure. That way of thinking defines women as objects for gratifying men's physical desires. Some cultures have tried to "embellish" women in ways that harm them physically and hold them down. (For example, the Chinese tradition of binding girls' feet in the past, and today's fashion of stiletto heels that damage the feet or the reemerging fashion trend of corseting.) That has never been the Jewish way. Torah acknowledges the nature of a woman and a man—two halves of the same essential being (remember in the story of creation, Adam was created male and female in one body)—and Torah honors those essences. The Torah approach to men and women is that of partnership. It's not that the roles are black and white. Of course, there is a spectrum of possibility.

There are also some boundaries that are set. Torah teaches that a man should not dress in women's clothing, and a woman should not dress with the "tools" of a man, meaning weapons, the tools of war. That does not mean that a woman cannot touch a sword or gun; the rule is not meant to hinder self-defense! Of course, any woman should preserve her life if threatened, and if it means using a weapon, she should use a weapon. The issue is that women are not meant to go to war. That would be the man's role. In Judaism, the woman's primary and honored role is that of nurturer. And of course, that does not mean a man cannot be nurturing.

It's important to understand that one role is not nobler, higher, more worthy, or more important than the other. Those who teach marketing and business to women have pointed out how women have a tendency to undervalue what they do. Some entrepreneurial teachers have noted this thinking in some women: if a talent comes easily or naturally, it must not be worth much to others. That means it's common for women in business to underrate their abilities. That may help put into perspective the general sense in the world we live in—not just in our generation—that women's role as nurturer is cheap. How easy it is for a woman to feel less-than if she isn't accomplishing something in addition to her role as mother or wife. Please be clear that this is not about limiting women. Women who have chosen a career track outside the home have often had to sacrifice parts of their nature to become more masculine in order to compete. There's a song from the 1940s musical *Annie Get Your Gun* that says: "Anything you can do, I can do better. I can do anything better than you!" It is all about the competition.

Our roles are not meant to be a competition, but rather, a complement.

What if we could be confident about the beauty and majesty, the inner power and strength of our feminine role in life? Devorah and Ya'el are eternal models that feminine does not mean weak. Feminine roles are not weaker. What if we could know that we are worthy in what we contribute to the partnership of masculine and feminine? Though we may have different roles, it does not mean we are not capable of doing what needs to be done. Certainly, childbirth is one of the most heroic acts, an act that, while it may seem common, is actually touching the Divine in one of the most extraordinary ways. Whether a woman has actually given birth or not doesn't even matter, because the menstrual cycle itself contains a knowing of the potential of birth and death.

Perhaps the most challenging question is on the inner level: Do we value ourselves? As it says in the "Woman of Valor" poem from Proverbs that we read at the Shabbat table,[13] "A woman of valor, who can find? Her worth is greater than pearls." One way to interpret this is as if it's an invitation: Look within and find *your* value; your worth is more precious than pearls. Can we find, honor, and treasure our truest nature?

Both Devorah and Ya'el expanded their roles and stretched to do what had to be done. The idea here is not for our roles to constrict us. Owning our femininity frees us to tap into our truest nature—and we can also, like Devorah and Ya'el, do whatever needs to be done. We are capable and brilliant. And so are our men, in different ways.

Ya'el might have chosen to use Sisera's sword. There was probably a knife in the house. But she chose to make another kind of statement about the tools she would use to get the job done, by using a tent peg and a hammer. Rebbetzin Leah Kohn (international teacher and director of the Jewish Renaissance Center) describes it beautifully: "Rather than taking up arms, Ya'el construes an unconventional murder in an effort to preserve her connection to the Divine source of her femininity, at the heart of this Torah commandment."[14]

In the Song of Devorah, Devorah herself proclaimed, "I rose as a mother of Israel!" She pronounced herself not as a leader, a judge, or a warrior, but as a mother. A mother. To be a mother of Israel encompasses an inner might and resourcefulness; those sparks reside within you. Devorah and Ya'el demonstrate that the feminine embraces a spectrum of possibility, that a woman constantly renews her connection with the spiritual realms by means of her actions in this world.

13. Proverbs 31:10 –31.
14. Leah Kohn, "Ya'el: A Righteous—Modest—Radical Part II," December 27, 2017, https://torah.org/learning/women-class54/.

Chana
Prayerful Spirit

The Story of Chana

Chana's (Hannah's) story is told at the beginning of the first Book of Shmuel (Samuel) the prophet.[1] This is the end of the time of the Judges and the dawning of the era of the Kings. Her name comes from the Hebrew word *chein*, which is usually translated as "grace." As we have seen with many of the other women and men in the Tanach, a name helps us understand something of a person's nature. The concept of *chein* encompasses and holds ideals of grace, compassion, kindness, beauty, refinement, poise, and dignity. Chana was all these things!

She was married to a righteous man named Elkana. They had a beautiful and loving relationship. Stories are told of their joy-filled travels four times a year to the Mishkan, the holy Sanctuary (which in her time was in Shilo—the Beit Hamikdash had not yet been built in Jerusalem). The Midrash paints a beautiful picture of their openheartedness.[2] Each time they traveled, they would take a different route so they could meet new people along the way and invite them to join in the journey and the festivities. They didn't

---

1. The story of Chana can be found in I Samuel, chapters 1–2.
2. Midrash, *Yalkut Shimoni* 77:5.

think only of themselves; they wanted to include others in the national celebrations.

While life for them was good in so many ways, there was something missing from Chana's life: as with several of the other women whose stories we have learned, Chana had no children. She ached for a child. At some point in a lifetime, most people can relate to that kind of intense yearning, such deep desire (whether for a life mate, a child, healing, or something else). It's a longing from the soul. This is the place from where profound prayers for help emanate.

Chana's longing was all-consuming. Knowing the stories of how the matriarchs Sarah, Rachel, and Leah each brought in another wife, Chana told her husband to take another wife.[3] Maybe then, she thought, God would have mercy on her and give her a child. Enter Penina. Penina (which means "pearl") was a good and righteous woman. And she was fertile. While Chana remained childless, Penina had baby after baby—ten in all.[4]

The Midrash tells us that Penina taunted Chana.[5] She flaunted her own motherhood to make Chana feel bad. Chana's empty womb and empty arms were all the more painful because of Penina's ridicule. But wait, we noted above that Penina was a righteous woman!

One interpretation said that Penina was trying to make herself look good, but another says that she knew that what Chana needed to do was pray. She knew that Chana must pray with all her heart. We're told that prayers are the most powerful when we are literally crying out to God. One midrash explains that Penina's intention was to get Chana to cry to God even more deeply. Herein lies Penina's fault: though her intentions may have been good, it was arrogant of her to treat Chana with such cruelty.

Elkana knew of Chana's longing. He loved her, and it didn't matter to him that she didn't have a child. But he didn't understand

---

3.   Malbim, I Samuel 1:2; Midrash, *Pesikta Rabbah* 43.
4.   Rashi, I Samuel 1:8.
5.   Talmud, *Bava Batra* 16a.

why she was crying, wouldn't eat, why her heart was grieved. He even asked, "Aren't I better than ten children?" Of course, none of his words could take away her burning desire for motherhood.

One day, Chana was in the Sanctuary of the Mishkan praying. She wept. She poured her heart out to God: "Every part of a woman's body has a purpose; how can you give me a womb and not fill it?" She pleaded and bargained with God: Chana promised God that if he gave her a son, she would dedicate his life to divine service.

When a Jew prayed in those times, it was always out loud.[6] There is power in your ear hearing the words that your mouth speaks. But Chana was so overcome with emotion, she whispered. The High Priest, Eli, saw her lips moving but did not hear her voice. In that sacred place, he accused her, "How long will you be drunken? Put away your wine!" She told him she had drunk no alcohol, and that she was pouring out her soul before the Eternal. Eli answered with a blessing that God would grant her request: "Go in peace; may the God of Israel grant what you have asked of Him." She continued her worship and was no longer sad.

Our text tells us that they returned home, that Elkana "knew" Chana his wife, and that God remembered her. Using the term "knowing" for sexual relations indicates that they were physically intimate in a way of depth and soul merging. When you know something, a connection is made. Knowing, in a spiritual sense, means unification.

Chana's prayer was answered. She gave birth to a son. She named him Shmuel (Samuel). Once he was weaned, Chana brought him to the Sanctuary with offerings. She brought Shmuel to Eli, the High Priest. She reminded him that she was the woman he had seen praying. She told him that God had granted her plea for a child, and that she was now giving him over to a lifetime of Torah and service to God. Shmuel became a great prophet. He eventually

---

6.   Rashi, I Samuel 1:13.

anointed King Shaul (Saul) and then King David.[7] A book in the Tanach is named for him.

The story of Chana does not end with the birth of her son. Chana, too, sings a song of praise to God, which is recorded for us in the text. Chana's song proclaims that our deeds and prayers can bring changes, that God can lift those who are broken and bring down those who are haughty. Chana's song of praise and gratitude echoes in our lives today.

Chana's Gift: Prayer

Chana set up a precedent for prayer that echoes all the way to our generation. Her prayers were whispered, the whispers of knowing that the Eternal is present and close by. Chana's prayer was mistaken for drunkenness. Can you imagine how desperate she must have felt to have given that kind of impression to the High Priest? Can you relate that to what it might look like today? Can you imagine talking to God as you walk down the street, and what people might think? Could you imagine shouting at God?

One woman who was the sole survivor of a boating accident in which her daughter died shared her intimate story. There in the sea, knowing she was the only survivor, trying to stay afloat, her daughter lost, she shouted at God. As angry, sad, and hurt as she was, she knew she was not alone.

God understands us. God knows where we're coming from. Even if you're mad at God, talk to Him. The idea of prayer is that you are in relationship with your Creator. When you're in any relationship, you need to communicate to keep the connection. The idea in prayer is to talk with God, no matter how you're feeling. You might feel lofty and close to the Divine, you might feel angry or small and in awe. Hopefully you'll express gratitude. There may be other times when you feel disconnected; you might feel alone. Reach out, reach in, and talk to God anyway. When you're well fed,

---

7.   I Samuel 16:13.

happy, with your loved ones, or even if you just find that perfect parking place, it's a good time to thank the Creator for the pleasures and gifts of life. You may not feel sublime or deep every time you pray. That's okay. Think about calling someone important in your life, such as a mother or father. Each call does not necessarily feel particularly deep and meaningful on its own, but the fact that you are calling, even to talk about the mundane, makes the connection and builds the relationship.

Some people worry about bothering God. The Almighty must be busy running the universe, after all. How could He have time for the little people? The thing is, God is, after all, God! You cannot bother God. King David assures us, "The Guardian of Israel never slumbers nor sleeps."[8] You can't wake God up, bore God, or put God to sleep; you aren't interrupting God from more important work. God's patience is infinite. His capacity to contain all that you are is infinite.

God knows where you are and keeps an open connection with you in every moment. Your connection to Him is better than being connected to a smart phone. You just need to pay attention; you can tap in to that connection twenty-four hours a day, seven days a week, right now.

What should you pray for? Rabbi Nachman of Breslov teaches that you should pray for everything from the biggest to the smallest.[9] Ask for all things major and minor, from a replacement for a torn garment to your entire livelihood; from peace in your relationships to the ability to forgive; from the wisdom to forget what needs to be forgotten to guidance in decision making; from that fluffy new pillow you've been wanting to crispy apples for breakfast; and from expressing gratitude for the warmth of the sunshine to the blessings that come with the rain—including the rain of tears, and even the hardship that is custom designed to help you grow and blossom. For more on how to pray, the parts of Jewish prayer,

8.   Psalms 121:4.
9.   *Sichot HaRan* 233.

and more, check out the "Spiritual Pathways" chapter at the end
of the book.

Reflections in Chana's Mirror: Growth from Pain

Pain brings us to growth. If you're in this world, pain is a part of
the package. It's not that we're supposed to seek pain, but we must
understand that it's a part of life. Pain comes in so many forms.
Often pain comes from a place of lack (barrenness) and the need
to fill the void, to fill the darkness with light. It could be the lack of
something materially, such as no warmth on a cold day; or it could
be the feeling of the lack of love. It is up to us to seek the solution
for healing what needs to be healed. Sometimes the healing is as
simple as a shift in perspective—but simple is not always so easy.
And here is where the journey to growth lies.

Had Chana conceived easily from the beginning of her marriage, she would not have been the same woman she grew into
after her trials. She needed to grow to become the woman who
would be able to bring through a soul at the level of Shmuel and
to mother him.

Penina's Hard Lesson: Sensitivity

Here, within the story of Chana, is the story of Penina as well.
Penina did conceive easily. While her effort to push Chana to
bring her prayers to a deeper place might have sprung from good
intentions, the way she made Chana suffer and cry was cruel. The
Midrash tells us her punishment was severe and incomprehensible:
most of her children died young.[10] This righteous woman made a
mistake that brought her the deepest grief imaginable. It's hard to
understand why her punishment was so severe. We want both for
ourselves and others to learn without pain, and this kind of pain
can seem out of proportion to us. One explanation that's repeated

---

10. Midrash, *Pesikta Rabbah* 43; Rashi, I Samuel 2:5.

here is that the Torah giants we are learning about, and that includes Penina, are held to a higher standard than we can imagine.

From the story of Penina comes a very powerful yet fundamental lesson in Jewish values *for us*. We have the chance to uplift this story by learning from Penina's insensitivity, which resulted in her own pain with the loss of her children. You can't understand another person until you've been in the same life situation. Since none of us can ever be in the exact life situation as another, we are never in a position to judge—not what someone else needs, not what others should be doing, not how soon anyone should be done grieving, not anything. We just don't know enough. This doesn't mean standing by when someone is in danger or holding back when what you know can help someone else's situation or perspective. However, the *way* we relate to others is critical. It's a theme that surfaces over and over again in the stories of our fathers and mothers. Loving others, treating others with compassion, and giving the benefit of the doubt are essential themes in all of Torah's teachings. After all, if we are made in God's image, if our very soul is the breath of God, we must see every soul as a manifestation of the Creator. How careful we must be not to trample another.

One beautiful and very simple way to move forward toward difficult conversations with others is to ask for divine guidance: "Please help me say the words that need to be said, from the heart, for the heart. Help me say what needs to be said, and to not say the things that do not need to be said." One source, *Mesilas Yesharim* (*The Path of the Just*) suggests that you take time at the end of every single day to do an accounting of your relationships.[11] Ask yourself, "How could I have said what I said with more sensitivity?" This accounting is most important on the days we know we had a short fuse, anger, or impatience. By asking yourself this question, you develop a plan for how you want to relate to others from the highest place. Having a plan makes it more likely you'll actually take action in that positive way.

---

11.   Rabbi Moshe Chaim Luzzatto, *Mesilat Yesharim* (*The Path of the Upright*) 3:12.

Meaning and Purpose

Pain has a purpose, even when we don't understand it. Sometimes the darkest parts of our lives reveal their purpose and sometimes not. Sometimes we build ourselves into something stronger or we become advocates for others. We have the power to transform the hard stuff of life. In the darkest places, we can strike a match and bring light. In the coldest places, we can build a fire to warm ourselves and others. Can you look through your own past and see something painful you have endured and understand how it has helped you grow to where you are now? Because if you can see how you've used pain to grow in the past, you can have faith that even if you don't understand your current pain, it's possible there will be meaning and purpose again.

We take our pain and we use it to rise.

There is a simple story of an old prospector who was walking in the desert one day with his donkey. The donkey fell into a deep, dry well. The donkey couldn't climb out, and the old man could not lift him. The old prospector felt bad that the donkey would have to suffer a slow death, so he decided to bury him and put the creature out of its misery. He shoveled some dirt and rocks into the well. The donkey did not like that a bit; he brayed and kicked. All the dirt fell off him and the donkey stepped onto it. As the man shoveled more dirt into the well, the donkey began to shake it off and then used it to step up higher and higher, until he could walk out of his hole. How many stories there are of men and women who survive unthinkable darkness and rise up to shine. The difficult and painful experiences can motivate us to go higher than we might have if we had remained comfortable.

Rising doesn't mean that you have to "get over it" so fast. Timing is different for everyone. Knowing you can use pain to grow gives you the power to look for the opportunity to grow and step into it. Other things are not worth fretting about, and the faster you let go, the faster you rise. There is a spectrum of life experiences, and so much of what happens will never be understood from our earthly perspective. There can, however, always be a level of healing when we bring meaning and purpose to our struggles and challenges. The mother who lost her child and started an organization that saves other children or comforts other families in pain has brought purpose to her loss.

Rising does not have to be on a grand scale to have deep meaning and purpose. The woman who is diagnosed with a disease visits another woman with the same diagnosis in her time of need. That act of comfort is the phoenix rising from the flame, majesty from the fire. You may not see from the midst of pain where it is taking you, but you can always know that there is a purpose and meaning to all pain—to bring you to your greatness. Use your challenges to grow.

Ruth and Naomi
Commitment and Persistence

The Story of Ruth and Naomi

The heroine of the Book of Ruth was a princess who went from riches to rags, then eventually became the matriarch of the Davidic dynasty.[1] She lived in the time of the Judges (that era began 1106 BCE).[2] Ruth was the daughter of a powerful but depraved king of the Kingdom of Moav (Moab). She abandoned her life as a princess to marry a Jewish man who was living in Moab. Widowed at a young age, she left her birthplace and accompanied her mother-in-law Naomi to the Land of Israel, a place foreign to all that she knew. She converted to Judaism and dedicated her life to living as a Jew. Ruth had the courage to seek what she knew to be the truth, and she was willing to give up her position and wealth to follow that path. She walked away from a life of royalty toward a life that might have appeared hopeless and lonely. But her courage and determination brought the birth of the royal lineage of King David to the House of Israel.

On the holiday of Shavuot, when we commemorate the giving of the Torah at Mount Sinai, we read the Book of Ruth. We remind ourselves that we are all converts, really, that we are choosing anew every day. We all need to make a choice to let go of some things in order to make room for something of greater value.

---

1. The Book of Ruth.
2. For a complete timeline of Jewish history, see Rabbi Ken Spiro, History Crash Course #68, "Timeline: From Abraham to the State of Israel," http://www.aish.com/jl/h/cc/48964541.html.

From Beit Lechem to Moav

Ruth's story really begins with her mother-in-law, Naomi. Naomi and her husband Elimelech were influential and wealthy. They lived in Beit Lechem (Bethlehem) with their two sons. Once again, a famine plagued the Land of Israel. Deprivation and hunger. Where do people turn in times of despair? They turn to those with the most resources for help. Elimelech was at the top of the list. Overwhelmed with so many poor and hungry people knocking at his door seeking relief, Elimelech made the decision to move to Moav with his family.[3] This was a painful choice for Naomi; she did not want to leave the Land of Israel, a place of holiness, to go to a place where life was depraved, selfish, and crude. But Naomi followed her husband to settle in Moav. There, her sons married Moabite princesses, daughters of Eglon the king of Moav; their names were Orpah and Ruth.[4]

The move to Moav was not a good one for Elimelech's family. First, they lost their entire fortune. Then the worst happened. Elimelech *and* both of his sons died. Naomi was left in poverty with her daughters-in-law. There was nothing left for her in the land of Moav. So when Naomi heard that the famine was over, she made the decision to return to her beloved homeland.

Naomi and Ruth

When Naomi began her journey home to Israel, Ruth and Orpah followed their cherished mother-in-law. Naomi discouraged them from coming with her. She blessed them that God would deal kindly with them, as they were so kind to her sons and to her. She blessed them with new lives and to have new husbands. Naomi kissed her daughters-in-law and they all wept. She told them to return to their mothers' houses and start over.

---

3.   Midrash, *Ruth Rabbah* 1:4.
4.   Midrash, *Ruth Rabbah* 2:9; *Yalkut Shimoni* 600:7.

But the two women wanted to stay with Naomi. How striking was the love between mother-in-law and daughters-in-law. She loved them like daughters. Still, Naomi told them that she had nothing to offer them. She told them that she had no more sons for them to marry, nor was it worth the wait even if she could bring more sons into the world. They raised their voices and wept again. At last, Orpah kissed her mother-in-law goodbye and turned back to return to her life as a Moabite princess.

But Ruth was tenacious.

Naomi tried again and told her to stay in Moav with her sister-in-law.

Ruth was clear about what she wanted, and it was not the life of a princess of Moav. It says in *Pirkei Avot*: "It's better to be the tail of a lion than the head of a fox."[5] It's better to be at the back of something great than the leader of something sly. Even as an impoverished widow, Ruth chose to follow the path of the life of a Jewess, and all that it encompasses: godliness, kindness, ethics, wisdom, righteousness, and purpose. She was willing to sacrifice all things material in order to fulfill her spiritual thirst.

Ruth poured her heart out to Naomi, her mother-in-law, in a deeply moving declaration of her commitment to taking on this new life and all it entails: "Do not urge me to leave you, to turn back from following you. For where you go, I will go. Where you lodge, I will lodge. Your people are my people, and your God is my God. Where you die, I will die. And there I will be buried. Thus may God do to me and so may He do more if anything but death separates me from you."

Ruth's moving statement is the source of many of the laws of conversion to Judaism.[6] Even today, a person who wants to become a Jewish convert is at first dissuaded,[7] as Naomi discouraged Orpah and Ruth.

5. Mishnah, *Pirkei Avot* 4:15.
6. Talmud, *Yevamot* 47b.
7. According to Jewish teachings, conversion to Judaism is not necessary to acquire a place in Heaven; this is promised for all who behave righteously (according to the

Naomi did not answer Ruth, and her silence was the signal that Ruth's plea was fully embraced. The two women journeyed back to Beit Lechem. As they entered the edge of town, people saw the two poor women entering on foot, and the murmurs began: "Is that really Naomi? Could it be? Naomi, is that really you?" Naomi told them not to call her Naomi (which means "pleasant") but to call her Mar (which means "bitter"), that her life had become bitter, and that the Almighty brought misfortune upon her.

Compassion

It happened to be harvest time for barley as Naomi and her daughter-in-law Ruth settled back in the Land of Israel. It is here in our story that we are reminded of some Torah laws that teach those who work in agriculture to have compassion and give to the poor so that the hungry may be fed without any temptation toward theft. When it was harvest time for the field owner, it was also harvest time for the poor. Torah law has three requirements for field owners regarding what to leave for the poor: *pe'ah*, to leave a certain corner of the field to be harvested; *leket*, to leave any grains that are dropped (called gleanings); and *shichechah*, not to go back for parts of the harvest that are left in the field.[8]

Ruth, the woman who had been royalty in her parents' home, was now a beggar, reduced to gleaning food for herself and her mother-in-law, Naomi. In a nation that treasures modesty, Ruth's modesty in the way she gleaned from the field is legendary. First, she was meticulous in following Torah law, taking no more than what was permitted.[9] And, when she gathered, she sat while

---

Seven Noachide Laws). For more information see "The 7 Noachide Laws," http://www.aish.com/w/nj/For_Non-Jews.html; see also Rabbi Yirmeyahu Bindman, "The Seven Laws of Noah," http://www.simpletoremember.com/articles/a/seven-laws-of-noah/. For a moving story about the journey of converting to Judaism, see Michaela Lawson, *Spark Ignited: The Difficult Journey to Orthodox Judaism* (Jerusalem: Menorah, 2016).

8. *Leket* and *pe'ah* derive from Leviticus 19:9–10 and *shichechah* from Deuteronomy 24:19.

9. Malbim, Ruth 2:7.

picking up fallen stalks, in order to avoid positioning herself in an immodest way.[10]

Enter Boaz, the owner of the field. Boaz was an older man[11] of stature and integrity. The Talmud says that he was the judge of the generation.[12] He was a Jewish leader in Beit Lechem. Boaz was greeting his workers when Ruth caught his eye. He inquired about her and was told that she was the Moabite girl who had returned with Naomi, and that she had asked to glean behind the harvesters. Boaz told Ruth to only glean from his fields, to stay close to the other women, and to feel free to drink from the jugs of water provided for them.

Have you ever had someone do something for you that for the giver was simple and easy, but because of the place you were in, it felt like the world? In this story, Ruth had left the only life she had ever known for a new land. The culture and people were completely foreign to her. She didn't know anyone besides her mother-in-law. Her gratitude to Boaz was deep. She asked why he was taking special note of her. He told her that he knew of all she had done for Naomi, how she had left her father and mother and her birthplace. He blessed her: "May the Eternal reward your deed, and may your payment be full from the God of Israel, under Whose wings you have come to seek refuge."

At mealtime, Boaz invited her to eat bread and vinegar with the harvesters. In Torah every nuance and detail is included for a reason. Herein lies a beautiful lesson. If Boaz had only known that this simple act of kindness and generosity—telling her to stay and glean from his fields, drink from his jugs, and eat bread with the workers—would be recorded for all generations, might he have laid out a feast for her instead of just bread and vinegar? On one hand a simple kindness can take on such huge proportions to the receiver. On the other hand, this could be a beautiful clue to us to

---

10. Talmud, *Shabbat* 113b. Midrash, *Ruth Rabbah* 4:6.
11. Midrash, *Ruth Rabbah* 6:2.
12. Talmud, *Bava Batra* 91a.

give kindly and with generosity. This story gives us an opportunity to consider what our lives look like from a distance, so we might do acts of kindness that are worth noting. You are "writing" your story in the Book of Life with each act, attitude, thought, and deed. How do you want your story to read?

When Ruth returned home with the barley, Naomi blessed the generous benefactor and asked his name. When she learned it was Boaz, she realized it was divine guidance that had led Ruth to those fields. Boaz was a close relative of Elimelech and one of their "redeeming kinsmen."

Why does this matter? What did she mean by "redeeming kinsmen"?

There is a practice described in the Torah (not in practice today) that when a married man died without children, his brother had a responsibility to marry his widow. The first child born to this couple would be considered as if it were the child of the deceased, and the deceased would then have left his mark through this child. (The intricacies of this mystical process are beyond the scope of this book.[13]) In this way he "redeems" his brother's name. However, the man is not required to marry his brother's widow. If he cannot or does not want to marry her, he performs an unusual ritual involving taking off his shoe, to indicate he is abdicating this responsibility. The search for a redeemer then follows the line of next of kin. This meant that for Ruth and Naomi, there was a possibility that Boaz, this kind, generous leader of the nation, was in a position to redeem the family as well as the family's land by marrying Ruth.

Ruth told her mother-in-law that Boaz had invited her to come only to his fields from then on, and with Naomi's encouragement, Ruth continued to glean from Boaz's fields until the end of the harvest. Naomi knew what to do next. She had a plan.

---

13. The halachic procedure here, known as *go'el*, is spoken about in Leviticus 25:25. Another aspect is called *yibum,* found in Deuteronomy 25:5–10.

The Plan

Naomi told Ruth to bathe and put on perfume and her finest dress. She instructed her to go to the threshing floor, where all the young girls who work on the harvest would be. Naomi told Ruth to wait until Boaz lay down to sleep (he stayed there during the height of the harvest season) and to uncover his feet and lie down by them. Then she was to wait for him to tell her what to do next.

This was such a peculiar direction for Naomi, so noble and respectable, to give to Ruth, who was known for her modesty. The intimacy and love between Ruth and Naomi was apparent. Naomi called her "daughter." Ruth's trust in Naomi's guidance was profound. Ruth agreed to do everything Naomi told her to do.

What was going on here? Why such unusual behavior?

The specific instruction to uncover his feet gives us a clue to this puzzle. Ruth did not lie *with* Boaz; she lay by his feet. This posed the unspoken question: Would he marry her and thus bring a child into the line of Ruth's departed husband? Or would he opt not to be the redeemer and instead perform the ritual that would relinquish this responsibility?

Boaz was startled awake in the middle of the night and saw the girl by his feet. "Who are you?" Ruth identified herself and asked him to spread his robe over her, as he was a redeemer. Boaz, who was a man of Torah, understood her meaning. He realized that he was in the position to redeem her husband's line. He praised her, but also informed her that there was someone else closer in the kinship line to Elimelech's family. He said he would first give that man the right to fulfill his obligation. If he chose not to, Boaz promised he would marry Ruth.

Boaz told Ruth to stay the night but to return home before anyone would be able to discern that a woman had come to the threshing floor. He gave her six measures of barley to take with her. There was so much symbolism in this one gesture. It was a promise of their union. One source notes that it was a hint to the six leaders that would come from her, each with six outstanding attributes perhaps represented by the Star of David.[14] (For example, it's written of King David that he was "skillful in playing, a mighty man of valor, a man of war, prudent in affairs, handsome in appearance, and God is with him."[15])

Boaz found the man who was before him in the family line (who is never named) and offered him the right to inherit Elimelech's land. At first, the man wanted to, but once he understood that it meant marrying Ruth, he thought otherwise. In front of eyewitnesses, he said he did not want to mar his own inheritance, and removed his shoe, signifying giving up his obligation and his rights. Boaz declared in front of the witnesses that he would take Ruth as a wife and thus inherit all that was Elimelech's. He promised to perpetuate the name of the deceased. The witnesses blessed the union.

Boaz came to Ruth and married her. She conceived and bore a son named Oved (which means "servant"). It was a time of great joy for Naomi. The women blessed Naomi and congratulated her on having a daughter-in-law who is "better to you than seven sons." Loving, steadfast, and loyal, beautiful Naomi took the child and lay him in an embrace on her bosom. She was there to raise him.

The story of Ruth is about a woman who sacrificed wealth and position for something that on the surface looked humiliating, but which truly was real and spiritually rich. In our generation we are so inundated with ads depicting romantic, beautiful people who are perfectly dressed, confident, and the ultimate in attractiveness. As Jews we pursue ideals and principles. While our lives are filled with delightful earthly pleasures, we seek to use those pleasures as tools to build something meaningful or elevated in the world. Ruth's heartfelt and dedicated decision to follow her mother-in-law Naomi back to Israel came with hardship; it came with the humiliation of being dependent on the kindness of others. But Ruth stepped forward over and over again, like her mother-in-law Naomi. That place of trust and faith brought Ruth to follow her role

---

14. Me'am Lo'ez, Ruth 3:15.
15. I Samuel 16:18.

model Naomi to the Jewish nation and to the Land of Israel. Oved became the grandfather of King David.

Indeed, Ruth was blessed and full. She became a great-grand-mother of King David and ultimately of his descendant, the Moshiach (Messiah), who is yet to come. She also became a matri-arch that the nation turns to for inspiration when we receive the Torah and its teachings anew every year at the holiday of Shavuot.

Moshiach

Ruth gave up the status of being a princess in a depraved society to convert and become a Jew. She is one of the predecessors of King David, from whose lineage the Moshiach will come.[16] The idea of a Messiah is a Jewish concept. Many people don't even know that the concept of Messiah originates in the Torah.

What is the Moshiach? In Hebrew the word simply means "anointed one." The Moshiach will be anointed as the leader of the Jewish nation and will usher in a time of peace on earth. There are prophecies written telling who Moshiach will be and what he will accomplish. The prophecies give us an idea of what the world will be like during that time. One of the more famous prophecies is that during the era of the Moshiach, the wolf will lie down with the lamb.[17] This is an amazing idea, to think that a predator will become so gentle that it will stop eating meat. This really means something more: that the humans who crave blood and death, those who bring about the destructive nightmares of this world, will also stop their craving for wickedness. We're told evil will be removed from the world.[18] This concept carries great hope for all of humanity. There is much written and speculated regarding the Moshiach. Even more is unknown.

What we learn from various stories throughout our texts and history is that our Moshiach will not be some perfect guy who

---

16. Talmud, *Sukkah* 52a.
17. Isaiah 11:6.
18. Zechariah 13:2; Malachi 3:19.

comes from a perfect lineage. He will not fit into any box we can imagine he "should" fit into. He will come from roots that are all over the map, including ancestors of impurity as well as purity!

One example of the sinister side of the lineage of Moshiach is the story of Ruth's father, King Eglon.[19] He was cruel. He was also enormously obese. A Jew came to assassinate him, saying he had a message from God for him. King Eglon knew who the Jews were, and though he was causing them to suffer, when the Jew walked in, Eglon exerted great effort to stand in honor of the message from the God of the Jews. With all of his despicable deeds, this one act of reverence earned him the honor of having the Moshiach in his lineage, and that came through his daughter, Ruth.[20]

Ruth and Naomi's Gift: Persistence and Trusting the Process

We study the Scroll of Ruth every year on the holiday called Shavuot, the holiday that marks the giving of the Torah at Mount Sinai and the birth of the Jewish nation. Why do we study Ruth to mark this one among the three festivals that God gave to the Jews? In one sense, we were all converts. Amid all the miracles and wonder that made up the Exodus from Egypt, our ancestors still had to make the choice to leave slavery. Then our ancestors at Mount Sinai chose again to stand and be a part of the nation that would receive the gift—and the yoke—of Torah. Every year, after the Pesach Seder (the ritual meal at which we remember the Exodus out of Egyptian slavery), we count seven weeks—forty-nine days—until the next festival, Shavuot, when we receive the Torah anew.

Torah is not meant to be like some cut crystal that gets set in a china cabinet to admire. Torah is really a relationship, like a marriage, that comes with commitment and accountability. This responsibility is sometimes called the "yoke of Torah." Why is Torah

---

19. Judges 3:12–25.
20. Rashi, Judges 3:20.

a yoke? (What is a yoke, anyway? A yoke is the wooden frame that was put on the necks of oxen or other animals when they were working, for example to plough a field or pull a cart.) A yoke is a metaphor for something heavy that seems to carry the energy of bondage and oppression. Not something we want to relate to. Who wants to sign up for a life like that? This is not a good marketing strategy! Yet all the Jewish souls stood at Mount Sinai and said yes to Torah. The reality is that it can feel like a heavy load, for the simple reason that it's human nature that we don't want to be told what to do and what not to do. No one wants to be commanded. Perhaps the metaphor by the poet Rabindranath Tagore can help frame the beauty of discipline: "I have on my table a violin string. It is free to move in any direction I like. If I twist one end, it responds; it is free. But it is not free to sing. So I take it and fix it into my violin. I bind it, and when it is bound, it is free for the first time to sing."

The matriarchs and patriarchs are said to have known through prophecy what Hashem wanted, and so they performed all the *mitzvot* (commandments; see also the chapter on Rachel and Leah). In a way it might actually be more challenging for the generations after the Torah was given. Some might consider it harder to take orders and to do what God commands us to do than to volunteer to do what God wants. Can you relate to this notion at all?

Now, if we can expand the thought that receiving the Torah is stepping into a beloved relationship, then it means that the paradigm shifts, too. In a bond of love and connection, the motivation to do what pleases the other is a beautiful thing. Relationship with God is sometimes likened to a relationship with a lover, and other times to that with a parent. The role of a parent is to help a child grow into the best she can be. "Don't go into the street without looking!" doesn't make sense to a very young mind. They cannot comprehend the danger, so we want them to trust us. In a relationship with the Divine, it is similar. We have been given a body of knowledge to guide us; are we willing to trust? The way you build trust is to show up in a relationship. You show up in relationships because there is a foundation of love, kindness, and compassion.

In addition to spring being the season of harvest, the setting of the story of Ruth, there is another reason we read and study the story of Ruth at the time of Shavuot: it is a deep story of love and compassion. Naomi's relationship with Ruth was so tender and so caring, and Boaz's actions were full of gentleness and empathy. Ruth's commitment was one of dedication and faithfulness. Even the community around them celebrated and blessed Ruth, her union to Boaz, and their child, when he was born. So, too, was Torah given to humanity in a phenomenal gesture of divine kindness, love, and devotion.

Life is not comfortable. It is fraught with difficulties and hardships. What if Ruth had given in and turned back for the "comfortable" life with her sister? What if Naomi had returned alone to the Land of Israel and just taken care of herself without the bother of finding a mate for her daughter-in-law? What if Boaz had backed out of the risk of getting involved in a marriage at his advanced age? Walking a spiritual walk of Torah is a commitment of eyes-wide-open love with the Creator. All of life's hard times can be faced with the idea of taking one more step forward. And then one more, not in spite of the discomfort, but because you know that the discomfort is shaping you and transforming you into something more magnificent than your comfort could ever bring you to. Ruth walked away from her life as a princess because she was attracted to the decency and nobility she saw in the family she married into.

Your steadfast walk in this world, like Ruth and Naomi's, can make way for immense greatness. Do not underestimate the meaning and purpose of even the smallest of steps you take with faith and trust. Trust that each one's journey unfolds with precision from a loving God as you do what is within your power: one more step.

Reflections in Ruth's Mirror: The Soul Journey

The concept that a man may "redeem" his deceased, childless brother brings our attention to the idea that a soul has a mission, and that if the mission is not fulfilled, there is another chance. This idea of the journey of a soul—reincarnation—was not something openly talked about in Western society until fairly recently.

So what about the journey of the soul? How is that relevant to you in your life right now? Have you ever felt that who you were ten years ago was a completely different person? Sure, there are similarities in your nature over a decade, but don't you feel you're in a totally different place? You've traveled through time and life experiences, and, God willing, there is more time ahead and more life experience to come. Who you will be in another ten or twenty years will be different yet again. The mistakes you learned the hard way are lessons learned that you wouldn't need to repeat. On the other hand, if it takes repetition to learn certain lessons, life has a way of bringing them on until you "get it." In a way, one lifetime can feel like many as you develop and refine.

The place to begin is to understand that there are mysteries of life; we are only in a position to see a small portion of this world. The Hebrew word for "world" is *olam*. It comes from the root word that means "hidden." If we can only see a small portion of this world, how can we expect to know more about other realms? Much more is hidden than is revealed to us. Yet there are teachings within the body of our Scriptures that reveal what is not easily seen by the eye. The soul is on a journey in life, and that may mean more than one incarnation. The concept of reincarnation is called *gilgul neshamot* (*gilgul* means "cycle" and *neshamot* means "[of] souls").

If you begin with the premise that there is a Creator Who runs the world, then nothing is by chance, and everything happens for a reason. Cosmically, things are revealed at the right time to any individual (or even to a whole nation). On one hand you can clearly see how this operates with children. Little children hear simplified versions of a story (such as "the birds and the bees," family history, biblical stories, or incomprehensible historical events such as the Holocaust). As they mature, they are given more information, more complex aspects of the same story, fleshed out. Now imagine the way we take electricity for granted: flip a switch, and there is light. Press a screen and a voice or video connection is made across the world in seconds. If someone had talked about technology like this a thousand years ago, that person would have been thought insane, a dreamer, or perhaps demonic. In the same way, the bearers of the secrets of the mystical realms of energy would have to keep things secret until a time when people would have a frame of reference to understand them.

The potential for technology always existed, and all the same resources were in the world a thousand years ago, but the knowledge was concealed. Today, technology has moved so fast that we are able to consciously grasp certain concepts because they are illustrated as part of our everyday life. The kabbalistic work the *Zohar* was written in a concealed way, often in riddles. Those who deeply studied Kabbalah understood what could be shared and what not to share. Jewish teachings have always called this world an "orb,"[21] but when the popular belief was that the world was flat, how would someone saying it was round have been viewed or treated?

There are those who say with confidence that there is nothing beyond this world. On the other hand, there are religions that promise an eternal hell of fire and brimstone to those who don't follow their program. Not so with Judaism. In Judaism there are certainly teachings of the soul's continuation after physical death.[22] Judaism teaches that there is a place of cleansing called Gehinnom, and that the embarrassment that the soul feels is like a burning, though there is not a body. There is the idea that a soul that does not completely fulfill its mission can have a chance to repair or fulfill its divine purpose. Yaakov Astor, in his book *Soul Searching*,

21. Isaiah 11:12; Ezekiel 7:2.
22. Talmud, *Pesachim* 50a; Arizal, *Sha'ar Hagilgulim* 29:2a.

writes: "The purpose of reincarnation is generally twofold: either to make up for a failure in a previous life or to create a new, higher state of personal perfection not previously attained."[23]

How is this relevant to our lives? Let's start by talking about how it's not relevant. Learning about your soul journey is not about satisfying curiosity about who you were in a past life. The important factor is to know that you are part of a continuity, of something bigger, something that is beyond our human comprehension.

The journey of the soul is for correcting, growing, repairing, or completing our soul mission. The journey of the soul is to rise and help others heal, repair, and excel. *Every soul has a mission, a purpose to step into with radiance.* When you're on track, you feel great about it. It is up to us to understand, to be still enough to center and connect, to hear the soul. The Talmud teaches us that each soul made a vow when it came into this world to serve its Creator.[24] Listen to the inner messages of what energizes you and makes your soul sing, whether it be parenting, teaching, sharing, art, learning a new skill, or service of any kind. *Every soul also has a challenge to refine aspects of itself.* The other mission to consider in the journey of the soul is improving character traits: anger, sadness, impatience, resentments, grudges, or arrogance. How honest can you be with yourself about what needs repairing? If your gift is generosity, do you know how to set healthy boundaries? If your nature is to seek knowledge, will you use it wisely and for the good? You can rise to your mission in this world even when you stumble or fall with the inevitable challenges and difficulties. Fall seven times and stand back up each of those seven times ("For a righteous one falls seven times and rises up again"[25]); the idea of being on a soul journey is that you have another chance, and another. And another. It's not all or nothing. It's never too late to take a step, to repair damage, or to build.

---

23. Arizal, *Sha'ar Hagilgulim*, chapter 8; Ramchal, *Derech Hashem* 2:3:10.
24. Talmud, *Niddah* 30b.
25. Proverbs 24:16.

Jewish liturgy gives us a bedtime prayer that includes the notion of reincarnation and connects it to a profound and liberating declaration of forgiveness. We declare that we forgive anyone who hurt us in any way, "whether in this incarnation or another incarnation."

The way you can use this knowledge of soul journeys, of souls (or offshoots of root souls) cycling through life is to understand that if God gives you the chance to come into another life to perfect or repair, that means that every soul has the chance to repair or to shine, right now. Every moment is another chance to return to the truth of your soul. There is another Hebrew word that touches on the breadth of the journey of a Jewish soul: *teshuvah*. It means "return" or "answer." The moment for *teshuvah*, the moment for returning to the truth of your soul, is always the present moment.

As you travel the journey of your unique soul, you can ask yourself: What lights you up? Pursue that (in moral, legal, just ways). What is your challenge? Work on refining that aspect of yourself and how you relate to the difficult character traits and relationships in your life.

Returning to the truth of your soul's journey brings meaning and purpose to life. Enjoy the journey!

Esther
Authentic Nobility

The Story of Esther

Megillat Esther (the Book or Scroll of Esther) tells the story of a Jewish woman who—against her own wishes—rises to become a queen. This is not a fairy tale; there is no glass slipper and no dashing prince. She does not want either the rank or wealth, but finds herself in the midst of a story where she is positioned to save her nation from certain destruction. The desire to save her nation triumphs in this story of twists and turns, palace intrigue, and "coincidences."

Megillat Esther is read every year on Purim, the holiday that falls in the spring, on the full moon, one lunar month before Pesach on the Hebrew calendar. It is a favorite holiday for many because it is full of merriment, costumes, parties, food, and drink. The jolly celebrations actually embody something deeply mystical. How wonderful that such a spiritually lofty experience is accompanied by such partying!

Have you ever heard the expression "the whole *megillah*"? The word *megillah* is Hebrew for "scroll." When we read Megillat Esther, we are supposed to hear every single word of it—"the whole *megillah*." During the reading, whenever the name of the evil character,

Haman, is mentioned, everyone makes noise as if to drown out the wickedness. It's riotous fun for kids.

In order to understand Esther and her legacy for us, we have to have her whole story in context. The key characters we follow in this story are:

- ❧ Mordechai: leader of the Jews, a good man
- ❧ Esther: Mordechai's cousin, who will replace Vashti as queen
- ❧ Achashverosh: king of Persia
- ❧ Haman: top advisor to the king, power hungry, rabid anti-Semite

Two other female characters play smaller but still significant roles:

- ❧ Vashti: the former queen
- ❧ Zeresh: Haman's wife

The story of Esther takes place in the city of Shushan, capital of the empire of Persia (known as Iran today) in 355 BCE. The First Temple in Jerusalem had been destroyed in 422 BCE.[1] The majority of the Jews were exiled from the Land of Israel. A large Jewish community had formed in Persia (perhaps resembling the large and prosperous Jewish communities today in London, New York, Los Angeles, Toronto, Sydney, and Johannesburg). The king's name was Achashverosh (Ahasuerus). King Achashverosh started as a stable boy but was clever enough to get into the kingship.[2]

Wanting to show off his wealth, King Achashverosh made a rich and lavish feast and invited all the people of the land, including the Jews. While this seemed inclusive, embracing all the citizens of the land, all was not as it seemed on the surface. There was a calculation going on in his mind regarding a Jewish prophecy. Some seventy years earlier, the prophet Jeremiah had warned the

---

1. For a complete timeline of Jewish history, see Rabbi Ken Spiro, History Crash Course #68, "Timeline: From Abraham to the State of Israel," http://www.aish.com/jl/h/cc/48964541.html.
2. Talmud, *Megillah* 12b.

Jews to stop being idolatrous or Jerusalem would fall.[3] The Jews did not heed the warning. The ruler of Babylon, Nebuchadnezzar II, conquered Jerusalem and destroyed the Beit Hamikdash, the First Temple, which had been built by King Solomon (more on that shortly), the heart of the Jewish nation. The Persian Empire then conquered Babylonia.

The Beit Hamikdash was the place where the revealed, palpable presence of God rested. It was clear to all who visited, from any nation, that it was a unique and sacred place. (The site of the destroyed First and Second Temples is known. The remnant of an outer courtyard wall— known as the Western Wall or Wailing Wall in Jerusalem, is all that was left standing after the destruction of the ancient holy place. It is visited by millions of tourists annually, many of them seeking spiritual sparks.)

When the prophet Jeremiah foretold the First Temple's destruction, he also revealed that the Temple would be rebuilt.[4] Achashverosh knew of this prophecy. He saw the Jews in Persia (those who had been captured in the Babylonian exile and their descendants) had settled in and become comfortable. He believed that they had abandoned the desire to return and rebuild. For this grand feast, Achashverosh used the sacred vessels that had been stolen from the Temple and even donned the garments of the High Priest.[5] For him, the feast celebrated and marked the assimilation of the Jews in his land, and a permanent victory over the Jewish nation.

On the seventh day of the festivities, Achashverosh called for his wife Queen Vashti to appear. Wanting to show off her remarkable beauty, Achashverosh demanded that Vashti appear wearing nothing but her royal crown. Vashti refused.

---

3.   Jeremiah 6.
4.   Jeremiah 29:10, 30:3, 33:7.
5.   Talmud, *Megillah* 12a, 19a.

Vashti

It might appear that Vashti was a great feminist, standing up to the king by not following his orders. Our Midrash gives other explanations: one story is that Vashti had skin eruptions of some kind. Another says that she had grown a tail.[6] Both conclude that she refused to appear because she was vain and haughty.

This allegory of the tail is important to pay attention to. It teaches us something deeper than the drawings that appear in children's Purim coloring books. On one hand, the idea of a tail may have a meaning that is not literal, in the same way that when we talk in today's slang about people's "love handles," we don't think that they suddenly grew handles. We don't think that someone with a "muffin top" is breaking out in muffins.

What's the truth about Vashti? She was a cruel woman who, in the footsteps of her grandfather Nebuchadnezzar and her father Balthazar, hated Jews. When Nebuchadnezzar destroyed the Beit Hamikdash, it was a bloody massacre of the nation. While some Jews were exiled to Babylon, over nine hundred thousand were executed and millions of Jews slaughtered. Vashti descended from these rulers.

The Talmud tells us more about Vashti. She used Jewish women as slaves, forcing them to strip naked and work in ways that would desecrate the Shabbat.[7] If you need images to help you envision the humiliating deprivation this was, consider our more recent counterparts to evil, the Nazis, and how they humiliated Jewish women on the streets by stripping them and worse. Jewish women throughout history have been known for dressing and behaving modestly. Vashti used the character trait of modesty against the Jewish women. She forced them to violate the Shabbat. What does that mean? Think of a relationship you treasure so much that you want to set up a boundary to honor the sacredness of it. There is a line you would not cross because it would be a betrayal of the

---

6. Talmud, *Megillah* 12b.
7. Talmud, *Megillah* 12b.

relationship. The Shabbat was a gift from God to the Jewish nation, a sacred gift that has kept us intimate with Hashem for millennia. In this generation, so many Jews have been cut off from the beauty of this intimate love relationship with Shabbat. In the time of Vashti, the Jews' love of Shabbat was palpable, and while Vashti stripped the women on the outside, she was also trying to strip them spirituality. Vashti is *not* a heroine of this story.

As for Vashti's refusal to appear, the Talmud fleshes out even more by revealing what Vashti really thought about the king in a nasty note she sent to the drunken Achashverosh, calling him the son of a stable boy who can't hold his liquor.[8] Achashverosh called his advisors to help him decide how he should respond. The king's counselors advised him to execute Vashti; it would stand as a warning to all women. And so, in his drunken state, he heartlessly ordered that Queen Vashti be executed. When Achashverosh came to his senses, he was saddened to have lost his trophy wife. He began a search among all the beautiful maidens for a new queen.

Mordechai and Esther

There was a Jew named Mordechai. The *megillah* makes a point of telling the reader that he was among the captives who had been forced to leave Jerusalem by Nebuchadnezzar, the king of Babylonia. Mordechai was the spiritual leader of the nation. He stood his ground on what was right, even when it was not popular. Mordechai raised his cousin, Esther, who was an orphan. We are told that Esther was among the most beautiful of all the women described in our Scriptures.[9] Esther's given name was Hadassah, which means "myrtle." Have you ever seen a myrtle flower? It is like a delicate white fairy with a subtle yet heady fragrance. The name Esther comes from the root "hidden." Much is "hidden" in the Scroll of Esther, not just Esther's identity. One understanding

---

8.   Talmud, *Megillah* 12b.
9.   Talmud, *Megillah* 15a.

of our story explains that Esther, while she was a cousin, was also actually Mordechai's wife.[10]

Achashverosh appointed officers to search among all the young, beautiful virgins of the land. We know that Esther was not interested in going to the palace or becoming queen, but she was brought to the palace. (How could that be if she was Mordechai's wife? Did the guards check? Did they even care? Perhaps for those taking the women, it was only about getting the beautiful "merchandise" to the king.) The maidens were gathered to the palace and treated like royalty. Each was given all the oils and finery she requested so she could prepare herself and impress the king. Esther asked for nothing!

But before the king would make his choice of who would become queen, he tested the goods—meaning he took each one sexually. And once he had taken a young woman, she was kept in his possession in a second harem as a concubine. She would never be free to marry or have a life of her own. She could only see Achashverosh again if he called for her. If she approached him and he refused, the penalty was death.[11]

Apparently gathering the women was not an easy process. Remember that Achashverosh had just executed his queen. Who would want to send their daughter to a man like that? Esther tried to hide, but eventually she was taken to the palace.[12] Mordechai told Esther not to reveal who she really was—not her family, nor her nationality.

Esther remained silent. Silence itself is not inherently good or bad. Silence can be the loftiest or most compassionate of responses or the cruelest, depending on the situation. The *megillah* tells us that everyone liked Esther, even the eunuch in charge of the women's house. So her silence was not about ignoring others or being aloof.

---

10.   Talmud, *Megillah* 13a.
11.   Ibn Ezra, Esther 2:14.
12.   Midrash, *Seder Olam Rabbah* 29.

Esther was guided not to tell about herself. She had been ripped from her Jewish home and put in the palace, where she witnessed the immoral behavior of a king who gathered young maidens and took each one to his bed in search of a queen. In the face of a lifestyle that was the antithesis of her modest ways, she had to keep secret her identity and all that it meant.

Perhaps her modesty and reserve made her all the more alluring. During the months of preparation, Esther asked for nothing. Perhaps the dignity with which she carried herself seemed befitting of royalty. When Esther's turn arrived, the king preferred her to all the other maidens and chose her to be the next queen, replacing Vashti.

Meanwhile, Back at the Gate...

In order to be near Esther, Mordechai spent his days by the gates of the palace. In one of many "coincidences" that make up this story, he overheard two guards plotting to murder Achashverosh. Mordechai revealed the plot to Esther, who then told Achashverosh in Mordechai's name. The two guards involved were executed; Mordechai's name was written in the king's record book as loyal and worthy of a reward. This will come into play later in our story.

Plot of Destruction

Haman, who had recently been promoted to be Achashverosh's top advisor, decreed that everyone bow down to him. Mordechai the Jew would not bow to him—he would bow in worship to no one but God. When Haman saw that Mordechai would not bow down, he knew it was because Mordechai was a Jew. Haman's rage flared, but he did not act on it in the moment.

Haman's lineage shows that he descended from Amalek.[13] Amalek is Israel's archenemy; it was in Haman's blood to want to

---

13.   Haman is referred to as the son of Hamdata the "Aggagite" throughout the Book of Esther (3:1, 8:3, 9:24). Agag was king of the Amalekites, as mentioned in I Samuel 15:8 (Agag son of Amalek son of Eliphaz son of Esav).

destroy the Jews. So Haman drew lots (as in a lottery) to decide on a date for the annihilation. The word *pur* (plural *purim*) means lot; hence the name of the holiday we celebrate around this story is Purim.

Haman approached King Achashverosh and offered to pay a huge amount of silver (the equivalent of 750 tons of silver) for permission to destroy the Jews. Achashverosh took off his signet ring to approve the plan. The Midrash tells us that Achashverosh also hated the Jews and wanted their destruction.[14] So he told Haman to keep his silver. A decree was sent to every corner of his expansive territory, in every relevant language, that on that one day all the Jews in the kingdom, young and old, women and children, should be destroyed, killed, and wiped out. The people who participated in the massacre would be allowed to keep the Jews' property.

Can you imagine the stir and the buzz around such a public decree? The confused Jews grieved. Mordechai tore his clothing (the sign of loss and grief) and cried bitterly. He sat at the king's gate. Esther's servants told her the news. She sent a messenger to Mordechai, who then sent her a copy of the decree and told her she must go to the king and plead for her nation. The time had come for Esther to reveal herself.

Esther considered what it would mean for her to approach the king and fully reveal her identity as a Jewess. As she reminded Mordechai, anyone who came before the king without being called could be put to death, and she had not been called to him in a month.

Mordechai told her that being in the palace was not a guarantee of protection against the decree to kill the Jews. He made it clear: "If you remain silent at this time, the Jews' rescue will come from someplace else. Who knows? Perhaps it is for this very purpose that you became queen."

Esther replied that she would go to the king. She asked Mordechai to gather the Jews of Shushan to fast for three days and

14. *Midrash Rabbah* 7:20.

nights in solidarity with her. She said, "Then I will go to the king even though it is against the law. And if I die, then I die."

That line, "and if I die, then I die," is so full of emotion. Esther was willing to make the ultimate sacrifice. She courageously risked her life for her nation, the Jewish people. Achashverosh had already showed that he could and would execute his queen. But it wasn't just her physical life that was at stake. If she survived the approach to the king, another part of her would die. Who was King Achashverosh to Esther? He was the one that stripped away her elevated life as a Jewess. In Jewish law if a woman is raped, she may return to her husband. But if she willingly initiates sexual relations with another man, her marriage is lost to her forever.[15]

Up until this point the sexual encounters she had endured with Achashverosh were considered rape. She was not a willing participant. As soon as *she* approached *him*, it would change her status. She would be forever forbidden to her husband Mordechai.

Mordechai left the gates to gather the Jews of the capital for a three-day fast, as Esther requested. Esther also fasted for three days. What went through her mind? What prayers were uttered from her lips? Did tears fall as she prepared herself to completely let go of the life she really wanted to live? Did she feel the unity of the nation that was fasting and praying for her to succeed on their behalf? Would her plan work? The *megillah* tells us that on the third day, Esther dressed "in her royalty." It doesn't say she dressed in her royal clothes, but that she dressed in royalty. The Talmud describes Esther as dressing in the divine spirit of inspiration.[16]

Of course, we imagine that she dressed in royal garments, but here we have the idea that we can also clothe ourselves in a kind of spiritual nobility. What must it have been like for Esther to prepare for this meeting? She had to prepare spiritually and physically for the spectrum of possible outcomes. What was it like for her to walk into the palace? Was she calm or was her heart pounding as

---

15. Talmud, *Yevamot* 56b.
16. Talmud, *Megillah* 15a.

she approached the royal courtyard and chamber? Did life seem to stand still as she saw Achashverosh sitting on his throne? Did she hold her breath, waiting to see the verdict, whether he would hold out his gold scepter, allowing her to approach? Or did she feel composed from her preparations and accepting of whatever the outcome would be?

Achashverosh extended his gold scepter. Esther came close to touch its crown. He asked what her request was and said he would give her up to half his kingdom. She did not immediately ask for the salvation of the Jews. Instead, she asked to invite the king and Haman to a banquet. The king agreed and rushed Haman to come to the feast she prepared.

At the banquet, the king asked Esther again what she wanted and again offered up to half his kingdom. She still did not get directly to the heart of the issue. Esther said, "If have found favor in the sight of the king, and if it please the king to grant my plea and to perform my request—let the king and Haman come to the banquet that I will prepare for them, and I will do tomorrow as the king has said." Esther would fulfill the king's request at last and reveal who she was.

Haman left the banquet feeling on top of the world for being included in the queen's private party with the king—until he "happened" to come upon Mordechai, who did not rise to honor him. Here he was, at an incredible peak of power and stature, and one simple Jew ruined it all for him. Haman was filled with wrath. Even in his rage, this loathsome man held his anger and headed home to his cunning wife, Zeresh.

Zeresh, the other female player in our story, was wealthy, the wife of the king's highest advisor, and lived the life of a noble. If you learned this story as a child, you might have seen an illustration of Zeresh with an ugly face to represent her malicious, heartless character. But perhaps we might imagine that Zeresh was more like the infamous French fashion designer and businesswoman

Coco Chanel, who appeared elegant and stylish but was known to support and have ties with the Nazis.[17]

Haman sat with Zeresh and shared the news of his great fortune and position. With all that he had—all the wealth, position, and influence—one thing still made him angry. He actually admitted, "All this is worthless to me as long as I see Mordechai the Jew sitting at the king's gate."

Zeresh told him to make a gallows fifty cubits high (that's nearly twenty-three meters or seventy-five feet high—approximately the height of an average seven story building). The plan was that in the morning they would get permission from the king to dispose of Mordechai by hanging, so Haman could fully enjoy the party. Pleased with the idea, Haman built the gallows.

At the Palace That Night...

That very night, Achashverosh couldn't sleep. He commanded his servant to bring and read his records and chronicles. There was Mordechai's name—for saving the king's life and being deserving of reward. Was this just another coincidence of interesting timing? He asked his attending ministers whether Mordechai had been rewarded and was told that he had not. What would the king do to reward Mordechai?

Lest you think that the king was altruistic in giving rewards, consider that he wanted to protect his position as king. He wasn't born into the kingship; he had somehow managed to take it from a lowly position. He was shrewd enough to understand that someone (say, Haman, for instance) might try to take his position. If the king rewarded those who were loyal to him, it would motivate others to be loyal so that they too might be rewarded.

In another strange "coincidence" on the night the king couldn't sleep, there was activity in the outer court. Haman had showed up to speak to the king about hanging Mordechai on the gallows he had just built. What timing! King Achashverosh invited him in and asked, "What should the king do to reward someone who has been loyal?" Haman, thinking that the king was referring to himself, elaborated his own fantasy of the type of honor he had his eye on. He suggested that a person the king wants to honor should ride the king's horse through the streets wearing the king's own clothing and crown, while a servant proclaimed: "This is how it will be done to the man whom the king delights in honoring."

Achashverosh told Haman to hurry (Esther's party was coming up, after all) and to do all that he spoke of *for Mordechai, the Jew* who sits at the king's gate (make no mistake about which Mordechai!). He ordered Haman not to leave any part of it out.

Haman had no choice. He did just that. He paraded Mordechai through the streets in royal garb with a crown on his head, shouting, "This is how it will be done to the man whom the king delights in honoring." Mordechai returned to his place at the gate. Haman returned to his wife and friends feeling humiliated.

Haman reported all that happened. They saw the writing on the wall and predicted Haman would fall. With this disparaging pronouncement from those closest to him ringing in his ears, Haman went off to the palace with the king's ministers who had arrived to take him to the second day of Queen Esther's private banquet. At the party, Achashverosh again asked Esther what she desired and offered up to half his kingdom. Finally, she spoke: "If I find favor in the eyes of the king, and if it pleases the king, my request is that my life be saved and that my nation be saved. I and my nation have been sold to be destroyed and killed."

The king asked who did this, and Esther answered that it was Haman. Haman shook with fear. The king stood up enraged and stormed out. It was clear to Haman that the king would have him executed. He literally fell onto Esther for mercy. When the king reentered the room, it looked as if Haman was assaulting the queen.

The *megillah* records that Haman's face was covered. The order was given to hang Haman from his own gallows.

Haman was gone, but what of the decree permitting the murder and plundering of the Jews? The story in the *megillah* continued. Since a decree of the king could not be rescinded, a new decree was sent out that the Jews were permitted to defend themselves against those who would perpetrate the extermination of the Jews. Haman's ten sons were hung. Mordechai recorded the whole story for the generations, including how the day would be celebrated: with festivities and gifts to the poor and baskets of food to friends.

There are several themes to this holiday. One significant idea about the holiday of Purim is that it is meant to unite the nation. Another lesson to note is that God is not explicitly mentioned even once in the whole story. Mordechai wrote the Book of Esther. It certainly had to be written in a way that would be acceptable to the ruling powers. As with any book of the Tanach, there is always the chance to delve deeper. While a first glance may not reveal God's presence, that does not mean that God is absent from the story. Even if God is not named, it is clear that all of the "coincidences" were not accidents or mere coincidences at all.

As anyone with much life experience knows, there is much in this world that is hidden—often more is hidden than is revealed.

Deepening Our Understanding of Esther

Interestingly, Esther was descended from King Shaul, the first king of Israel, so royalty was in her blood. Although she was called one of the four most beautiful women of the Tanach,[18] sources say she was not that young, and other sources say she wasn't all that beautiful. Perhaps aging was different in that generation, but Esther's age is cited as somewhere between thirty-five and even as old as eighty-five.[19] She was not a young child. The aspect of Esther's appearance is full of paradox and mystery.

---

18.   Talmud, *Megillah* 15a.
19.   Midrash, *Genesis Rabbah* 39:13.

Have you ever met someone who, as you get to know him or her, seems to become more and more attractive? Suddenly you start to see something beautiful that you didn't notice at first. That is an inner radiance that, once seen, grows to make people seem very attractive. Whatever the level of Queen Esther's exterior beauty may have actually been, her inner beauty, kindness, and modesty made her outer beauty glow and shine even more.

But what made her so magnetic? Not just her beauty alone. Perhaps the silence she kept about herself created the space for listening. It's human nature to feel cared for if someone is hearing what you have to say. It's a comfort. Is it possible that her silence was the compassion that others hungered for? *Silent does not equal passive.*

Esther kept her background to herself. What do we have to talk about if we're not talking about our own lives and life experience? Yet, this was part of her power. She knew exactly who she was and what her values were, but she held in silence about that. Herein lies a paradox. At one stage of life the goal is to find your voice, to know what you want to say and to have the courage to say it. Then there is another aspect: knowing what to say, knowing you can say it, and knowing that *not* saying it may be the highest road. Can you find your voice and still hold your tongue?

Esther's Gift: Finding Your Voice

At some point in a woman's life, there seems to be a struggle to "find her voice." What does that mean? Maybe being able to stand up for yourself (setting a boundary, for example) or being able to articulate what is true for you, or being able to voice what you need or want. It might be in your relationship with yourself or a relationship with another. If you're walking a spiritual path, there is also finding your voice in prayer—how you connect with the overwhelming, unfathomable divine life force.

A reality of life is that struggle to learn how to speak up for ourselves or advocate for others. At some point in life everyone gets teased, taunted, belittled, blamed, or lectured to some degree. Learning how to speak up is part of life. Then there are the people who, for whatever reason, be it caring or controlling, want to give you their opinions. Consider the source, because some of them may truly have your best interests at heart, but some just like to project their own choices and feelings onto others. One abrupt response, "I'm not open to other opinions at this time," will work to turn down the volume. A more polite way to deflect unwanted opinions is something like, "Thank you for caring enough to share that with me." There's a balance between saying what is true for you and being gracious to another. When people ask probing or intimate questions, it's perfectly gracious to inform them that you don't talk about that with most people.

Consider that there is another level to finding your voice that can be even more powerful than speaking out—and even more powerful than speaking out with grace. That is the attribute of silence—not a stonewalling or angry silence, which can cause much hurt, but a silence of patience, kindness, or deferring to peace. This kind of silence actually comes from a place of fortitude, because it means that you have to push your ego aside. It's not about expressing your power; it's about *being* your power—whether the "other" sees it or not. You know who you are.

Power is not about overpowering another. Grace is not a weakness. Taking power to the highest level is not about others perceiving it. It's not about yelling, and it's not about punishing. There's a place beyond the need to prove your power to others.

The story of the destruction of the Second Temple in Jerusalem two thousand years ago may well be one of the most powerful stories for our generation to learn from and integrate. Understanding this one is genuinely life changing.

During the time of the Second Temple, there was a man who threw a big party.[20] He sent an invitation to his friend Kamtza, but it mistakenly went to the wrong guy—his enemy Bar Kamtza—who

20. Talmud, *Gittin* 55b–56a; Midrash, *Lamentations Rabbah* 4:3.

showed up at the party as a guest. The host saw Bar Kamtza and got very angry. He acted like a big jerk, with an emphasis on really BIG jerk. He ordered Bar Kamtza to leave. The guest, Bar Kamtza, offered to pay for his meal so he could stay without being humiliated, but the host would not relent. Bar Kamtza offered to pay for half the party if he could just be spared the embarrassment of being thrown out. The host was adamant and insisted Bar Kamtza leave. Ultimately Bar Kamtza offered to pay for the entire party in order to be spared the embarrassment. But our jerk of a host (remember, his true identity is never revealed in the story!) threw Bar Kamtza out.

The plot thickens. Apparently, there were a bunch of rabbis sitting nearby when this all happened, and they stayed silent! We are heartbroken because they should have known better. As Jews, aren't we taught that humiliating someone is like murder? We all relate to the guest who's been abused in this situation because we've all felt that embarrassing sting of humiliation.

Here's the twist: the guest, Bar Kamtza, is *the one who is blamed for the destruction of the Holy Temple in Jerusalem*! What? Why? How can that be? The behavior of the host was obviously wrong. And it was wrong of the rabbis to remain silent in the face of that kind of insult—they didn't even make an effort to make peace or mediate.

Bar Kamtza is blamed because he *reacted to the hurt he received by wanting revenge*. Here's what he did: He told the Romans, who had great military power in the region, that the Jews would not accept a sacrifice in their Holy Temple from the emperor. When the Roman emperor sent a cow to test this, Bar Kamtza slashed the cow's lip, rendering it ritually impure and thus unfit for Temple use. Otherwise, the Roman sacrifice could absolutely have been received. The Romans rage at the refusal of their sacrifice fed into a series of events that eventually led to them destroying the Temple, and this hate-filled episode is said to be an example of why God would let that happen.

We are taught that if the Temple is not rebuilt in our generation, it means we have yet to correct the damage of baseless hatred. To lots of us, Bar Kamtza's hatred doesn't actually seem so baseless, but the idea here is that *each* one of us has the power to let it go, get over it, move forward, and rise, keeping silent in the face of insult.

It's difficult to understand, but the original friend who didn't get the invitation, Kamtza, is also blamed for the destruction of the Temple. His responsibility was that, with such a big event as his close friend's party, when he didn't get the invitation, he should have gone to his friend and asked if all was well between them. His silence in the matter of clearing the air between friends is considered destructive.

Silence can have a spectrum of effects. Esther was silent when she first came to the palace not because she did not have or could not find her voice, and certainly not out of weakness. The timing simply wasn't yet right to express what would come to light in the perfect time. When it was right to use her voice, Esther bravely did so in the ultimate service of saving her nation.

Reflections in Esther's Mirror: Beauty

As we learned at the beginning of this book, the Israelite slave women used copper mirrors to beautify themselves and keep their husbands close (see the introduction, "In the Merit of the Righteous Women," and the chapter on Miriam). Our foremothers' copper mirrors give us a foundation of knowing that highlighting our beauty has worth, but it is not just physical, exterior beauty standing on its own. Esther won a "beauty" contest to become a queen. Although it was her internal beauty that saved the Jewish people, she arrived at her place of influence through the beauty that others were able to see.

What is that interplay between internal and external beauty? Is it possible to relate to beauty in an elevated way? What is true beauty, inside and out? How can we relate to our own beauty? How do we honor the beauty each of us carries?

Beauty is a universal issue for women everywhere and in all times, because God placed within us a desire to be beautiful. We have the opportunity to use that beauty in wonderful ways, as the Israelite slaves did with their copper mirrors in order to come closer to their husbands, and as Esther did to save the Jewish people from her position as a desired queen. The desire to be and feel beautiful is in and of itself a holy desire, beloved to God, especially when focused with love and intention.

Women have expressed this desire in a variety of ways, depending on their culture and outer influences. Some take it to an extreme. Some women intentionally avoid stepping into their beauty, creating a kind of invisibility. There are women who are challenged with medical conditions that affect their looks, and some women experience deformity from accidents. For those who are blessed with long life, there is the aging process and the way it affects our relationship to what we see in the mirror's reflection. No matter where anyone is on the spectrum of physical looks, there is a lot of noise to get through to explore the heart of the topic.

To say "beauty is in the eye of the beholder" is to hand over the power of beauty, and maybe even the perceived worth of a woman. We know when we feel beautiful, and that does not need to be dependent on any beholder. We don't need some vogue fashion designer or cosmetics manufacturer to set a standard or declare anything about us. We are not called to ignore the outer beauty, but ignoring inner beauty and only focusing on the outside leaves beauty without substance.

In a dramatic and descriptive verse, King Solomon wrote, "Like a golden ring in a pig's snout is a beautiful woman who lacks discretion."[21] Maybe there's a message for us in the idea that beauty itself is like a golden ring, and if it's not used for good, it's as if it's being worn in the snout of a pig. The golden ring has value, but where

---

21. Proverbs 11:22.

you put it—the context of where the golden ring is placed—makes a difference. What a potent metaphor to help us consider the way we develop that golden ring, the physical body, and how it adorns the spiritual body, the soul. A loving partnership between the body and the soul is beauty inside and out. When developed with intention, this practice of self-nurturing radiates out to heal and nurture the world.

Outer Beauty

Starting with the physical, consider your unique color, shape, features, size, age, and stage of life. This is *not* the time to allow the voice of any critics into your head. The voice of your celestial soul will only speak in a loving, kind, compassionate voice. If the voices you hear, whether inner self-talk or the voices of other people around you, are unkind in any way, don't accept them. Stamp those messages "not at this address" and let them go to the unclaimed pile.

There's certainly something real to making up and dressing up, so this is not about throwing these adornments out as if they have no value in the beauty process; rather, doing so is something to consider *with perspective*. When an actor plays a role, he or she goes through the process of makeup, hair styling, and costuming. All the resources that are put into the "look" create an image that gets the actor into character. If you look closely, it's not hard to see that most actors and actresses are pretty average-looking people who spend time (and often a lot of money) on their looks. They are creating something when they play a role, even if it's the role of movie star or singer in the spotlight. When it's time to step onstage or in front of the camera, they don't go in front of the public eye alone. Wardrobe, makeup, hair, use of lights (and shadow), filters, and even the camera angle are used to create the image.

Offstage, well-known stars find themselves in the limelight, or with an image to keep up so they can get the next job. The entertainment industry is about the look and the attitude. Money is spent on just the right products, personal trainers, and high-end embellishments, from watches to sunglasses. Pretty much anyone with the resources of the rich and famous can have "the look," at least to some degree. Nearly every image we see in print has been manipulated with computer programs that widen eyes, broaden lips, and cinch in waistlines. These photos alter the natural human textures and proportions of the body or the face, so that models and actors don't even look like themselves. There's been an outcry of sorts, and the fashion industry now occasionally uses models in a variety of sizes, colors, and ages. Still, by its nature, the focus of the beauty and fashion industry is external, with many casualties of women who have been hurt along the way.

Even without the budget and resources of the rich and famous, the influence of the beauty industry and fashion trends reach into the corners of our lives and thoughts. Consider where the dictates of eyebrow shape or hair color are coming from and how they change over time. One year something is the "in" category of beauty, the next it's somehow outdated and unacceptable.

In particular, consider that women's beauty and sex appeal are often commodified. Driven by a market that hungers for more and more skin, those with something to sell use what is titillating to get attention. How much attention and what kind of attention do you want to attract? Every woman has to face these issues in one way or another.

Explore the following questions if they are relevant to you:

- When you have the look you're after—and the attention that goes with it—what do you aim to do with that attention? What is the purpose that attracting this attention is serving?
- Are you attracting attention you want or don't want?
- Are you trying to fill certain needs through the way you present your beauty?
- Do you need attention in order to validate your worth?
- Is trying to get attention really a way to get someone to give you *affection*?

ॐ Are you looking for companionship? And if so, what kind
    of companionship?

ॐ Are you going for what is authentic, or are you caught up in
    the counterfeit?

ॐ What is your self-talk about your looks? Are you kind to
    yourself? Are you comparing yourself to others?

ॐ Do you default by saying you don't care at all?

As our bodies change with time, and even as life experience broadens our perspectives, our answers to these questions will also shift. One of the key lessons Esther teaches us emerges from how she prepared herself before inviting the king and Haman to her feast. When she "dressed in royalty," she gave us all access to the spiritual garments we have available when we direct our attention and intention to connecting with the Divine.

Still, the way we dress, how we present ourselves physically, makes a difference, not just in how the world sees and judges us—and that is a reality of life—but also in the way we see and judge ourselves. You know the difference between wearing sweats and wearing a gown, the difference in the way you carry yourself and how you feel.

Beauty from the Inside Out

Stepping into your essential beauty is not about ignoring your body. Those who study beauty and what makes others rate someone as more beautiful clearly list health as a factor of beauty.[22] These simple and utterly loving actions keep the body beautiful. Care for your skin, eyes, teeth, and more, by nurturing yourself with the following key elements:

ॐ **Water.** Drinking fresh water, and plenty of it, helps the
    body to flush out toxins from the system. Hydration of the

---

22. James Erskine, *The Human Face*, BBC documentary, 2001.

inner organs means that the skin can also be hydrated to look its best.

- ❧ **Food.** Nourishing food gives your body energy and vitality. If you support your body with wholesome foods, this too will be reflected in your overall appearance.
- ❧ **Sleep.** Rest is one of the most important elements of health on every level. It improves your mood as well as your appearance (and of course, your mood affects your appearance—more on that below). The industry of cosmetic surgery and chemical treatments considers results to be successful if the outcome of the treatment gives the patient a more rested look. Do not underestimate the importance of getting enough rest.
- ❧ **Oral hygiene.** Taking care of your teeth has a significant impact on your health and beauty. A clean mouth contributes to a healthy body and beautiful smile. One Torah source says it's better to give the milk (meaning the white—a smile) of your teeth than money to someone in need.[23] Your smile is that important.
- ❧ **Movement.** Moving your body—whether you lift weights, swim, go walking, stretch, or dance around the house—has benefits that all agree are important. Staying fit and strong means you can shine fully into this world.

The body and soul are a partnership, a sisterhood. Taking care of the health of your body is crucial to fully utilizing the gift that is life; it's also the foundation for the longevity of beauty. Your physical body is a vessel, a gift from God. Honor her by taking care of her, delight in her beauty and strengths, and be tender and loving with her frailties.

---

23. Talmud, *Ketubot* 111b.

Enhancing Your Beauty Factor

In wanting to look your best, there is a spectrum of choices from makeup and hair colors to skin treatments and even surgery. There is no shortage of options, and it's up to each woman to determine what she needs and wants to do to enhance (or alter) her natural physical beauty. Torah challenges us to consider something more. In the traditional poem sung every Friday night called "A Woman of Valor,"[24] there is a strong line toward the end that says, "Beauty is fleeting." The descriptive word translated here as "fleeting" is *hevel* in Hebrew. It doesn't have an adequate English translation, but one way to describe *hevel* is this: when the air is cold outside and you exhale, it's that puff of steam that lasts but a fraction of a moment. So while we honor our outer beauty, it is not who we are. There is something more, and that something is the character from which the truest, most essential beauty radiates. Some see it and some will never see it.

Have you ever looked at people who gave a beautiful first impression, but then, as soon as they opened their mouths and showed you who they really were, they suddenly were not so attractive anymore? Or have you experienced the opposite: someone looks unremarkable, but as you get to know him or her, you see something attractive?

What are the qualities that build beauty from your essence (with or without makeup)? How do you use these inner qualities to step into a deeper level of beauty? Here are some beauty secrets that sprout from the inside:

- **Posture.** It's no secret that the way you hold your body creates a state of being. Humiliation, arrogance, or joy has a posture that telegraphs what's happening inside a person's psyche. There are scientific studies that show different

---

24. Proverbs 31:10–31, called in Hebrew "Eshet Chayil."

hormones are released based on your physical stance.[25] Posture sends a message to the outside, and it also sends an actual chemical message to your insides. This is a tool you can use to step up your appearance.

- ❧ **Confidence.** The posture of your body can influence your attitude, and the reverse is also true. Your inner posture, your confidence, influences the outside. Confidence is knowing who you are. You are a daughter of the King. You contain a spark of the Divine. You are created with unique gifts to bring to this world just by your very being. This is truth. And while modesty of spirit is a beautiful quality, it does *not* allow for the demeaning of the self.

- ❧ **A generous smile.** Scientists who study beauty give a mathematical ratio to the proportions commonly considered beautiful in both nature and the human body—a sort of geometry of the face. The smile is considered the most attractive configuration of this analysis.[26] The opposite of a sour face that no one wants to come near is a smile. A smile can show caring for another. It can telegraph compassion or let others know you're happy to see them. A sincere smile is often contagious, and sharing one means you are likely to get one back. (A note to consider: not sharing your smile can also be a way of setting a boundary that needs to be set.)

- ❧ **A sparkle in your eyes.** What does that mean? Be present, smile with your eyes, and your eyes will shine. Inviting happiness to be a part of your nature is perhaps the most attractive beauty treatment available. A joyful heart is irresistible. (Review "Leah's Gift—The Secret to Happiness" about gratitude, or "Live in Joy" in the Spiritual Practices chapter.)

---

25. See "Powerful Posturing," *Association for Psychological Science*, October 4, 2010, https://www.psychologicalscience.org/news/releases/powerful-posturing.html.
26. James Erskine, *The Human Face*, BBC documentary, 2001.

❧ **Overall facial expression.** Find the facial expression you want imprinted on your face in your old age and use it regularly now to make it real. This is a lifetime's work.

Our relationship to beauty is worthy of deeper consideration. Likewise, our relationships with others begin with a first impression, but there's so much more to it. First impressions can be important; how you present yourself will definitely impact what people look for or expect to see. A put-together image makes a difference.

Now, what about the relationships that last longer than a glance? Love is not dependent on appearance. It should not be ignored; it certainly matters, but it is not all that matters. Honest love is based on building trust over time. The beauty of youth fades with age, but the beauty that glows on the faces of an elderly couple touches us deeply. A baby looks at his mother with eyes of love no matter her weight, hairstyle, or complexion. When a dear friend is sick, our love for her does not fade because she lacks the luster of health. Love comes with time, trust, bonding, and compassion.

Can you be compassionate to yourself and look with eyes of kindness instead of the filter of disdain, self-loathing, or even false modesty? Are you willing to look at yourself in the mirror and call out the purest and most beautiful part of your soul?

Soul Beauty

The Torah gives us instruction for the soul, most of which is action in the world: setting appropriate boundaries, moving with dignity, expressing awe and gratitude, acting with kindness and justice, cultivating a generous heart, nurturing a joyful mindset, speaking to build, and using silence in wisdom. We're not always in a position to actively do the things we want to. Most of what happens in the world is out of our control. And when life situations are beyond our control, the Talmud teaches, "All is in the hands of Heaven but the awe of Heaven."[27] We may not have control of what's happening on

---

27. Talmud, *Megillah* 25a; *Berachot* 33b.

the outside (that's in the hands of Heaven) but we always have the choice about what's happening on the inside (the awe of Heaven). Essentially, we are in a constant relationship with our Creator. Each moment brings us an opportunity to move closer to the unfathomable love available. Love creates the glow of a bride, and we can tap into that as the most soul-beautifying experience.

We're told that every mitzvah we do creates an angel.[28] When the time comes to leave this world, it is those angels that accompany our souls to the World to Come. The good we bring to the world beautifies us at the soul level. Transforming mundane routines into ways of blessing the world allows light, healing, and joy to ripple out and impact others. The beautiful smile you flash as you help a lost child find her mother; the protein bar you give to the homeless man at the grocery store; the money you donate to build a school, hospital, museum, or park; or the tissue you give to someone shedding tears all beautify your soul. As we live this physical life, knowing that the soul is eternal, we're in a unique position to collect the true diamonds worthy of soul pleasure in the World to Come.

May you live fully in the splendor of your soul as you shine your beautiful, unique, precious spark—in good times or hard times, beyond understanding, shine!

---

28. Mishnah, *Pirkei Avot* 4:11.

SPIRITUAL PATHWAYS

What has the deepest meaning in life is not revealed for free. This has nothing to do with money. The depths of any relationship are revealed with time, effort, and commitment. This is also true of walking a spiritual path. Whether you consider marriage, parenting, the arts, sports, academics, gardening, building, mechanics, or any other activity, the possibilities are infinite. A master in any skill knows that being a master reveals how much more is yet unknown. Any one of the pathways explained in this chapter may or may not *feel* as you hope or expect it to, but these pathways actually open profound spiritual connections.

Rabbi Nachman of Breslov said, "All the world is just a narrow bridge…"[1] What does that mean? This world that we see around us is only one of many spiritual realms, and only a passageway between worlds. This idea helps us focus in on who we are as souls. Our manual, the Torah, gives instructions on how to grow in spirituality. Interestingly, it's all about our *actions* in this physical world—what we do and what we do not do. That's what elevates the human spirit.

The way of our tribe is that the action (as well as the intention) creates the spiritual sparks. Spirituality deepens with the practice of actions and deeds. If you are a Jewish spiritual seeker, then the path, the way, and the practices of Jewish spirituality have been divinely given and are constantly available to you.

This chapter is by no means a complete or comprehensive list, but it is a place to begin or review. To take any step in this mini-guide, you don't have to be affiliated with a synagogue or with an organization, and you can live anywhere on the planet. It doesn't matter whether you grew up not knowing you are a Jew or going

---

1. *Likutei Moharan* 2:48:2.

to a religious Jewish school. These are practices that began with your matriarchs and have been an integral part of your lineage for thousands of years. If you are a Jewish woman, you do not have to go back many generations to find the grandmother or great-grandmother who held fast to these simple practices. These are rituals you can perform, simple actions you can take as a Jewish woman to nurture your spirit, honor your soul, connect with God, and bring more light into the world. Each time you do any of these *mitzvot*, you have the opportunity to be present, with intention, and breathe life into your connection with yourself, others, and the Eternal.

Each one of the seven spiritual pathways listed here is literally life-changing. Any one of these pathways, or *mitzvot*, will lift your spirit and change your world. Each of these practices will also impact and improve at least one of the three relationships you have: with yourself, with others, or with God. Each of these simple (some easy, some not as easy) actions has infinite meaning, and your interactions with them can deepen over time. All of life has a pulse, including a spiritual journey, so don't expect to do all of this all at once. Pace yourself and move forward gently.

Candle Lighting: A Deeper Level of Peace in the Home

Perhaps the easiest spiritual practice, lighting candles on Friday evenings, is one of the most profound rituals for Jewish women. It is an utterly simple action—it takes very little time or effort to light a couple of candles—and the significance is tied to the deepest depths of the Jewish home, starting with our first matriarch, Sarah. Don't mistake easy for insignificant or unimportant. Lighting these little candles is a literal passing of the flame from generation to generation.

Friday night at sunset ushers in a sacred time for the Jewish people. We bring the workweek to a close; we change gears. It's a time to take a deep breath and bring another level of soul into your life and a deeper level of peace into your home. Shabbat (the

Sabbath) is connected to the feminine and is also referred to as the Shabbat Queen. The Shabbat is also like a bride,[2] so pure, so beautiful and loyal. In preparation for Shabbat, it's customary to bathe and don our finery, ready to greet the majesty of our Beloved. When a Jewish woman lights her Shabbat candles, she brings light into her home, both literally (through the physical action of lighting candles) and spiritually (with her intention and the blessing she recites).

Many women feel the change in atmosphere once their candles are lit. I had one meaningful experience just after I began experimenting with this idea of lighting candles. I was having dinner with some girlfriends from graduate school on a Friday night. Before we sat down to eat, I explained that I had taken on lighting Sabbath candles and asked for a moment to light before we began the meal. I didn't think much of it. It was a small ritual I was trying out. I circled the light, covered my eyes, and said the blessing. When I uncovered my eyes, all three of my girlfriends, not one of them Jewish, were *crying*! What touched them so deeply about that simple act? It was a defining moment and a wake-up call for me to understand that there was something moving in this basic Jewish action.[3]

HOW TO LIGHT SHABBAT CANDLES

❧ Set up two candles well before sunset on Friday afternoon. You can use any type of candle: beeswax or paraffin, tapers or tea lights. Some women use olive oil in small glass cups with floating wicks (you can partially fill the cup with water; the oil will float on top). The candles will need to burn out completely and should not be extinguished, so be sure you place them in a location and on a surface that is

2.   Yehuda Shurpin, "Four Reasons Shabbat Is Compared to Bride and a Queen," http://www.chabad.org/library/article_cdo/aid/3753326/jewish/Who-Is-the-Shabbat-BrideQueen-Four-Answers.htm.

3.   For more about why we light Shabbat candles, see Tzvi Freeman, "Where Does the Torah Say to Light Shabbat Candles?" http://www.chabad.org/library/article_cdo/aid/767153/jewish/Where-does-the-Torah-say-to-light-Shabbat-candles.htm.

safe for them to burn all the way to the end. Never leave lit
candles unattended! If you will be going to sleep or going
out soon after lighting, use candles that won't burn for long,
such as tea lights.

- Before you light, drop a coin or a few coins into a charity
  box (see "Cultivate a Generous Heart" below).

- Check the time of sunset for that week and your location;
  you can find this with a simple online search (there are also
  Jewish calendars available in Judaica stores that have local
  candle-lighting times printed in them). Before the sun goes
  down, stand before the candles. Use this moment to take
  a breath and to feel settled and calm. Now is your time to
  connect with God through the gift of the Sabbath, as you
  ignite the flame and touch the wicks of the candles!

- Circle your hands near the flames as if you're pulling the
  light into yourself. Cover your eyes gently with your palms.

- Say the blessing: (the "kh" is the guttural sound; if you have
  trouble saying that, just use a "k" sound.)

Bah-rookh Ah-tah Ah-doe-nai,	**Blessed are You Lord,**
El-o-hey-noo Mel-ekh ha-o-lahm,	**our God King of the Universe,**
ah-shehr kid-de-shah-noo	**Who sanctified us**
beh-mitz-vo-tav	**with His commandments**
ve-tzee-vah-noo	**and commanded us**
le-hahd-leek nehr shel Shah-baht.	**to light the Shabbat candles.**

- You can hold this moment. There is no need to rush out of
  this sacred space. You can add your personal prayers for
  yourself, your family, your nation, and the world.

- Uncover your eyes and behold the radiant light!

Allow the candles to burn completely. Be sure to put them in a safe
place so you won't have to put them out or move or touch them
until after sunset on Saturday night.

Live in Joy

At first glance it might seem unusual that living in joy is a spiritual practice. Yet the Torah actually instructs us to serve God with joy.[4] The path of a Jewish woman is powered and illuminated through gladness. Power grows exponentially through *joy*. Did you know that in order for a prophet to receive prophecy, he or she had to be in a state of joy?[5] Of the women written about in this book, Sarah, Miriam, Devorah, Chana, and Esther were prophetesses, and if you read about them, you know the hardships they endured, from being kidnapped to infertility to war. Yet while the heavenly gate of tears is always open, the clearest access to the spiritual realms is in a state of joy.

Joy is something that you have to commit to intentionally. This is not the "as long as you're happy" of the ego self. That would be something like "I'm happy because things are going the way *I* think they should be going." The ego self does not acknowledge that *God* is running the world. True happiness can't get thrown off balance when things don't look a certain way, because true joy is generated from within. So the mitzvah of being happy means that while you're fulfilling the things that are not so easy to do, you find a way to do them with joy. When your baby is keeping you up at night and all you want to do is go to sleep, you find a way to be joyful for the opportunity to be a mother. Or when you don't feel like washing dishes again (or whatever the work at hand), you find a way to tweak your thinking so that you see the higher purpose of that mundane act. You find ways of bringing love and purposeful intention into all you do and all you are in the world. The most profound acts, and also the smallest of deeds, approached with an attitude of joy, are lifted higher.

No matter what the job, repetitive tasks can seem mundane. An award-winning silversmith shared that even in creating unique and beautiful works of art, there are mundane and repetitive tasks,

4.   Deuteronomy 28:47; Psalms 100:2.
5.   Radak, Genesis 45:27.

such as polishing and shaping. It's part of life, even in work that appears to be more glamorous.

Can you turn suffering into celebration? Sometimes. Sometimes you just have to grieve though. That's part of life, but it does not need to be an hourly, daily, or weekly event. Most of the stuff that Western, first-world readers call suffering isn't really suffering in the big scheme of things. If you can take a step back and see the big picture, you see how very blessed you are in so many ways. More often than not, it's our own inner voices that get in the way of our seizing the present moment joyfully. What does that mean? We've been bombarded with media, most of it meant to sell you something: you *need*—that latest phone, car, pair of shoes, or whatever it might be. We're shown photoshopped models with lots of sex appeal and then spend a lot of effort and money trying to shape our bodies, hair, and clothing so we can be happy with ourselves. You don't have to ditch your desires to be your most beautiful, but what if you make being joyful a bigger priority? What if you started right now? What if joy is the most effective beauty treatment available?

How do you build, expand, create, allow, increase, develop, excite, multiply, magnify, intensify, grow, escalate, attract, invite, and deepen joyfulness in your life?

- ∽ **Practice.** The way to move toward mastery of anything is through practice. You make up your mind and take action. In this case, you have the opportunity in every moment, again, and again, and again. It makes sense. Being joyful increases joy. Being delighted with simple or small things builds delight. Taking pleasure from things you might have taken for granted increases pleasure.

- ∽ **Give meaning to the mundane.** One way you can do that is by asking yourself: "Why is this important?" and "Who is it serving?"

ﾋ **Choose your thoughts.** Instead of ruminating on the nasty thing so-and-so said (we're always trying to make sense of the things that hurt us), have a short go-to list of the thoughts you will use to replace the unwanted thoughts. What's a favorite memory or great accomplishment? What is a happy visualization of your near future? Who loves you? What is your favorite quote or happy song?

ﾋ **Express gratitude for the details.** Give yourself the experience of constant, deep gratitude for the smallest details in your life. What if you could even be grateful for your challenges and the opportunity to grow? Be very detail oriented in expressing gratitude in your daily life. One technique is to make a list *every day* of ten things you are grateful for. The catch is that you can never list the same thing twice (see "Leah's Gift: The Secret to Happiness").

ﾋ **Sing!** Sing songs that nurture your spirit, songs that lift you. King David, who had crazy, scary, heartbreaking challenges all his life, composed most of the Psalms, and he sang *all* of them! The Levites would sing Psalms during the Temple service. This timeless line is often quoted and sung: "Serve God with gladness, come before Him with song."[6]

On a really hard day, I posted on social media: "I woke up. I got dressed. I fed myself. That is all." A friend responded, "Try doing those things without waking up." I shifted my attitude. Maybe that's why our sages gave us a foundation with a few words of gratitude to say upon waking every morning. (Check that out in the next pathway below.)

You may be asking, "How can I feel joy when there is so much suffering in the world?" One of the most important things to know about true joy is that it can actually be a weapon against evil. It is a light in the darkness. Terrorists want people to feel terror. It's how evil dominates.

---

6. Radak, Genesis 45:27.

When you can choose to step into a joyful state even in the face of challenging circumstances, you do not lift yourself alone. You lift others as well, and that diminishes the darkness. By choosing joy, you are bringing light into the world.

Connect with the Divine

Never underestimate the power of a sincere prayer. Prayer changes you, and it changes the world. Just talk to the Creator. Rabbi Nachman taught, "Pour your heart out to God as if you're talking to a good friend."[7] Pray using a prayer book or in your own words.

What prayer is not: it is not treating God as a vending machine, putting in a coin and pressing a button to get what you want (though we do want to make requests, as you will see shortly). Prayer is a way to connect to the Creator. And it impacts you and this world in ways that are beyond what we can comprehend. Experiment and see for yourself the differences prayer brings. Sometimes prayer is about what you are asking for, and sometimes it's about what you want to be rid of: anger, resentment, arrogance, and so on.

HOW TO PRAY

Pray out loud so that your ears can hear the sounds of your words; it can even be the smallest whisper. Pray from the heart in your own language. Don't worry if it feels awkward.

There are three basic components of prayer.[8]

~ **Know.** Know with Whom you are speaking. Call out one of God's names that you're comfortable with: Dear God, God of My Understanding, Hashem, Father, Abba, Merciful One, Master of the World… Use whatever name resonates

---

7. *Chayei Moharan* 439.
8. The three components of prayer are identified by Rambam, *Mishneh Torah*, Laws of Prayer 1:2: "first uttering praises of God, then, with humble supplication and petition asking for all that one needs, and finally offering praise and thanksgiving to the Eternal."

for you, because this is *your* intimate relationship with
your Creator. Recognize the sovereignty of God. (Do you
see the word *reign* in there? It's a hint to Who governs
this universe.) You are standing before the Almighty. You
have connections, since you're with your heavenly parent
Who loves you infinitely. *God does not need to be praised.*
Actually, the praise we express here opens the channels
within *us* to connect.

ॐ **Ask.** Ask for what you want. Ask for what you think you
need. God needs nothing from us, but we need everything
from God. Don't worry that you will bother God with
details or small things, or that you ask for too much.
Asking for what you need and want is a powerful way of
acknowledging that we know everything comes from God.
Asking is an important aspect of prayer, so ask! Here are
some things you can ask for:

- Help with your life issues—healing, finding a mate,
  conception, education, relationships, success

- Material needs—anything from increased income or a
  home to that perfect item you've been wanting, or even
  a parking place

- Spiritual needs—understanding, feeling closer, divine
  guidance

- For others—healing, finding a mate, conception,
  income, success

- For your family—the well-being and success of spouse,
  children, parents, siblings, extended family

- For your friends—healing, finding a mate, children,
  income, peace

- Clarity—resolving issues, increased wisdom, ideas

- Help—with growing spiritually, becoming a deeper person, guarding your speech (see below), parenting, relationships, projects, finding a lost item

❧ **Thank.** Gratitude is very powerful. It opens the channels to receiving all the good that is available to you. Again, *God does not need our gratitude.* Our gratitude builds *us* and deepens our experience of prayer. We do this for our own understanding, to open the channels to receive, and to deepen our relationship with the Creator.

It is good to know why you are asking for things. You can make a case in your plea and say why you want what you are asking for. Be specific. Tell God what you will do if your prayer is answered. This part of our conversation with God actually changes *us*. As we grow, we open ourselves to receive more (in the world of the material or in aspects of understanding, acceptance, energy, inspiration, compassion, and so on). God is the King. God can do it all. Ask. The answer may be "yes" and it may be "not yet," or it could be, "I have something better for you!" Ask.

There is one prayer that will always be answered positively. When someone prays to feel closer to God, that prayer will be fulfilled. So, ask.

TWO SIMPLE PRAYERS

The following two simple statements are short prayers that can increase your spiritual connection with God. (You can find videos on the Internet that will teach you tunes with which to sing them.)

❧ **Shema.** The Shema (pronounced *sheh-mah*) is the one prayer every Jew should know. It is said before retiring at night, it is part of the daily prayers, and it should be the last utterance before death. The Shema declares the Oneness of the Eternal, All-That-Was-Is-and-Will-Be, and that is what we are connecting with.

Once you can say this without reading it, cover your eyes with your right hand when you recite it. This focuses your consciousness inward, toward your inner, spiritual, elevated awareness of God.

Sheh-mah Yiss-rah-el,	*Hear, O Israel,*
Ah-doe-nai El-o-hey-noo,	*the Eternal is our God,*
Ah-doe-nai Eh-khad.	*the Eternal is One.*

(Then, uncover your eyes and say in a whisper:)

Bah-rookh shem	*Blessed is the name*
ke-vohd mal-khoo-toe	*of the glory of His kingdom*
le-o-lahm vah-ed.	*forever.*

~ **Modeh Ani.** Jew is Yehudi in Hebrew, and that means "grateful." The following short sentence in Hebrew is said upon awakening in the morning. What a simple sentence, yet a profound way to set the tone of the day. (There are a variety of tunes you can sing this to.)

Mo-deh ah-nee le-fah-neh-khah,	*I am grateful before You,*
Mel-ekh khai ve-kai-yahm,	*living and existing King,*
sheh-heh-kheh-zar-tah	*that You returned*
bee neesh-mah-tee beh-khem-lah.	*my soul to me.*
Rah-bah eh-moo-nah-tekh-ah	*Your faith [in me] is great.*

One of the ways to deepen in faith and prayer is to acknowledge that God has the big picture. This means that all is seen, and that there is ultimately good in every situation. Another idea to consider is the expression that "God has broad shoulders." You are never alone in life. "Enter His gates with gratitude, His courtyard with praise, thank Him and bless His name."[9] It's so natural to take waking up for granted. Understand that each breath, each day, every talent, all

---

9.   Psalms 100:4.

knowledge, and all our senses are gifts from our Creator. We have much to be thankful for.

Ask that all our prayers be answered for good.

New Moon Celebration

The women were given a holiday (holy day) that marks the new moon: Rosh Chodesh.[10] The civil calendar (January through December) that we are so accustomed to is a solar calendar; it is based on the sun's rotation. The Hebrew calendar is based on the cycles of both the sun and the moon, so it is both a solar and a lunar calendar. Each Hebrew month begins on the new moon, and that first day (sometimes two) of the new month is called Rosh Chodesh. *Rosh* means "head," and *chodesh* means "month." *Chodesh* shares its root with the word *chadash*, which means "new."

While the whole nation celebrates this holiday, it was specifically given to the women.[11] Why a holiday for the women? After leaving Egypt, when the Israelites were in the Sinai Desert, the men wanted to create something, a golden idol in the shape of a calf, to worship. As the men gathered gold jewelry to be melted and used for this golden calf, they tried to get gold from their wives, but the women refused. The women did not participate in the creation of the golden calf.[12] Lest you think that the women were just attached to their gold, later in the story when it came time to donate toward the building of the Mishkan (the Tabernacle), the women gave generously.[13]

A beautiful teaching helps us notice something we can use every day. When the moon is new and beginning its cycle, we only see the smallest sliver of a crescent reflecting the light. There is no doubt, however, that the moon is whole and round; it's just not easily visible to our eyes. This is a metaphor for life. Our matriarchs

10. Talmud, *Sanhedrin* 41b–42b.
11. Rashi on the Talmud, *Megillah* 22b.
12. Midrash, *Pirkei d'Rabbi Eliezer* 45:4.
13. Ramban, Exodus 35:22.

were strong in their faith: no matter how bleak life seemed in any moment, they knew the light would be fully revealed. This is the faith that our mothers carried and the reason Rosh Chodesh was given to the women. When things seem dark in our lives, when we're not seeing the full light, we know with certainty that life is moving in the direction of whole and full.

The observance of Rosh Chodesh is simple but rich, sensitizing us to the calendar. It's a time to celebrate the feminine, and it's a time for women to ascend together with joy. The idea is to back away from mundane work if possible (like let go of laundry and other chores on that day). Dress a little nicer. Gather with other women to celebrate an inspiring and enriching time together. For some, that means creating a space for women to get together in unity and praises for the Creator. For some communities, it might look like women gathering to learn words of Torah. You can pretty much count on lovely culinary delights being included.

Each month has its unique energy, gifts, and awareness. For example, the springtime month of Nisan is when the holiday Pesach occurs, when the Israelites came out of slavery into freedom. Often that's a time to reflect on what is holding you back (enslaving you) in life and how you might free yourself from those limitations. Fall brings us the month of Tishrei, the month of heavenly judgment and forgiveness. Exploring how to take forgiveness to the next level—both in asking for it and giving it to yourself and others—is a beautiful study. The month of Kislev is the month of Chanukah, the time when the ancient Temple in Jerusalem was rededicated. It is the time of year when the days are the darkest, and we consciously bring light into the world with our modest but persistent candle lighting.

Rosh Chodesh is an opportunity to gather and celebrate the feminine focus that marks time and life cycles and that accents the spiritual cycle of the seasons. Tap in to your radiance with the new moon celebration. As the following piece describes the process of transformation and reflection, know that you, too, shine as a divine expression.

> The moon, when she was first created, was a glistening jewel. She did not merely reflect light, but rather trans-formed it and brought out its inner beauty, much as a precious stone glistens with a secret, hidden light all its own. In her own way, the moon was greater than the sun—for the sun only shines from its surface, whereas the moon shone from its inner essence. The sun holds the light that extends outward, whereas the moon holds the light of being.
>
> And so will be, once again, and much more so, in the time to come, once we have transformed the world with the Torah and its mitzvahs.[14]

Cultivate a Generous Heart

In a world where accumulating is the norm, it may seem counter-intuitive to cultivate a generous heart. Yet, it is the action of each individual's generous heart that will change and build worlds.

Maybe you've seen the viral video one father made of his daughter.[15] While looking out the window of the restaurant where they were having lunch together, the young daughter saw a home-less man sitting on a bench. She asked her father if she could bring the man her lunch. The father started his video camera and followed his daughter bringing her plate to the slumped man. The video shows the man receiving the food and beginning to eat. The little girl then comes back in and peers out the window to see the results of her giving. "How does it feel?" the father asks. The girl is visibly moved, and the father expresses his pride.

---

14.   Rabbi Yitzchak Isaac of Homil, *Shnei Me'orot*, cited in Tzvi Freeman, "The Moon and Us," Chabad.org, http://www.chabad.org/library/article_cdo/aid/247861/jewish/The-Moon-and-Us.htm; used with permission.

15.   "Kind Little Girl Gives Her Food to a Homeless Man Video 2016," https://youtu.be/T2-no_KWMVM.

How do we teach our children to be like that? By modeling. We model the behavior we want to see in them. So how do we model a generous heart? How can we cultivate that within ourselves? As with other spiritual practices, learning the mindset is part of it, and the other piece is practice. You start where you are, right now. Here are some thoughts to help you get into the frame of mind of cultivating a generous heart.

We're told the good deeds we do in our lifetime are what accompany us as we enter the World to Come. In that world our souls will stand before our Creator to be judged. The good deeds we have done in life are our defenders in that heavenly court.[16] One such act of goodness, and the topic at hand, is *tzedakah*.

What is *tzedakah*? This Hebrew word is usually translated as "charity," but it really means so much more. The root word *tzedek* means "justice," as in something ethical, honest, right, or good.[17]

Giving is such an essential part of our world. Every Jewish home should at least have a small "*tzedakah* box" (also called a *pushka*, if you grew up in a home where Yiddish was spoken). Any money that goes into the coin box is earmarked for charity. The money you give can, for example, feed people, help build a Jewish institution that cares for orphaned children, buy glasses or shoes for underprivileged children of poor families, or help fund the wedding of a needy couple. The idea of having a *tzedakah* box in your home is to make the idea of giving a daily part of your life. Of course it's not just about the coins.

The idea of social justice and taking care of others is a foundational Jewish value. The Torah teaches us: "If there is a needy man, one of your brothers within your gates, in the land which your God gave you, don't harden your heart or shut your hand from your impoverished brother."[18]

---

16. Mishnah, *Pirkei Avot* 4:11.
17. See Rabbi Lord Jonathan Sacks, "Rabbi Jonathan Sacks on Tzedakah Defined," YouTube, https://www.youtube.com/watch?v=meEK4dUf3Os.
18. Deuteronomy 15:7.

We are taught that everything comes from God. Everything: all the circumstances of your life, the abundance of talents you possess, and your material resources. The idea is that ultimately, whatever you possess, you do not own. How so? We all know that when it comes to material wealth, "You can't take it with you." There's a lively little bit that follows this saying, and it isn't as well known: "…but you can send it on ahead!" What does that mean? "Sending it ahead" refers to the acts you do from your generous heart and the contributions you make.

Those who have much materially are being entrusted with it to do the right things. It's a very lofty deed to give money to house, feed, clothe, or educate the poor. While it is overwhelming to think of all that needs to be done, you don't have the weight of the world on your shoulders; you simply do your part, from coins to large checks. You know the resources you have from which to give. You know if your philanthropy muscle needs to be strengthened with the smallest acts of giving or bigger acts of generosity.

How is this a Jewish spiritual pathway? The idea of tithing comes from the biblical commandment to bring a tenth of one's crops to the Temple.[19] The produce could also be sold and the money brought. The act of giving charity is even simpler than tithing. Technically, the minimum one should give to charity each year is the value of about seven grams of pure silver.[20] At the time of this writing that comes to less than four dollars a year! That is the minimum. But, what if…? What if more hearts began to practice generosity? How many lives would that change? How many hungry people would be fed, clothed, or educated?

The great sage Maimonides outlined eight levels of giving, in ascending order of spiritual greatness.[21] All eight ways of giving are good—the idea is to give—but this list is a way to ascend from good to better, and to the highest level. Explore. If you are at level

19. Deuteronomy 14:22.
20. Rambam, *Mishneh Torah*, Laws of Charity 7:5.
21. Rambam, *Mishneh Torah*, Laws of Charity 10:7–14.

eight, see how it feels to give, and then to move up the giving ladder to a higher rung.

(8) Giving grudgingly.

(7) Giving cheerfully.

(6) Giving after being asked.

(5) Giving without being asked.

(4) The receiver knows where the charity came from, but the giver does not know who received the gift.

(3) The giver knows who the receiver is, but the receiver does not know who is giving the gift.

(2) Giving in a way that the giver and receiver are unknown to each other (that means there's someone helping to facilitate the giving).

(1) Helping others to receive in a dignified way, such as giving them employment or a loan to help them establish a business.

This list shows that even if you don't *feel* such a generous heart right now, but you give anyway, *you're still doing something profound.* You're on the ladder to increase the richness of the experience of giving. If you did not grow up with the concept of giving in this way, start small. Experiment and see what happens.

Giving *tzedakah* is such an important concept that even the poor person who lives by receiving charity himself is required to give.[22]

Most of the commandments given by the Torah don't speak of reward, but this act of donation comes with the promise that God will reimburse you. We're even told we can test God on this one. Being lofty is sublime, but getting rewarded for your generosity is

---

22. Rambam, *Mishneh Torah*, Laws of Charity 7:5.

promised. God said, "Test Me now with this, says the Lord of Hosts, [to see] if I will not open for you the windows of heaven and pour down for you blessing that there shall be more than sufficiency."[23] At the same time, we are guided not to give so much that we ourselves become needy (one guideline is not to give more than a fifth of what we have, but there are exceptions).

Now, go exercise that glorious, glowing philanthropic muscle!

Guard Your Speech

While the topic of how we speak is also addressed in the chapter on Miriam, it is so important—and life changing—that it is worthy of emphasis as a spiritual pathway. Indeed, the positive power of speech is highlighted as one of the qualities of a "woman of valor": "The teaching of kindness is on her tongue."[24]

Why all this attention to speech? The world was created with speech, and since we each contain a spark of the Divine, we have the power to create our reality, affecting others and ourselves, with our speech. While some spiritual practices hold silent retreats or have silent monasteries, Judaism does not ask for silence in order to ascend to heavenly realms. Judaism asks for something much harder: use speech constructively, and guard speech from destructive uses.

Simply: don't talk about other people. This goes beyond refraining from gossip. There are volumes written that teach the subtleties of guarding your speech. While the mindfulness of the words you use will save others, you will find that implementing this powerful mitzvah and life strategy will improve your life dramatically.

How can this change your life? Your spirits will be higher, which makes sense since you expand that which you talk about. When you stop complaining about others, you will likely find that your relationships improve. Can you imagine the lift in your own

23. Malachi 3:10.
24. Proverbs 31:26.

sense of well-being that could come with a change of focus in your speech?

Even speaking about someone in a way that seems neutral could actually be harmful. How so? Let's say you're talking about someone in a way that you think could not possibly be harmful. If the person you're talking to doesn't happen to like the one you thought you were harmlessly talking about, it could prompt the listener into an avalanche of negativity in order to "set you straight" about the subject.

Guarding your speech is a lifetime process. We spend our lives around people and interact with others all the time. At the end of the day (or after the wedding, work, school, and so on), it's pretty natural to want to share or process our experiences. Very few will truly master this practice. People fall. The idea is to work on using speech for building or repairing—so when you fall, you don't give up, you rise up. As you walk the walk of watching your talk, you'll find that the falls are less frequent and not as deep.

These guidelines acknowledge that sometimes people need to blow off steam. Again, if you want to study this more deeply, there are books that address in great detail how to let off steam safely. As a very short summary, here are some basic guidelines for blowing off steam:

- **Talk to a neutral party.** Find someone to talk to who doesn't know (and is not likely to meet) the person who has you upset. With phone calls as cheap as they are, you can talk to someone in another state or even another country.

- **The harder, the higher.** The harder it is to hold your tongue, the loftier your self-restraint. The heavenly realms are cheering you on!

- **Blowing off steam is overrated.** Consider that venting will usually not help change the situation or, more importantly, the way you relate to the situation. Decreasing or eliminating negative "replays" of hurts or slights means happier times. Here's an example you might have experienced: Did someone say something rude or thoughtless and you did the same back so they could "see what it feels like"? It doesn't work, because people will never see that you mean it as a reflection of their own behavior.

Speaking of reflections, there's a scientific name for the way gossiping will backfire. It's called "spontaneous trait transference."[25] What that means is that listeners will attribute to you the qualities you describe about others! While this hasn't been given much attention, it is a real phenomenon. And it's worth considering: When you're speaking negatively about others, what are your listeners associating with you?

GUARDING YOUR TONGUE

Consider the following tips and guidelines for creating life-changing and positive results in your quality of life and the lives of all around you. If you can improve even in one small area, it's a big deal.

(1) Keep it minimal. Decrease talking about people under the following circumstances:
- even if you would say it to the person's face
- even if it's true
- if the person you're talking *to* can't do anything to help the person you're talking *about*

(2) No sarcasm. Sarcasm comes from the Greek for "to tear flesh" and can cause hurt or humiliation, even when it's presented as humor.

---

25. J. J. Skowronski, D. E. Carlston, L. Mae, and M. T. Crawford, "Spontaneous Trait Transference: Communicators Take on the Qualities They Describe in Others," *Journal of Personality and Social Psychology* 74, no. 4 (April 1998):837–48, https://www.ncbi.nlm.nih.gov/pubmed/9569648.

(3) **Body language matters.** Rolling eyes, sighing, making the crazy sign of twirling your finger next to your head are all ways of hurting people.

(4) **No "pillow talk."** Just because you're talking to your spouse doesn't mean it's okay to talk about another person. It's healthier for this most precious and intimate relationship to leave out as much gossip as you can. Sometimes it feels like the safest place to blow off steam, but perhaps it does more damage than the comfort it may seem to bring.

(5) **Have compassion and give the benefit of the doubt.** No one knows the whole story of another. You don't know who's hurting or why or for how long. Striking out and doing harm is not justified, even if you are hurting, and in many situations, compassion can diffuse the hurt much more swiftly than lashing out in kind (to someone's face or otherwise). Also, consider that sometimes things said and done were not meant to harm at all, but were misunderstood. This is especially possible in the world of social media, where tone often doesn't come across accurately. If you're not sure, give yourself a better chance at good health by assuming that something didn't come across as it was meant.

(6) **Guard these people.** Begin with the innermost circle and radiate outward.

- Don't talk about your spouse. Get permission to tell stories *before* you tell them. If you need to process something, make sure you limit who you talk to and that you're choosing people who will support you and your marriage.
- Don't talk about your children. Don't talk about other people's children either!
- Don't talk about your parents.
- Don't lump a whole group together (all liberals, all conservatives, all men, all Jews, etc.).

- Don't say negative things about yourself. There's a difference between being modest and putting yourself down.

What if someone asks you questions about others? You have permission to not answer questions about yourself or others. You can simply say, "I don't know." Or, "Maybe you can ask them that directly." Or, gracefully respond with a sincere smile, "I don't answer those kinds of questions," and that is enough said.

If you need advice about your relationship, or how to parent a child, ask only one or two trusted sources. If you need advice about your marriage, talk to someone who is happily married and has a track record of longevity. If you need parenting advice, talk to someone who has experience with your issues, and who will help you in supporting your child's growth. The idea is to seek the counsel of those who will help you in practical ways so that you can have as positive an outcome as possible.

GUARDING YOUR EARS

Save the speaker from damaging himself or herself. Save the subject of the gossip from being damaged; a destroyed reputation may be difficult or sometimes even impossible to fix. Save yourself from the negativity, even when it doesn't seem as if it will be negative. There are lots of ways to get out of hearing talk about others:

- Change the subject. Have go-to topics ready (something you've just learned, for example).
- Ask a question to change the subject ("Have you done any traveling lately?").
- Excuse yourself and walk away.
- Share honestly what you're learning about changing speech.
- Get creative to decrease or eliminate gossip from your world.

When you grow in these areas, you are not just eliminating harmful speech. You're increasing joy and peace.

Peace in the Home

One of the most foundational and profound things we can do in life is to create a home of *shalom*. The word *shalom* is translated as "peace," and it is interesting to look a little deeper at the root of the word, which means "completeness" or "wholeness." When your home is filled with welcoming warmth and love, it becomes a safe place for those within the home to flourish. That means we should focus on what is positive, and not on the criticism and complaints that can come to us all too easily. It can seem especially tricky to do this when spouses or children often reflect back to us to show us the areas where we need to grow!

Challenges are a natural part of life. Having peace in the home can mean sacrificing being "right" for joyfully being together. It's about making the connection between members of the family more important—and more frequent—than the corrections. While the correcting moments or "teaching moments" are helpful for growth, connecting with your family more than correcting will help bring *shalom* and make love itself the lesson.

The Hebrew term *shalom bayit* (peace in the home) is something that has many teachings attached to it regarding both the marriage relationship and also parenting. It is worthy of further study. There are both Jewish books and secular books that teach about making relationships thrive. One small change in the way you respond to your family can make the difference between pushing a spouse or children away or drawing them nearer.

While the concept of *shalom bayit* includes children, siblings, and parents, the foundation for peace in the home is between husband and wife. Here are some tips (mindset *and* actions) you can incorporate into your relationships right now. Bringing in even one of these will bring about a positive change:

- **Set your intention.** Make a conscious plan to increase the peace in your home, because it begins with the inner

course you set for yourself. Your commitment to wanting a
home of peace will bring you the tools and opportunity.

- **It's 100 percent.** It's a mistake to think that marriage is
  50/50. A marriage works best when you take one hundred
  percent responsibility for your relationship: the way you
  give and receive, how you respond, what you do, the way
  you treat others, and even the way you're treated. The
  hardest thing—and the most empowering—is taking
  responsibility. When you blame your spouse, you take zero
  percent responsibility, which is only a great strategy if you
  like being a victim.

- **How you speak matters.** How you talk about and to
  your spouse builds or destroys the relationship. Your level
  of patience is often expressed by your tone. This isn't a
  call to be fake, and it's not about ignoring problems. It's
  about meeting your spouse eye to eye and compassionately
  working through the hard stuff.

- **Be forgiving.** Challenges are part of marriage. In
  fact, it is exactly the challenges that bring us to growth.
  Misunderstandings happen. Bad moods are part of life.
  Sometimes it's easy to see that one of you was hungry, tired,
  hurt, or whatever, and sometimes it's not so easy. Open
  your heart one more time. Be quick to apologize and
  easy to appease. Be willing to accept apologies. (Abuse is
  another matter and should not be ignored or rationalized.
  If you are in an abusive relationship, know that you are not
  alone. Get the help you need.)

- **Faithfulness is essential.** Infidelity destroys, usually
  irrevocably. The highest levels of unity are built over time
  and in faithfulness. Faithfulness in action and also thought
  builds the strongest bonds of trust.

❧ **Be generous with expressing affection, admiration, and appreciation.** Affection can be a loving touch or a love note. The things you do and say communicate "You are worth my time and energy" or "I treasure you" or "I acknowledge the thought and effort you put into my life." Don't underestimate the power of consistent, simple acts of kindness in your marriage. Don't underestimate the power of "thank you," for even the simplest of gestures.

❧ **Take time to enjoy life together.** It's all too easy to fall into taking care of business. Make it a priority to date each other (no business, no talk about the kids or your jobs). It doesn't need to be complicated or expensive. Some ideas: take walks together, take a fun class together and learn something new (art, cooking, or clowning class, for example), go bowling, or sit in a coffee shop over a cup of tea and ask each other questions to deepen your knowledge and understanding of each other (do a quick search online to get some great questions and other ideas of ways to date your mate).

❧ **Set the mood.** Create an environment in your home that signals peace to your family. This will be different for every couple and family. It could be music, candles, a basket of fruit, or keeping current, happy photos of your family in sight. Whatever that is for you, your effort to create it will make a difference.

❧ **Pray.** Never underestimate the power of prayer. You can:
- Pray to learn the skills to build a happy marriage.
- Pray for the strength to do what you know is right.
- Pray to be humble and strong in your marriage.
- Pray for your spouse's well-being, success, happiness, patience, *shalom,* work situation.

Building trust and *shalom* within the home has rewards that ripple into and affect the world in magnificent ways. Little by little, piece by piece, over time, each small action can have a big impact.

AFTERWORD

How can it be that our mothers were so dedicated to the continuation of the Nation of Israel, the Jewish People? Why did they care? Why do we? What's the difference?

When an old woman plants a fruit tree that will come to bear fruit only after she is gone, she is passing on something that will nourish those who come after her. The same is true for the seeds you're planting when you build a family, stand for justice, clean a corner of the world, teach, care for the health of others, create art, feed people (physically, emotionally, or spiritually), share a kindness, or crochet a blanket. We are leaving more of a legacy than we can comprehend. Every woman has the potential to bring light into the world and to share that light with all those she touches. That touch ripples out to others and shapes generations to come.

The spiritual well-being of this world matters. Our mothers knew this. The Torah and its values, ethics, morals, and teachings are a guide for spiritual consciousness and conscience. The world without a conscience is a place where anything goes, a place without boundaries. Torah brings God consciousness and conscience into the world through compassion, justice, generous hearts, and prayer.

A cashier who was among the hostages held in the January 2015 terrorist attack on a kosher grocery store in France shared her memories of praying during the traumatic experience. The terrorist let her speak by phone to her parents, who told her to pray and have faith in God. Another of the hostages stayed calm and said that everything was in God's hands. The cashier recited the first psalm that came to her mind:

> I look to the mountains; from where does my help come?
> My help comes from the Lord Who made heaven and
> earth.[1]

---

1.   Psalms 121:1–2.

Where did this young woman, her parents, and the other hostage find that strength? They are standing on the shoulders of those who came before. We gird ourselves and pull through the hardest of times with faith and trust. Often it is only in retrospect that we see the good that comes out of the most difficult of situations. But we always seek the good, even when we don't have access to the "big picture." Something great is at work here, reaching beyond survival of the self.

The transmission of Torah wisdom was traditionally conveyed from parent to child, father to son, and mother to daughter. But recent generations have seen a breakdown of that connection to the learning and life passages. Movements arose that promised a better life if only we would abandon our spiritual roots, the very source of our nourishment. In the end they were empty promises. In a passage in the Book of Hosea,[2] the prophet talks about such a time, when we are seduced away from our connection and find ourselves in a wilderness, a desolate valley, which leaves us yearning. With all the resources we have materially, we want more. And the Eternal promises to be in that valley when we wake up, there with a portal of hope, so that we can return to the union of majesty and love with the sublime Oneness.

There is an inherent goodness and kindness in the way of the Torah that touches every aspect of our being. Life is precious. The Torah's light—including a relationship with the Creator and a life guided by ethics, morals, and kindness—is for the entire world, not just members of the tribe. You are part of a chain that crosses time and space to connect generations. It is not random; it is full of meaning, and with a mission to bring goodness and light into the world through action. Your presence impacts the world, your dance brings joy to the world, your song brings comfort, and your very being brings a unique and precious light.

May you be blessed with joy, humor, grit, gratitude, and health. May your grief be comforted, and may your growth come gently. May you live in *shalom*—completeness, trust, and peace.

May you be like Sarah, Rivka, Rachel, and Leah.

---

2.   Hosea 2:15–21.

ACKNOWLEDGMENTS

Dear reader, I pictured you as I wrote. I heard your questions, and I also heard you arguing with me so that I could refine or clarify. My prayer is that you might find a piece of what you were looking for in this book. Some of you asked me via notes or in person when the book would be ready. You helped me stay on track. You are my inspiration. You are my sisterhood. Thank you.

I'm not sure what possessed me to want to teach about the women of the Tanach, but I could not have even thought about writing this book if Tova Weingot hadn't believed in and trusted me to teach at Sharei Bina Seminary (aka Darchei Emunah) in Tzfat (Safed). My amazing, adventuresome, courageous, and beautiful students loved the topic and encouraged me to write this book. One student said, "Oh, you *have* to write a book; we don't know the difference between Sarah and Cinderella, and *that* is retarded!" The most recent class asked me how the writing was going. I winced and told them it was going, but slowly. Seeing I needed encouragement, they cheered, "Write, write, write!" Ladies, you have no idea how that really inspired me. Thank you to all my students for showing up, asking questions, arguing, and sharing your thoughts and feelings.

Thank you to Sara Eidelshtein of Teatree Design for the stunning cover design and to S. Kim Glassman for typesetting the cover and the exquisite interior. Your art blessed this book infinitely. To Annette Amir and Micki Gersht for lovingly proofing the manuscript at the end of the process. To Fern Seckbach for the comprehensive index.

The women who read chapters and gave me feedback along the way about my writing were each an important part of the process to keep me on track. Thank you for investing your time and contributing to this process in such a meaningful way: Ronit Gourarie, Hyla Kompel, Haleila Nusinow, Julie Zunder, Deb Shadovitz, Rachel Shifra Tal, and the beta readers.

The women of my community in Tzfat are my bedrock. Thank you for being my role models for giving, kindness, and support. In particular, thank you to Ariella Bracha Waldinger, Chaya Bracha Leiter, Judy Paikin, Micki Gersht, Rebecca Rahlbag, Jodi Sugar, Chaya Ben Baruch, Tova Weingot, Ruth Zimberg, Geula Tova Streisand, and to all the women who have taught me or come to my classes, asked questions, challenged and encouraged me. Elina Shcop Naseck, my wonderful writing buddy, I'm so grateful for the hours we spent together to put words to paper. The friends who were not local but who encouraged and comforted me during the birth pangs of this book, Chany Scheiner, Hagay and Annette Amir, Eli and Naomi Kalfon, Sol and Martha Grazi, Brett and Susan Kramer, Jeffery and Shira Reiss, Shifra Weisman, Tzipora Hoynik, Rhonda Greene, Emily Katz—thank heaven for you, seriously!

To those who are unnamed in this outpouring of gratitude, I beg your forgiveness that I didn't name each of you. The heavenly accounting of your support is surely recorded on high.

When that daunting, critical inner voice told me I could not, should not write this book, it was the Lubavitcher Rebbe Menachem Mendel Schneerson and Rabbi Noach Weinberg whose voices came to me through their emissaries who have taught and encouraged me. "If you know *alef,* teach *alef,*" said Rebbetzin Chany Scheiner, one of my greatest encouragers. You gave me the chutzpah to write. At least I know that there is *alef,* and so I'm teaching what I have learned. To Lori Palatnik, for believing I could write this book—you have no idea how that nourished me. Thank you.

Many of my teachers are books and online classes. Rebbetzins Holly Pavlov, Tziporah Heller, Chana Juravel, Chana Weisman, Chana Bracha Siegelbaum, Shira Smiles, Orit Esther Riter, Leah Kohn, and others have taught me much on the topic of women in Tanach.

Real-life teachers Rabbis Ari Kahn and Avraham Arieh Trugman; Rebbetzins Chaya Bracha Leiter, Chana Bracha Siegelbaum, Leah Engel, and Rivky Kaplan; and Ellyn Hutt added to this book with their input, which brought it to a higher level. Thank you also to Susan Kramer for feedback about giving from a generous heart.

Only one midwife usually attends to a birth; I am privileged and honored to have had three. You are the ones who polished my words and helped them shine. You filled in the chipped or cracked parts. This book would not be what it is without you. Kezia Raffel Pride, a dear sister-friend and a most dependable, loving, busy, cheering, and expert editor: knowing you would be there to help with this project was so strengthening. You are also one of my most wonderful encouragers ever. Your guidance throughout the years and your wisdom and expertise helped make this book what it is. Allison Ofanansky, I don't know how I could have done this without your help, getting me unstuck and on track and then speeding up the process to get to the finish line. Your insights and heart brought clarity and refinement. Our conversations during the process were wonderful. Sabrina Lightstone, your contribution to the polishing and editing of this book supported me in ways you may never understand. Your encouragement, comments, and questions helped me shape and birth this book. And you saved me from my enthusiastic overuse of italics, exclamation points, and misplaced commas. I deeply thank you.

Moshe Epstein lifted this book in a solid, heroic way by listing sources. You are really a hero of our nation on so many levels, and you're a significant hero in getting this book to print.

My rabbi and teacher, Rav Ari Kahn, there will never be enough words to express my gratitude for all you've taught me and continue to teach me, for answering the phone when I called with a burning question before teaching a class or while working on this book, and for answering all my emailed questions. I could never have taught this topic or written this book without your guidance. You were my online teacher for years before I found you in "real life" (www.RabbiAriKahn.com and www.aishaudio.com). Thank you, infinite thanks. And to your beautiful wife, your *eshet chayil*, Naomi, thank you, too!

My son Yermiah Shaul heard me talk about the women of Tanach so often and challenged me to communicate that it's not *only* about the women. Thank you for asking the difficult questions and helping me refine the message. My daughter Avital Hana showed me what I couldn't understand until I watched you as a child, that a very young girl has the capacity for greatness. Serach Ravitch, my thanks for listening to me read parts of the book out loud and for your patience in the process.

My parents, Matitayhu Mendel ben Yehoshua Leib HaLevi and Matah bat Shimshon Berish, this book is in your memory and for your merit, because I would not be writing a book on Torah without your prayers and timeless support. You will always be the wind beneath my wings. To my grandparents and great-grandparents, your journeys got me here and give me strength.

My husband, Yaron Jackson, confidently envisioned the book tour before the book was halfway done. Thank you for listening to me read out loud, for telling me the truth when it wasn't clear, and for cheering at the parts you liked. Thank you for believing I could do this. Thank you for being my life partner.

For the gift of Torah, the ability to write, the support of so many, for the technology to transmit teachings at my fingertips and the desire to go deeper, I can only meekly echo the psalmist and ask the Eternal to look into my heart to know my gratitude for opening this journey. *Rabbah emunatecha.*

GLOSSARY
OF HEBREW WORDS AND NAMES

A

Achashverosh. Ahasuerus. In the Book of Esther, he was the King of Persia. He is often identified by historians as Xerxes.

Aharon. Aaron, the High Priest, brother of Moshe (Moses).

Akeidah. The Binding of Yitzchak (Isaac). As described in the Book of Genesis, God commands Avraham (Abraham) to bring his son Yitzchak as an offering, but he is not required to actually sacrifice his son.

Amalek. The most evil force in the world, which works to destroy the Jewish nation.

Amram. Husband of Yocheved, father of Miriam and Moshe.

anavah. Humility.

averah. Sin; missing the mark; from the root "to pass over."

Avraham. Abraham, the first of Judaism's three patriarchs, who introduced the concept of monotheism to the world; husband of Sarah.

B

Beit Hamikdash. The Holy Temple in Jerusalem. *Beit* means "house of"; *mikdash* comes from the root *kadosh*, meaning "holy" or "sanctified."

Binyamin. Benjamin, youngest son of Yaakov (Jacob) and Rachel, who died giving birth to him.

Bnei Yisrael. Children of Israel; the Hebrews.

brit (also pronounced *bris*). The ritual covenantal circumcision (removal of the foreskin) of Jewish baby boys, ideally performed at eight days old.

C

Calev. Caleb. One of the two scouts or spies sent into

241

Israel by Yehoshua (Joshua, another of the twelve spies, whose story is not covered in this book). Miriam's husband (Talmud, *Sotah* 12a).

chanukiah. Nine-branched candelabra lit during the holiday of Chanukah, also called a menorah by many people since it reminds us of the miracle of oil in the Temple Menorah.

Chava. Eve, the first woman, the mother of all life.

chesed. Loving-kindness.

chuppah. Marriage canopy. It is open on four sides, representing the home of the couple and that they are emulating Avraham and Sarah, who had a door on each side of their tent.

D

Dina. Daughter of Yaakov (Jacob) and Leah.

dudaim. Plants known for their fertility-enhancing or perhaps aphrodisiac properties, often translated as mandrakes.

E

Edom. A descendant of Esav (Esau), whose offspring eventually gave rise to the nation that became the Roman Empire. Edom is the father of Amalek.

emunah. Often translated as faith or belief, *emunah* more accurately means trust or affirmation (*emunah* is related etymologically to the word *amen*, which refers to affirmation or verification). The word appears in Genesis 15:6 to describe the relationship of Avraham (Abraham) to God.

exile. Expulsion of the Jewish nation from the Land of Israel, although some Jews have always maintained a presence there.

F

festivals. There are numerous Jewish holidays, but there are only three festivals that are commanded by God directly in the Torah: Pesach, Shavuot, and Sukkot.

G

Gehinnom. In the afterworld, an intermediary place of suffering for the purpose of cleansing the soul.

gematria. Jewish numerology; study of the way numerical values of Hebrew letters add up and suggest additional meanings and correlations.

gilgul neshamot. Reincarnation; literally "cycle of the soul."

H

halachah. Jewish law; literally "the Way."

Hashem. God; literally "the Name."

Holy of Holies. The innermost chamber of the Beit Hamikdash or Mishkan, which contained the Ark of the Covenant. In Exodus 25:8, God told the Jewish nation to build this holy place, and the Divine Presence would live in them (that is to say, not in the object itself but within the people themselves).

K

Kabbalah. Jewish mysticism. Teachings for the finite mind of man to grasp some bit of understanding about the infinite and indefinable essence of God. (Be cautious: there are teachings claiming to represent Kabalah that are not true to the Torah way.)

ketubah. Marriage contract according to Jewish law. It contains the material, physical obligations and promises that a man makes to his wife.

Kinneret. Sea of Galilee.

kosher. Biblical dietary laws (includes permissible and forbidden foods and mixtures of foods).

L

lashon hara. Gossip, slander; literally "evil tongue."

Lavan. Laban. Brother of Rivka (Rebecca), father of Leah and Rachel, corrupt father-in-law of Yaakov (Jacob).

M

Me'arat Hamachpelah. Cave
of the Patriarchs, literally
"cave of the doubled," where
Adam and Chava (Eve),
Avraham (Abraham) and
Sarah, Yitzchak (Isaac)
and Rivka (Rebecca), and
Yaakov (Jacob) and Leah
are buried (Rachel is
buried elsewhere). It is in
the city of Hebron and can
be visited today; many Jews
come to pray there.

megillah. Scroll. This usually
refers to the scroll of the
Book of Esther, although
there are four other texts
called megillot (Ruth, Song
of Songs, Ecclesiastes, and
Lamentations).

Menorah. Seven-branched
candelabra in the Beit
Hamikdash (Temple in
Jerusalem). Its construction
was commanded by God.

Midrash. Body of interpretive
rabbinic literature in
the form of stories that
illuminate the Torah text.

mikveh. Ritual bath for
spiritual purification—
either a natural body of
water or a constructed,
spa-like pool that is
connected to a natural
source of water. Women
immerse in it before
resuming sexual relations
following the time of
separation (niddah—see
below) during the monthly
cycle. Jewish men may also
immerse in a mikveh for
ritual purification before
holy days (or even every
day, for some Chassidim).

Miriam. Sister of Moshe
(Moses). A prophetess in
her own right, she helped
lead the Children of Israel
out of Egypt; water was
provided for them in her
merit via Miriam's well.

Mishkan. Holy Sanctuary,
usually translated as
Tabernacle. The Jewish
people were commanded to
build it as a dwelling place
for God. The Mishkan
was a temporary, portable
structure that preceded the
Beit Hamikdash.

Mishnah. Jewish law which,
according to our tradition,
was given orally by God to
Moshe at Mount Sinai. See
also Talmud.

mitzvah. Commandment in Jewish law.

Moshe. Moses, the Jewish prophet and leader who lead the Jews out of slavery in Egypt, brought down the Torah from Sinai, and led the Jews through the desert bringing them to the entrance of the Land of Israel. He spoke directly with God and yet is considered the humblest of all men.

Moshiach. Messiah. Technically this term means "the anointed one." There are teachings that the Moshiach will usher in an era of peace for all humanity.

N

niddah. Time during a woman's monthly cycle (generally from the first spot of blood until seven ritually "clean" days have passed) when a married couple refrains from sexual intercourse and physical contact.

P

Passover. See Pesach.

Pesach. Passover. Festival in the spring at which we recount the Exodus from Egypt, especially during the Seder (ritual meal). The festival lasts seven days, during which Jews abstain from eating leavened grain products (bread, crackers, cereals, etc.) and eat unleavened bread (matzah) instead.

pikuach nefesh. Preserving life. This refers to the Talmudic concept that for the purpose of saving a life, most commandments are overridden.

Pinchas. Phinehas. One of the scouts sent into Israel by Yehoshua (Joshua). He was also a leader of the nation.

Pirkei Avot. Ethics of the Fathers, a collection of wisdom that relates to living a righteous life.

R

Rachav. Rahab, from the Book of Joshua, who sheltered the scouts in Jericho, and

ultimately became a Jew
and married the leader of
Israel, Yehoshua (Joshua;
Megillah 14b).

Rambam. Maimonides
(1135–1204), an influential
rabbi, physician, and Torah
scholar of the Middle Ages
whose full name is Moshe
ben (son of) Maimon.

Ramban. Nachmanides (1194–
1270), a leading medieval
rabbi and scholar whose
full name is Moshe ben
(son of) Nachman.

Rashi. Rabbi Shlomo Yitzchaki
(1040–1105), one of
the most important
commentators on the
Torah, whose commentary
is usually printed together
with the Torah text.

Rivka. Rebecca, wife of the
patriarch Yitzchak (Isaac),
mother of Esav (Esau) and
Yaakov (Jacob).

Rosh Chodesh. The first day
of each month in the
Jewish calendar, which
begins when the first sliver
of the new moon is seen
(sometimes includes the
last day of the previous
month).

Rosh Hashanah. The Jewish
New Year, the Day of
Judgment, the first two
days of the Hebrew month
of Tishrei (falling generally
in September or October).

S

Sabbath. See Shabbat.

Shabbat. The Sabbath, the
seventh day of the week
and the day of rest. It lasts
twenty-five hours from
Friday night just before
sundown until Saturday
night after sundown.

shalom. Peace. It comes from
the root word that means
complete or whole.

shalom bayit. Peace in the
household.

Shavuot. Festival when we
commemorate the giving of
the Torah at Mount Sinai.
It is also called the Festival
of Weeks. It occurs in late
spring at the time of the
grain harvest in Israel.

Shechinah. The feminine
aspect of God; Divine
Presence.

shivah. Traditional one-week
grieving period observed
by the deceased's close

relatives, who wear a torn garment, sit on low stools, and do not wear leather shoes. Visitors come and sit with the mourners. (For more on Jewish mourning, read *Remember My Soul* by Lori Palatnik.)

T

Talmud. Compilation of the Mishnah (Jewish laws which, according to our tradition, were given orally by God to Moshe [Moses] at Mount Sinai), along with rabbinic commentary on the Oral Law (called the Gemara).

Tanach. Acronym for Torah, Nevi'im, Ketuvim—the Torah, the Prophets, and the Writings (which include the Scroll of Esther and the Scroll of Ruth, as well as Psalms, Proverbs, Ecclesiastes, and more).

teshuvah. Literally means "return," meaning returning to God or to Jewish tradition. It is sometimes translated as "repentance," but that translation carries

a weight that is not a Jewish way of thinking.

tikkun. A repair or fix for damage we have done in the world.

Torah. The Five Books of Moses, also called the Pentateuch, given by God to Moses at Mount Sinai; literally "teaching."

tzara'at. A skin disease or eruption that appeared on clothing or walls resulting from *lashon hara* (gossip). It is usually translated as "leprosy" but this is not accurate.

tzedakah. Charity, from the root for "justice."

Tziporah. Daughter of Yitro (Jethro), wife of Moshe (Moses).

tzniut. Modesty in dress or behavior.

Y

Yaakov. The patriarch Jacob, son of the patriarch Yitzchak (Isaac) and Rivka (Rebecca), brother of Esav (Esau), husband of Leah and Rachel, father of the twelve tribes of Israel. He

was also given the name
Yisrael (Israel).

Yehoshua. Joshua. Successor to
Moshe, he led the Children
of Israel as they entered the
Land of Israel after forty
years in the desert. He
married Rachav (Rahab).

yichud. The private "seclusion"
of a man and woman
(forbidden in Jewish law
unless they are first-degree
relatives).

yirat Shamayim. Awe of
Heaven. The related
term *yerei Shamayim*
(literally fearers of Heaven)
describes people who
live according to the
understanding that there is
a heavenly accounting and
so live in integrity with the
laws of the Torah.

Yisrael. The Hebrew word
for Israel. It is the name
the angel gave to Yaakov
(Jacob) after they wrestled.
There are many meanings
to the name, including.
"to wrestle with God" or
"straight to God."

Yehudi. Jew; literally "grateful."

Yitzchak. The patriarch Isaac,
son of the patriarch
Avraham (Abraham) and
Sarah, husband of Rivka
(Rebecca), father of Esav
(Esau) and Yaakov (Jacob).

Yom Kippur. Day of
Atonement, the holiest day
of the Jewish year, a day to
stand humbly before our
Creator and take account
of our actions having made
amends with the people in
our lives.

Yosef. Joseph, son of Yaakov
and Rachel. Cast out by his
brothers, he ended up in
Egypt and became viceroy
to Pharaoh, in the process
earning the title of Yosef
Hatzaddik (Joseph the
righteous one).

Z

zerizut. Alacrity, swift action.

Zohar. Book of teachings
in Kabbalah, Jewish
mysticism.

RESOURCES

Websites

There are so many resources to dip into the infinite well of learning Torah. This short list of trustworthy websites is by no means exhaustive. Here are a couple of tips for continuing the journey:

- Learning Torah can lead you to different interpretations and seemingly conflicting ideas. Finding balance in the paradox is part of the journey.
- Time will bring you more answers as well as more questions.
- Happily there are so many resources, but at the same time it can seem overwhelming. One place to begin is to choose a topic or text you want to learn and begin with that, or choose just one of the websites below and explore.
- There are many teaching styles. You will likely resonate with some teachers and not with others. It doesn't mean the ones you don't connect with are not good. Simply move on, and you might be surprised to find that you'll connect with them later.

For primary sources (biblical and other Jewish texts in English translation), try the following:

www.mechon-mamre.org
www.sefaria.org/texts

For stories, information about the holidays, inspiring video content, and more, try the following sites:

www.aish.com	www.hatanakh.com
www.alephbeta.org	www.jewishclarity.com
arikahn.blogspot.co.il	www.JewsForJudaism.org
www.chabad.org	www.jewishvirtuallibrary.org
etzion.org.il/en	www.thejewishwoman.org

jwa.org   www.rabbiarikahn.com
www.myjewishlearning.com   www.thetrugmans.com
www.naaleh.com   www.torah.org.il
www.OU.org   www.torchweb.org
www.partnersintorah.org   www.simpletoremember.com

If you're a Jewish mom, check out the Jewish Women's Renaissance Project at www.jwrp.org

Books to Read for Continued Learning

Aaron, Rabbi David. *Inviting God In: Celebrating the Soul Meaning of the Jewish Holy Days*. Durban, South Africa: Trumpeter, 2007.

Ansch, Tamar. *A Taste of Challah*. Jerusalem: Feldheim, 2007.

Bell, Yitzchok Leib. *Between Me and You: Heartfelt Prayers for Each Jewish Woman; Compiled and Adapted from the Prayers of Rav Noson Steinhartz*. 2nd ed. Jerusalem: Nachas Books, 2014.

Jungreis, Rebbetzin Esther. *The Committed Life: Principles for Good Living from Our Timeless Past*. New York: HarperCollins, 1999.

———. *The Committed Marriage: A Guide to Finding a Soul Mate and Building a Relationship through Timeless Biblical Wisdom*. New York: HarperCollins, 2002.

Kaplan, Aryeh. *Waters of Eden: The Mystery of the Mikvah*. New York: Union of Orthodox Jewish Congregations of America/ National Conference of Synagogue Youth, 1993.

Pavlov, Holly. *Mirrors of Our Lives: Reflections of Women in Tanach*. Southfield, MI: Targum, 2000.

Pliskin, Rabbi Zelig. Anything with his name on it! Rabbi Pliskin has written many books on the practical application of Torah teachings to grow in areas of happiness, letting go of anger, speech, connecting with the Creator, and many more.

Palatnik, Lori, with Bob Burg. *Gossip: Ten Pathways to Eliminate It from Your Life and Transform Your Soul.* Deerfield Beach, FL: Simcha, 2002.

Palatnik, Lori, with Rabbi Yaakov Palatnik. *Remember My Soul: What to Do in Memory of a Loved One; A Path of Reflection and Inspiration for Shiva, the Stages of Jewish Mourning, and Beyond.* New York: Khal Publishing, 2008.

Scherman, Rabbi Nosson, ed. *The Stone Edition Chumash: The Torah, Haftaros, and Five Megillos with a Commentary from Rabbinic Writings.* New York: ArtScroll Mesorah, 1993.

———. *The Stone Edition Tanach: The Torah/Prophets/Writings; The 24 Books of the Bible Newly Translated and Annotated.* New York: ArtScroll Mesorah, 1996.

Siegelbaum, Rebbetzin Chana Bracha. *Women at the Crossroads: A Woman's Perspective on the Weekly Torah Portion.* New York: Lambda, 2010.

Telushkin, Rabbi Joseph. *Words That Hurt, Words That Heal: How to Choose Words Wisely and Well.* New York: HarperCollins, 2010.

Trugman, Rabbi Avraham Arieh. *Orchard of Delights: The Ohr Chadash Torah Commentary.* Moshav Mevo Modi'in, Israel: Ohr Chadash, 2011.

Weisberg, Chana. *The Crown of Creation: The Lives of Great Biblical Women Based on Rabbinic and Mystical Sources.* Oakville, Ontario: Mosaic Press, 2010.

Weissman, Moshe. *The Midrash Says: The Narrative of the Weekly Torah-Portion in the Perspective of Our Sages.* 5 vols. Rev. ed. New York: Benei Yakov Publications. 1995

INDEX

A

accountability, 3, 106, 118, 123

Abraham. *See* Avraham

Achashverosh (Ahasuerus),
183–84, 186
decree against the Jews, 189,
194

action: represented by Rachel,
80

Adam, 128, 154
buried in Me'arat
Hamachpelah, 45
in Garden of Eden, 20–23
name, 19
naming Chava, 20
relationship with Chava, 29
See also Tree of Knowledge
of Good and Evil

age, 113

Akeidah, 44–46, 55

alacrity. See *zerizut*

Amalek, 62

Amram, 108–9

anavah, 47–49

anti-Semitism, 149, 151

assimilation, 149–53

Avimelech, 65

Avraham (Abraham), 33–34
and angels' visit, 40
buried in Me'arat
Hamachpelah, 45
in Egypt, 36–37

Land of Israel promised to,
39
and monotheism, 35
name change, 39
relationship with God, 34
and search for Yitzchak's
wife, 54–55
told of son to be born to
him, 40–41

awe of Heaven. See *yirat
Shamayim*

B

Barak, 143–44, 146

barrenness, 95, 162
the matriarchs', 83
Rachel's, 83, 84, 87
Sarah's, 36, 38
Yitzchak and Rivka's, 61

Batya (Egyptian princess), 109

beauty, relating to, 131, 198–207
care, 202–3
internal and external,
198–202
outer, 200–202
of righteous women in
Egypt, 10, 110, 112
soul, 206–7

Beit Hamikdash (Jerusalem
Temple), 29, 31, 224
and Chanukah, 150, 221
and copper mirrors, 11
destruction of Second,
196–98

A Slice of Laya's Story

In my search for meaning and purpose, I made the decision to abandon Jewish traditions in my twenties. I experimented and explored for some years, but I got a wake-up call from a job I took while in graduate school in 1989. I had applied to work at a residential facility for boys that happened to be run by the Catholic Church. The job required taking the boys into the chapel every morning for a quick prayer. The administrator who interviewed me, having read my resume and seeing that I had been to Israel, asked if I could go into the chapel. What flashed through my mind's eye was the history of my nation: visions of men and women—my ancestors—who were persecuted and even murdered for not bowing or kneeling to the gods of others. I wasn't practicing Judaism, yet why would I act as if I were practicing something else? I wanted the job, however, so I answered that I'd respectfully take the boys into the chapel but that I would not kneel. I was hired and began work.

One morning a couple of boys misbehaved in the chapel. My job was to "give a consequence." What grew from that simple event took me by storm. Some of the boys started a campaign against me: "Miss Saul should *not be allowed* into the church, she's a Jew!" Then notes with swastikas started appearing. A couple of boys even shouted "Heil Hitler" as I drove off campus. What surprised and disturbed me was that not one staff member backed me up. I was told I was being "overly sensitive." I was in shock as I watched this scenario unfold. Then a secretary from the administration pulled me aside and in secret told me that she was also a Jew but that no one there knew it. She assured me that the administration was anti-Semitic. I didn't know what to make of this.

Then the director of the facility approached me. We took a little walk in the beautiful evening air of northern California to talk. He shared that I was a very valued staff member and that he didn't want to lose me over this, that the boys were just looking for my Achilles heel. It did feel nice to be acknowledged. But after a brief silence he added, "Anyway, when are the Jews going to get over the Holocaust? I mean, it happened nearly fifty years ago."

I could not even speak.

As I tried to make sense of what had happened and how I could respond, the message came through clearly: *Laya, you were born Jewish for a reason.* It was a defining moment for me. Having studied Jewish history, I could see what it meant to die as a Jew. Now I needed to find out more, and so began my quest to find out what it meant to *live* as a Jew. It has been a long road with twists and detours, wonder and awe, trials and tears, and even what I would call some mystical experiences. I have reunited with the path that brings meaning and purpose to my life. My search ultimately brought me back to the essence, connections, and mission of my soul as a Jew. I'm so grateful to be on this journey. It is not always easy, but walking in the path of my foremothers always nourishes my heart and soul.

GIVE THE GIFT OF

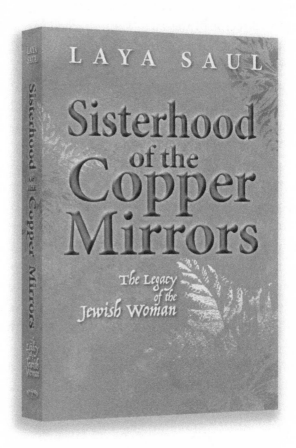

to family and friends
or donate copies to schools, synagogues, and libraries

Please write a book review on your favorite site
such as Amazon or Goodreads;
it will help others find this rich resource.